A MAP OF THE DIVINE SUBTLE FACULTY

The Concept of the Heart in the Works of
Ghazali, Said Nursi, and Fethullah Gülen

A MAP OF THE DIVINE SUBTLE FACULTY

The Concept of the Heart in the Works of
Ghazali, Said Nursi, and Fethullah Gülen

Mehmet Yavuz Şeker

TUGHRA
BOOKS
New Jersey

Published by Tughra Books
345 Clifton Ave., Clifton,
NJ, 07011, USA

www.tughrabooks.com

Library of Congress Cataloging-in-Publication Data
Seker, Mehmet Yavuz.
A map of the divine subtle faculty : the concept of the heart in the works of Ghazali, Said Nursi, and Fethullah Gülen / Mehmet Yavuz Seker.
pages cm
ISBN 978-1-59784-340-9 (alk. paper)
1. Heart--Religious aspects--Islam. 2. Religious life--Islam. 3. Ghazzali, 1058-1111. 4. Nursi, Said, 1873-1960. 5. Gülen, Fethullah. I. Title.
BP190.5.H38S45 2015
297.2'25--dc23
2014039403

ISBN: 978-1-59784-340-9

Printed by
Çağlayan A.Ş., Izmir - Turkey

Contents

PART II
GHAZALI, SAID NURSI AND FETHULLAH GÜLEN'S
APPROACHES TO THE HEART

Foreword

I n the Islamic understanding, the honor of a human being and the quality rendering them superior to all other beings in existence is their belief in God and their knowledge of Him. A person who believes in God and is subsequently able to adorn their life with the manifestations of this belief becomes the most esteemed of all creation. Otherwise, they cannot avoid falling to the basest of states. For this reason, considering the human being as candidate to this highest of positions, in lieu of seeing them as the most honorable of all creation would perhaps be a more prudent approach. A person who believes in God, knows the God in Whom they believe, loves Him as they know Him, are loved by Him and who are faithfully devoted to Him can fulfil what is expected of them, can realize God's will in relation to them, only in this way. And the human being accomplishes all this with not another bodily limb or organ, but only with their heart. In other words, that which believes in God, knows Him, draws near to Him, obeys Him, acts in His Name, feels and perceives His presence, discovers secrets pertaining to Him and ascends to the position of as though seeing Him, is perpetually and solely the heart.

Just as the heart is thus, it is also predisposed to being in the exact opposite position; it can stoop to a position of denial and ignorance of God and be deprived of love and nearness to Him, and rebel against Him. All of these are important in terms of their demonstrating the neutrality and the changeability of the heart. Indeed, just as the heart has been created with an aptitude for all goodness, it is simultaneously amenable to every kind of vice and is open to all forms of positive and negative development. In the same way a person's advancing to perfection and attaining the level of true humanity is contingent upon their heart, their descent to the position of the lowest of creation is again related to it. While the heart, which purges itself of everything other than God so as to host Him, is that which is willed and beloved by God, a heart that does not believe in Him is subjected to His disfavor and wrath.

From another perspective, the heart is in a position of dominance over all the other bodily organs and faculties. When considered as a sultan, the other organs are its servants and chattels and when regarded as a commander, the other faculties are as though its troops. This being the case, everything ensuing from the human being, whether good or bad, is the product of the heart. That is to say, all the beauty and vileness pertaining to the human being stem completely from the heart's radiance or darkness, with everything harbored therein being reflected outwardly via every word and action of the human being. This is why it is possible to suggest that a person is 'as human as their heart.'

The heart is the expression of a person's spiritual existence. A believing heart is a Divine gift bestowed upon the human being, a Divine subtle faculty. It is a polished mirror reflecting God, a mirror opening onto truth and reality, the projection of the realms beyond in the corporeal world, the spiritual dimension of the physical heart and the bridge between the corporeal or visible realm and the world of the unseen. The mind is its dimension, which pertains to cognizance and knowledge, and conscience is its other dimension wherein its feelings and perceptions are reflected. With is inner depths of *sirr* (secret), *khafi* (arcanum) and *akhfa* (super-arcanum), it observes God like an 'observatory,' and with is points of reliance and seeking help, continuously seeks and points to God.

When purged and purified and with due care and maintenance, the heart is that which believes, comprehends, thinks, becomes conscious, grasps, understands, conceives, knows, sees, hears, feels, perceives, intends, resolves, does, acts with sincerity, rejoices, comes to rest, is rewarded, is overjoyed with guidance and esteemed. When sullied and neglected, however, it becomes that which disbelieves, becomes sealed, blinded, hardened, afflicted, heedless, and duplicitous and that which is punished, which falls astray and which is scorned. It is a lake into which both crystal clear waters cascade and muddy, murky waters are poured; it is both a bosom receiving angelic inspiration and a target of Satan's virulent arrows. The heart is such a luminous, two-faceted jewel that, in contrast to carrying to the body the spiritual effusion it receives when it enters into the spirit's service, and producing breezes of tranquility therein, when exposed to satanic and carnal urgings, it can also become an instrument of every kind of hazardous venture. It is precisely and perpetually this heart which is the means for humanity's surpassing the angels as well as their becoming a plaything of Satan.

It is perhaps by virtue of this delicate position that the Qur'an teaches Muslims the supplication, "Our Lord, do not let our hearts swerve after You have guided us," and the Messenger of God reminds them of this vital safeguard with the words, "O God, O Converter of hearts! Establish our hearts firmly on Your religion." Moreover, the Qur'an's approaching the heart as though it were a living being in describing it, attributing to it such positive and negative qualities as malady, soundness, heedlessness, tenderness, hardness and repose, is also rather striking.

The Sufis' views in relation to the heart naturally hold primacy. It is interesting that scholars in other Islamic disciplines, however, also too spoke like the Sufis when the heart was in question and formulated their views and interpretations from the same vantage point. This perhaps serves to explain why I did not encounter erratic interpretations, approaches and views from individuals of differing disciplines with respect to the heart in my research. Due to the Sufis' assuming a central position in the matter, they naturally scrutinized and tried to understand the heart more closely. An attempt was made in this book, to obtain the views and insights of scholars prominent in virtually all branches of the Islamic sciences. With a view to achieving a holistic approach of the topic, I opted to present the various interpretations and views as separate subheadings, as opposed to dividing up the various disciplines.

Subsequent to the introduction, I approached the topic in two central sections. In the introduction, I focused on the literal meanings of the Arabic word for heart, *qalb*, the points of similarity and divergence between the material and spiritual *qalb* as well as related concepts such as *fuad*, *lubb*, *sadr*, *aql*, *hilm*, *hijr* and *nuha*.

Referring to the functions of the heart in the first section, I evaluated the heart's being—as mentioned above—the locus of perception, understanding, feeling, knowledge and action. I examined God's disposal over the heart as well as the Qur'an's positive and negative characterizations concerning the heart.

In the second section of the book, moving to the more specific, is a discussion and interpretation of the evaluations and insights of Imam Ghazali, Said Nursi and Fethullah Gülen with respect to the heart. In an exploration of Imam Ghazali's works, I encountered his marvelous definition of the heart as a "Divine, spiritual faculty" and examined his descriptions of the heart as sovereign and master over all the other bodily limbs and faculties.

I observed Nursi's characterization of the heart by means of distinct and unconventional metaphors. These include his attributing to the heart such terms as spiritual map, center, mainspring, seed and, in discussing its functions, employing such words as telephone, eye, ear, feet, wing and sustenance.

That Gülen also deals at length with the heart and that he ascribes the heart a mission different to that of the first two scholars, is also discussed in this work. His emphasis on the development of the heart at the individual level is elucidated, in addition to the importance he attaches to the contribution and value of such spiritual development on a societal plane.

One of the main aims of this work is to explore the spiritual aspect of the human being in the Islamic understanding and to draw attention to the extent to which this aspect holds sway over them. It is my earnest hope that such a consciousness is inspired in the reader. My utmost hope, however, is the acceptance of this endeavor before God and its earning His endless favor and approval.

Mehmet Yavuz Şeker
Istanbul, 2014

Introduction

The term *qalb* is an Arabic word derived from the letters q-l-b. The term takes plural forms such as *qulub, eqlab, qilaba* and *'aqlub*. The term denotes turning something inside out, inverting and transforming[1]. Raghib al-Isfahani (d. 502/1108) defines *qalb* as "changing something from its existing state to another one."[2] Al-Firuzabadi (d. 817/1414) states that the word *qalb* refers to "turning and rotating an object [and] changing its direction" and notes that "such rotating involves turning something upside-down, inside out, left-to-right, right-to-left and front-to-back."[3] The Arabic idiom, *rajulun qullab*, literally means "a man who takes all forms," referring to the proverbial 'chameleon.'[4] In addition, the term is also defined as *fuad, 'aql*, the essence, center or truth of a thing.[5]

As such, is has been said that this word being used to denote the human heart is due to the heart's constantly being in a state of flux and change, and being the center of both material and spiritual existence.[6]

It can also be said that the term *qalb* has been used to denote the heart because of its carrying out the function of blood circulation throughout the body and actualizing such spiritual elements as willpower, perception, feeling and knowledge. Lane refers to *qalb* being synonymous with the word *damir*, "meaning the mind or the secret thoughts," as well as

---

[1] Abu Nasr Ismail Jawhari, *Taj al-Lugha wa sahah al-'Arabiyya*, 2 vols. (Beirut: Dar al-Fikr, 1998), 204; Ibn Manzur, *Lisan al-'arab*, 'q-l-b'; Muhammad Ibn Ya'qub al-Firuzabadi, *al-Qamus al-Muhit* (Cairo: Mu'assasatur-ri'salah, 1951), 163; Murtada al-Zabidi, *Taj al-'Arus min Jawahari'l Qamus*, 10 vols. (Cairo1888), 68.

[2] al-Isfahani, *Al-Mufradat*, 411.

[3] Muhammad Ibn Ya'qub al-Firuzabadi, *Basa'ir dhawi al-tamyiz fi lata'if al-Kitab al-'Aziz*, 6 vols. (Beirut: al-Maktabah al-'Ilmiyyah, n.d.), 281; 82.

[4] Salman Zayd Salman Yamani, *al-Qalbu wa Wazaifuhu* (Dammam: Dar Ibn al-Qayyim, 1994), 44.

[5] al-Firuzabadi, *Al-Qamus*, 163; Asım Efendi, *Translation of Al-Qamus*, 4 vols. (Istanbul: Cemal Efendi Matbaası, 1305), I:446.

[6] al-Isfahani, *Al-Mufradat*, 411; al-Zabidi, *Taj al-'Arus*, IV:70; Abu 'Abd Allah Qurtubi, *al-Jami' Li-ahkam-il Qur'an*, 20 vols. (Beirut: Dar al-Kutub al-'Ilmiyya, 2004), I:131.

damara, "meaning the intellect, or intelligence."[7] The Qur'an uses certain verb forms derived from the root q-l-b. The following verses can be cited as examples:

> ... Assuredly, they sought to stir up sedition before, and tried to turn things upside down to frustrate you.[8]
>
> ...they are in fear of a Day on which all hearts and eyes will be over-turned.[9]
>
> ...The wrongdoers will come to know by what a (great) reverse they will be overturned.[10]
>
> ... We confound their hearts and eyes...[11]

Prophet Muhammad, in his most frequent oath, "By the turner of hearts!'" used the word *muqallib*, and used the same word again when making an oath, "O turner of hearts!"[12]

The word *qalb* in the Qur'an is used to express three meanings. These are the mind, thought and perception, as well as the physical heart itself. The following three verses indicate these meanings respectively:

> Surely in that is a warning reminder for anyone who has a heart (that is truly alive), and who gives ear (to the one conveying this reminder), with eyes able to see well.[13]
>
> You think of them as one body; but, in fact, their hearts are at odds with one another. This is because they are a people who do not reason (and come to an understanding about the situations they face).[14]

---

[7] Edward William Lane, *An Arabic-English Lexicon*, 8 vols. (Lebanon: Librairie Du Liban, 1968), VII:2554.

[8] (9:48) In this verse, the term translated as "turn things upside down" is *qallabu*.

[9] (24:37) The word expressing the meaning "on which all hearts and eyes will be overturned" in the Qur'an is *tataqallabu*.

[10] (26:227) The phrase in this verse translated as "what a (great) reverse they will be overturned" is expressed on the original Arabic as *munqalabin yanqalibun*.

[11] (6:110) Here, the meaning of the verb *nuqallibu* is "we will turn."

[12] Bukhari, Tawhid, 11; Badr al-Din al-'Ayni, *'Umdat al-Qari*, 25 vols. (Beirut: Dar Ihya' al-turath al-'Arabi, 2001), XXV:94; al-Asqalani Ibn Hajar, *Fath al-bari sharh Sahih al-bukhari* (Beirut: Dar al-Kutub al-'Ilmiyyah, 1997), XIII:389; Muhammad Anwar al-Kashmiri, *Fayd al-Bari ila Sahih al-Bukhari*, 6 vols. (Beirut: Dar al-Kutub al-'Ilmiyyah, 2005), VI:552.

[13] (50:37)

[14] (59:14)

For indeed, it is not the eyes that have become blind; it is rather the hearts in the breasts that are blind.[15]

The first verse clearly states that the one who takes heed and learns lessons is the heart. It is always the heart that hears, understands, takes lessons from and gains experience from those things that it hears and comprehends.

The second verse entails an evaluation of the hypocrites, who look well-coordinated and unified on the outside from the perspective of their hearts, and describes how their external appearance does not correspond with reality. They appear outwardly to be unified. Those who see them assume them to be in complete accord. However, their hearts are not in agreement in relation to helping the Jews. That is, they differ significantly from one another in terms of thought, understanding and approach.

The final verse draws attention to the distinction between the physical eye and the spiritual one and maintains that the eye which actually needs to 'see' is not the one in the body, but instead the eye of the heart and explains that the deniers are in fact blind because this particular eye cannot see the truth.

Heart in the Islamic Context

When the word *qalb* is examined in the religious context, the material heart is considered before describing the spiritual one, and information is provided therein, albeit brief. Accordingly, the heart—on the left side of the chest, beneath the left breast, resembling a pine cone—is different to all other bodily organs with respect to its composition, tissue, and self-functioning nature, is a piece of flesh that ensures the continuation of human life by means of its pumping blood to all parts of the

---

[15] (22:46) Raghib has also stated that *qalb* denotes life and perception, and has supported these definitions with the relevant verses for the Qur'an. In his view, the term "hearts" in the verse, "(Remember) when they came upon you from above you (from the east), and from below you (from the west), and when (your) eyes turned dull, and (your) hearts came up to the throats, and (those of weak faith among) you were harboring vain thoughts about God" (33:10) means "lives." Similarly, the term "their hearts" in the verse, "...We have laid veils over their hearts so that they do not comprehend it" (6:25) means "their understanding" (al-Isfahani, *Al-Mufradat*, 411).

body and is the corporeal heart that the science of medicine has as its subject matter.[16]

With respect to definitions of the spiritual heart, it is important to note at this point that they are considered from a broad spectrum. With there being many definitions on the subject, in general each of these approach the immaterial heart from one or more different perspectives. In addition, it is also important to state that there is no single definition that encompasses all of its facets. For this reason, I will attempt to combine all these definitions rather than offering one general description.

Some of the definitions of the spiritual heart are as follows:

The spiritual entity that is the center of human consciousness, conscience, feeling, perception, mind and will, what Sufis refer to as the Human Reality[17] (*haqiqa al-insaniyya*) and philosophers to *nafs al-natiqa*, or the Reasoning (or articulating) Soul; the luminous jewel addressed by God, held responsible for their actions, punished and rewarded;[18] the sum of all human potential[19], a human being's inner world,[20] the resplendent vehicle through which humanity is actualized vis-à-vis the soul and the carnal self;[21] the mirror on which the meanings of the unseen are reflected and on which wisdom descends;[22] the hidden force distinctly perceiving Divine realities;[23] the Divine subtle faculty, Divine jewel, source or

---

[16] al-Ghazali, *Ihya,'* III:44; Elmalılı Muhammed Hamdi Yazır, *Hak Dini Kur'an Dili*, 10 vols. (Istanbul: Azim Dagitim, 1979), I:10. Yamani, *al-Qalbu wa Wazaifuhu*, 45.

[17] Massignon, *Essay on the Origins of the Technical Language of Islamic Mysticism*, 134.

[18] Sayyid Sharif al-Jurjani, *Kitab al-Ta'rifat* (Beirut: Dar al-Kutub al-'Ilmiyya, 1983), 178; Yazır, *Hak Dini Kur'an Dili*, I:209-11. al-Ghazali, *Ihya,'* III:113; 'Abd al-Razzaq al-Kashani, *Istilahat al-Sufiyah* (Cairo1981), 162; Asım Efendi, *Translation of Al-Qamus*, I:445.

[19] Hüseyin Aydın, *Muhasibi'nin Tasavvuf Felsefesi* (Ankara: Pars Yayıncılık, 1976), 47; Kabir Helminski, *The Knowing Heart: A Sufi Path of Transformation* (Boston: Shambhala Publications, 1999), 11.

[20] Hakim al-Tirmidhi, *Bayan al-Farq bayn al-Sadr wal -Qalb wal-Fu'ad wal-Lubb* (Cairo: Dar Ihya' al-Kutub al-'Arabiyya, 1958), 33.

[21] 'Abd al-Razzaq al-Qashani, *Istilahat al-Sufiyah* (Cairo1981), 162.

[22] Jürgen Wasim Frembgen, *Journey to God; Sufis and Dervishes in Islam*, trans. Jane Ripken (London: Oxford University Press, 2008), 5.

[23] Nicholson, *Studies in Islamic Mysticism*, 115, 238.

vehicle of knowledge and thought,[24] the locus of faith and piety as well as of disbelief,[25] that which is guided, shows mercy and compassion, is enlightened, contented, finds peace, the arena of struggle for both between angelic and satanic forces;[26] that which distinguishes between truth and falsehood, right and wrong, can choose between good and bad, the center of knowledge, awareness, thought and belief;[27] the point at which Divine light descends, the subtle faculty through which human beings attain their humanity, the target of arrows of grace and retribution, the object of beauty and glory, the source of openness (*bast*) and contraction (*qabd*), the origin of spiritual annihilation (*mahw*) and spiritual sobriety (*sahw*), the source of diseased morality and base conduct,[28] the site of both knowing and perceiving God,[29] the place wherein resides the potential of profound awareness and understanding of God,[30] the Divine gift bestowed—like the mind, eyes and tongue—to allow the acquisition of the wherewithal for eternal life and happiness;[31] the mechanism given to human beings by God, through which Divine realities are discerned;[32] the wellspring of Divine Names and Attributes, the vantage, observation point enabling remembrance (*dhikr*) and experience of utmost astonishment (*hayra*) of God;[33] the expression of a person's spiritual existence.[34]

As can be gleaned from these descriptions, while some emphasize the composition of the heart and 'what' it is, the others—and most of them at that—focus on its function and purpose as distinguished from its make-

---

[24] Reynold A. Nicholson, *The Mystics of Islam* (London: Routledge And Kegan Paul Ltd, 1970).

[25] William C. Chittick, *Faith and Practice of Islam* (Albany: White Cloud Press, 1992), 6; Toshihiko Izutsu, *Creation and the Timeless Order of Things* (Ashland, Oregon: White Cloud Press, 1994), 161.

[26] Türkiye Diyanet Foundation, *TDV Encyclopedia of Islam*, 37 vols. (n.d.)., "qalb."

[27] al-Razi, *Mafatih al-Ghayb*.

[28] Mahmud ibn 'Abd Allah Alusi, *Ruh al-ma'ani fi tafsir al-Qur'an al-'Azim wa al-sab' al-mathani*, 30 vols. (Beirut: Dar al-Fikr, 1997), I:134.

[29] Ismail Haqqi Bursawi, *Ruh al-Bayan*, 10 vols. (Istanbul: Mektebetu Eser, 1969), I:30.

[30] 'Abu Hafs 'Umar al-Suhrawardi, *'Awarif al-Ma'arif*, ed. Adib al-Kamdani and Muhammad Mahmud al-Mustafa (Mecca: Al-Maktaba al-Makkiya, 2001), 10.

[31] Said Nursi, *The Words*, trans. Şükran Vahide (Istanbul: Sözler Publications, 2008), 38.

[32] Said Nursi, *Signs of Miraculousness: The Inimitability of the Qur'an's Conciseness*, trans. Şükran Vahide (Istanbul: Sözler Publications, 2007), 100.

[33] M. Fethullah Gülen, *Prizma 6* (Izmir: Nil Yayınları, 2006), 80.

[34] M. Fethullah Gülen, *Kalbin Solukları* (Izmir: Nil Yayınları, 2009), 40.

up, as is the case in the Qur'an and the Prophetic Traditions. That is, 'what it does' is expressed, more so than 'what it is.' For instance, the heart's unknowability has been stressed, with reference to it as a "spiritual entity," while calling it "luminous" highlights its essence. The heart's being "the sum of all human potential" alludes to its dominance over all the other bodily organs and faculties and constitutes a different expression of this notion. By referring to "a human being's inner world," Tirmidhi (d. 320/ 922) offers in a succinct manner, his definition. Ghazali (d. 505/1111), the towering personality of Islamic thought and spirituality and famous with his title *Hujjat al-Islam* (The Proof of Islam), aspires to explain that the heart belongs to God rather than the human being, by defining it as the "Divine subtle faculty." It is perpetually the heart that knows, perceives, comprehends, interprets, sees, hears, thinks, believes and denies and it is, as such, a Divinely bestowed gift to human beings. And again as is evident from these definitions, while the point of departure for some of these depictions is a person's relationship with the Creator, others approach the topic directly from the perspective of the Creator's relationship with human beings.

Relationship between the Physical and Spiritual Heart

As is evident, scholars have defined *qalb*, in two ways: physical and spiritual or corporeal and immaterial. Diverse views have been propounded as to the nature of the relationship between the heart that is the piece of flesh and that which is defined as the "Divine subtle faculty." Ghazali refers to the close connection between these two hearts, but states that minds are in astonishment when it comes to the nature of this connection.[35] In addition to reference to the existence of a strong relationship between the heart's physical and spiritual facets, Ghazali, in brief, stresses the complex nature of this relationship.

It is possible to see many scholars espousing similar approaches both before and after Ghazali. One noteworthy example from the modern period is Muhammed Hamdi Yazır (d. 1361/1942)—twentieth century Turkish scholar of Islam who is most renowned for his Qur'anic interpretation—who also presents views along these lines. While Yazır states that scholars and philosophers have expressed amazement with regard to

---

[35] al-Ghazali, *Ihya,'* III:11.

this connection, its nature and the locating of the precise point in the body at which it is based, he also draws attention to the mysterious nature of the matter via a series of questions: "Is this connection to the physical heart first? Is it to the mind? Is it to just the nerves? Or to the complete body with its heart and conscience, veins, nerves, muscles and organs? Is it the relationship between one who sits and the place at which they sit? Is it akin to the relationship between a captain and a ship, between a head of state and their nation?[36]

In a similar vein, Adem Ergül's observations are also worthy of note:

> Just as the piece of flesh that is the heart is known as such because of its being located in the body's central region and being the very important essence ensuring the continuation of our material being, the luminous and spiritual intellect has been given the name due to its also being the essence of our spiritual being and the center of human reality. There is no doubt that the outer heart, the piece of flesh in the shape of a pine cone, and the spiritual heart that is the wellspring of life for all human feeling and perception are so inter-connected that they can be said to be two faces of a single truth. As can be understood from the verse stating, "it is rather the hearts in the breasts that are blind"[37] and the Prophet's saying that "piety is here" [38] while indicating his chest, it is virtually impossible to sepa-rate the spiritual heart from the physical one. It can also be said that the *hadith*, "There is piece of flesh in the body, the nature of which is that when it is sound, the entire body is sound, and when it is corrupt, the entire body is corrupt—it is the heart,"[39] too, indi-cates the association of physical and spiritual heart. Only, it is con-siderably difficult to reach a satisfying conclusion as to the exact nature of this connection and relationship.[40]

---

[36] Yazır, *Hak Dini Kur'an Dili*, I:211.

[37] (22: 46)

[38] Muslim, Birr, 32; Tirmidhi, Birr, 18; Muhy al-Din Abu Zakariyya Yahya b. Sharaf al-Nawawi, *Sharh Sahih Muslim*, 18 vols. (Beirut: Dar al-Qalam, 1997-1993), XVI:356; Muhammad Abdul Rahman b. Abdul Rahim al-Mubarakfuri, *Tuhfat al-Ahwazi*, 10 vols. (Beirut: Dar al-Fikr, 1995), VI:33.

[39] Bukhari, Iman, 39; Muslim, Musaqat, 107; Ibn Maja, Fitan, 14; Ahmad b. Muhammad al-Qastallani, *'Irshad al-Sari li Sharh Sahih al-Bukhari*, 15 vols. (Beirut: Dar al-Ku-tub al-'Ilmiyya, 1996), I:211.

[40] Adem Ergül, *Kur'an ve Sünnette Kalbî Hayat (Spiritual Life in the Qur'an and Sunna)* (Istanbul: Erkam Yayınları, 2000), 99.

Ergül thus approaches the matter in question via reference to Qur'anic verses and *hadith* and offers his interpretations based on the definitions transmitted above. But he admits, at the same time, the impossibility of making any final, clear word on the nature of the connection between these two hearts.

Words Close in Meaning to the Notion of *Qalb*

There are other words used in the Qur'an and the Prophetic Traditions synonymously with the word *qalb*. The extent to which these words overlap with *qalb* and the points at which they diverge in meaning has engaged linguists as well as exegetes and commentators interpreting the verses and *hadith* where these words appear. These terms are *fuad*, *lubb*, *'aql* and *sadr*.

Fuad

The root letters f-a-d forming the word *fuad* denote warmth and extreme heat. Its plural is *af'ida*. In Arabic, fried meat is referred to as *faid*.[41] According to Raghib, the heart's being referred to with this word is due to its being burnt through the different pains that it experiences.[42] With one of its dictionary definitions being movement and provocation, Zabidi, with reference to Firuzabadi, has preferred this meaning due to the dynamic nature of the heart.[43]

Just as there have been those who have referred to *fuad* as the heart itself, there have also been those who have referred to it as its outer casing. As such, the heart constitutes the essence and seed within that outer shell.[44]

Tirmidhi's following observation is significant in terms of its demonstration of the nuances above:

> Being the third of the stations belonging to the heart, *fuad*'s relation to the heart is as the pupil is to the eye, as Masjid al-Haram[45] is to Mecca, as the room within a house is to that house, as the walnut ker-

---

41 Ibn Manzur, *Lisan al-'arab*, 'f-a-d'; Asım Efendi, *Translation of Al-Qamus*, I:1232.
42 al-Isfahani, *Al-Mufradat*, 386.
43 al-Zabidi, *Taj al-'Arus*, IV:68.
44 Ibid., IV:69.
45 The Grand Mosque in the city of Mecca housing the *Ka'ba*, the 'House of God.'

nel is to the walnut. It is the site of *ma'rifa* (experiential knowledge of God), memories and dreams. When a person encounters something of benefit, first their *fuad*, and then their heart benefits. Just as a pearl is in the center of an oyster, the heart is in the middle of the *sadr* (bosom), and the *fuad* is at the center of the heart.[46]

While Tirmidhi devotes little time to the *fuad* due to its close alliance with *qalb*, he refers to it on the most part in terms of its relation to *qalb*[47] and in particular to how it differs therefrom.

The term *fuad*, mentioned in sixteen places in the Qur'an, is that which is accountable, which confirms or denies, is inclined or predisposed and punished. A few of these are provided below as examples:

> Do not follow that of which you have no knowledge (whether it is good or bad), and refrain from groundless assertions and conjectures. Surely the hearing, the sight, and the heart—each of these is subject to questioning about it.[48]

In this verse, the word translated as heart is *fuad*.

> God brought you forth from the wombs of your mothers when you knew nothing, and endowed you with hearing and eyes and hearts (*afida*), that you may give thanks.[49]

> "Our Lord! ... make the hearts (*afida*) of people incline towards them, and provide them with the produce of earth, so that they may give thanks.[50]

The plural form of the word *fuad*, *af'ida* has been employed in the last two verses. The Prophet, in one of his narrations, mentions these two terms in juxtaposition:

> "The people of Yemen have come to you, whose hearts (*af'ida*) are tender and are kind-hearted (*qulub*)."

---

[46] al-Tirmidhi, *Bayan al-Farq*, 38.

[47] Natalie A. Pavlis, "An Early Sufi Concept of Qalb: Hakim al-Timidhi's Map of the Heart" (McGill University, 2001), 57.

[48] (17:36)

[49] (16:78)

[50] (14:37)

The incident which led to his making such a statement unfolded as follows: When the Qur'anic chapter entitled *Nasr* was revealed, Prophet Muhammad was to recite it to his Companions, as he always did. The Companions gathered for this reason. When he started reciting with the first verse, "We have surely granted you a manifest victory,"[51] a delegation from Yemen had come and entered Islam as a group.[52] In another version of the *hadith*, Prophet Muhammad said the following as an expression of this verse: "The people of Yemen have come to you, and they are more soft hearted and gentle hearted people. The capacity for understanding religion is Yemenite and Wisdom is Yemenite."[53]

The word *riqqat* in the *hadith*, translated as 'tender,' means the opposite of hardness of heart, while the word translated as 'soft,' *lin* in the original, means tranquility, solemnity and reverence.[54]

All these meanings are those pertaining to the actions of the heart. Thus, it is possible to say that *fuad* and *qalb* share the same meaning, or that *fuad*, in certain situations, is a dimension of the heart that possesses its qualities.

Lubb

The word *lubb* means the essence of something, its most pure component. It for this reason that *'aql* has also been referred to using this term.[55] According to Imam Nawawi (d. 676/1277) the meaning implied in this word is the "mind's perfection."[56]

Some scholars, stating that the term *lubb* refers to the illuminated mind free of all kinds of stain and blemish, have emphasized the general difference between *'aql* (the mind) and *lubb*. As such, just as every person who possesses *lubb* is intelligent, every intelligent person cannot be said to possess *lubb*. Those who with the Qur'anic expression are *ulu al-albab*, or the People of Discernment, are those who best use their ability

---

51 (48:1)
52 Bukhari, Maghazi, 74; Muslim, Iman, 90.
53 Bukhari, Manaqib, 9; Maghazi, 74; Muslim, Iman, 84; al-'Ayni, *'Umdat al-Qari*, VIII:71.
54 Ibn al-Athir al-Jaziri, *an-Nihaya fi Gharib al-Hadith*, 2 vols. (Cairo: Dar al-Ihya' al-Kutub al-Arabiyya, 1963), 'r-g-g' and 'l-y-n.'
55 al-Zabidi, *Taj al-'Arus*, IV:474.
56 al- Nawawi, *Sharh Sahih Muslim*, I:146.

for sound thought and reasoning and are those with mastery in discerning between the beneficial and the harmful.[57]

In the view of Tirmidhi, *lubb* is analogous to the light of seeing in the eye, the light of the wick within the lamp, and the hidden oil within the kernel of the walnut.[58] He also describes *lubb* as the mind illuminated with Divine guidance.[59] Accordingly, a mind that has not discovered God is something other than *lubb*. Through this approach, Tirmidhi takes *lubb* a step further, directly associating it with belief. More interesting is the point that intellect, heart and belief become united through *lubb*.

Abdurrazzaq al-Kashani (d. 730/1329), describing *lubb* along similar lines as that of Tirmidhi, draws a connection between *lubb* and belief and defines it as "the mind freed from imagination and delusion and illuminated with Divine light."[60]

As a result, the term *lubb* is the mind illumined with guidance as opposed to the common mind. The following Qur'anic verse indicates that such a discerning mind can be found, not in those who disbelieve, but in believing people:

Who, when they hear speech, follow the best of it. Those are the ones whom God has guided, and those are the ones who are people of discernment.[61]

Even if the heart can be said to be synonymous with the notion of *lubb* due to its being the center of perception and feeling and constituting the essence of a person's corporeal and ethereal existence, *lubb* remains the name of the state of the mind—the faculty whereby the heart's most important function of belief, awareness, understanding and discernment is realized—illumined with belief in God.

Sadr

The word *sadr*, appearing in the Qur'an more than forty times in both its singular and plural forms, refers to such meanings as the forefront or

[57] al-Isfahani, *Al-Mufradat*, 446; Yazır, *Hak Dini Kur'an Dili*, IV:2939.
[58] al-Tirmidhi, *Bayan al-Farq*, 38.
[59] Ibid., 72.
[60] al-Qashani, *Istilahat*, 90.
[61] (39:18)

uppermost part of something,[62] its section, a side that one faces, the front section of the body from the neck to the navel. In addition, the term also encompasses the meanings chief and commander.[63]

Tirmidhi states that the *sadr* is the outer section of the heart. In his view, *sadr* is the starting point of the heart. It is the dwelling place of whisperings or suspicion, arrogance, enmity, carnal desire, and emotions of desire and need. It has a disposition that at times becomes contracted and expands.[64] At the time, *sadr* is the place where the light of belief and knowledge is safeguarded and protected.[65]

Verses which state that God knows all that the bosom contains constitute the references where the Qur'an most uses the term *sadr*. In one of these verses it is stated: "Keep from disobedience to God in reverence for Him and piety. Surely God has full knowledge of what lies hidden in the bosoms."[66]

In summary, it can be said that there is virtually no difference between *sadr* and *qalb*. These two concepts are very closely connected. Even when used distinctly, they are, nonetheless, very similar. For instance, the openness of the heart comes to mean the same thing as the heart's guidance

---

[62]   For instance, the head of a spear, a valley, a meeting-place or the start of the summer or winter months is referred to as *sadr*. (Ibn Manzur, *Lisan al-'arab*, 's-d-r'; Asım Efendi, *Translation of Al-Qamus*, I:464.)

[63]   al-Isfahani, *Al-Mufradat*, 276.

[64]   In describing the expansion and contraction of *sadr*, Hakim al-Tirmidhi presumably takes these verses as a reference: "Thus, whomever God wills to guide, He expands his breast to Islam, and whomever He wills to lead astray, He causes his breast to become tight and constricted, as if he were climbing towards the heaven. Thus, God lays ignominy upon those who do not believe (despite many signs and evidences)" (6:125). "Is he whose breast God has expanded to Islam, so that he follows a light from his Lord?" (39:22).

[65]   al-Tirmidhi, *Bayan al-Farq*, 35; 36. Tirmidhi bases these words too on Qur'anic verses. The Qur'an clearly states that hearts are located in the *sadr*: "...For indeed, it is not the eyes that have become blind; it is rather the hearts in the breasts that are blind" (22:46). The Qur'an indicates that knowledge is protected in the heart through the following verse: "It (the Qur'ān) is indeed self-evident, enlightening Revelations in the hearts of those endowed with knowledge" (29:49).

[66]   (5:7) The following verses also express this same matter: (3:29, 119, 54); (8:43); (11:5); (27:74; (28:69); (29:10); (31:23); (35:38); (39:7); (40:19); (42:24); (57:6); (64:4); (67:13).

and tranquility. The contraction and tightening of *sadr*, moreover, is synonymous with the heart's blindness and deviation.[67]

'Aql

The Qur'an places much value on the mind and makes frequent mention of it. In contrast to Western philosophy's sentimentalization of the 'heart' since the Cartesian turn, it should be noted that "the Qur'an assigns a clearly epistemic and intellectual function to the heart."[68] Although the word *'aql* (the mind, reason, intellect) itself is not used, it is mentioned, in its various verb forms, in forty-nine different places in the Qur'an. As far as the Qur'an is concerned, what matters is not the mind itself, but instead its functions. The heart too is considered from this standpoint and, as mentioned earlier, its functions as opposed to its composition are emphasized.

In the definitions that will be provided henceforth, the mission and functions of the heart are more so taken into consideration and presented, and not its structure.

The word *'aql*, with the derivation a-q-l, denotes something that deters from evil speech and action, the opposite of ignorance, preventing something from happening, prohibiting and persevering in something. In addition, knowledge with its beauty or repulsiveness, perfection or deficiency has also been described as *'aql*. There are also linguists who maintain, in short, that "knowledge is the mind."[69]

Raghib states that the power which serves the purpose of gaining knowledge, is *'aql* (reason). Again, he states that the knowledge one acquires through this means can also be called *'aql*, and supports his view by using the fourth caliph and cousin of Prophet Muhammad, Ali (d. 40/660) as a point of reference. Ali divides the mind into two components, namely *matbu'* (imprinted, innate) and *masmu'* (acquired). The first is the mind that one is born with and the second is that which is acquired later. Rea-

---

[67] Abu al-Fida Ibn Kathir, *Tafsir ibn Kathir*, 10 vols. (Riyadh: Darussalam, 2000), II:175.

[68] Ibrahim Kalın, "Reason and Rationality in the Qur'an," in *The 2nd Muslim - Catholic Forum* (The Baptism Site, Jordan2011), 15; Martin Lings, *What is Sufism?* (London: Unwin Paperbacks, 1988), 48, 49; William Stoddart, *Sufism: The Mystical Doctrines and Methods of Islam* (New Delhi: Taj Company, 1994), 63.

[69] al-Zabidi, *Taj al-'Arus*, 'a-q-l'; Ibn Manzur, *Lisan al-'arab*, 'a-q-l'; al-Firuzabadi, *Al-Qamus*, 1336.

son that is reproached in the Qur'an for not being used properly is *'aql masmu* and that which the lack thereof relieves a person of accountability is *'aql matbu*.[70]

One of the most renowned personalities of Sufism, Muhyi al-Din ibn al-'Arabi (d. 638/1240) states the following in his interpretation of this verse:

> Truth changes from one state to another, taking on various semblances and characteristics. The verse does not state, "there is counsel for one who possesses a mind," because thought is a limitation. The mind limits truth to a single quality. The truth, however, resists limitation. For this reason, the Qur'an is not counsel for one who possesses a mind. Those who think are the believers. As such, God ordains for "those who have a heart." In this way, just how the Truth changes from one form to another becomes clear.[71]

Through such an approach, Ibn al-'Arabi emphasizes that the heart does not merely consist of the mind. It contains much greater depth than the mind alone. Human beings receive counsel by means of their hearts. They evaluate and comprehend the realities they hear according to the level at which they experience the 'life of the heart.' Therefore, Truth and Reality are perceived and understood at differing degrees and depths in each person.

In addition, Ibn al-'Arabi also describes the sound mind as "a heart purified from false beliefs and remaining in the state in which it was first created."[72] This approach indicates that the mind can, for various reasons, lose its way and experience deviation.

At the time in which the early Sufis were delineating various spiritual systems, such as *qalb*, *nafs* and *ruh* in trying to make sense of human spirituality, Abu al-Husayn al-Nuri (d. 295/908) "saw in man (*sic*) four different aspects of the heart, which he derived in an ingenious way from the Qur'an."[73] According to Nuri, the heart has been created by God, as the center wherein human beings can meet with Him. The heart from the outside in is comprised of the nested layers *sadr*, *fuad* and *lubb*. These harbor Islam, belief and experiential knowledge of God, respectively. Islam

---

[70]   al-Isfahani, *Al-Mufradat*, 341; 42.

[71]   Muhy al-Din Ibn al-'Arabi, *Fusus al-Hikam* (Algiers: Mufam li al-Nashr, 1990), 122.

[72]   Ibid., 264.

[73]   Schimmel, *Mystical Dimensions of Islam*, 192.

mobilizes the outer layer, *sadr*. Righteous action activates the heart—the safe haven of belief. This process of spiritual development continues until only God's love remains in *fuad*.[74] Through bringing together the above-mentioned meanings, Nuri has attempted to establish unity in meaning.

Ghazali, maintaining that *'aql* encompasses myriad meanings, emphasizes two meanings in particular. The first of these is the mind's potential to know the reality of things, such that through this meaning, it is the name given to the attribute of knowledge contained in the heart. The other is the jewel within human beings which perceives knowledge. In such case, the mind is synonymous with the heart.[75] Linguists such as Ibn Manzur (d. 710/1311) and Zabidi (d. 1205/1791) have also defined *'aql* as the heart.[76]

Sharif Jurjani (d. 816/1413) also defines the mind and loads it with various meanings. The following definitions of the mind are some of those that overlap with those of the heart:

The jewel, albeit not material, which regulates and directs the activities of the body, the thing through which the reality of matter is known, and the jewel, which perceives the unseen through certain channels and the apparent through observation. He has defined the mind, moreover, as the light located in the heart, through which right and wrong, truth and falsehood are known.[77] Shah Wali Allah al-Dihlawi (d. 1175/1762) describes the mind as "the thing through which, by means of the senses, a person's feeling love and enmity, choice and resolve are realized.[78]

In Yazır's view, however, the mind is a Divine light whose substance is in the heart and spirit and whose radiance is in the intellect, and which perceives things that cannot be perceived by the sensory organs.[79]

As a final point, before an examination of the place and value that the Qur'an affords the mind, it is useful to note some of the meanings that Said

---

[74] Ahmet T. Karamustafa, *Sufism: The Formative Period* (Los Angeles: University of California Press, 2007), 15.

[75] al-Ghazali, *Ihya,'* III:114.

[76] Ibn Manzur, *Lisan al-'arab*, 'a-q-l.'

[77] al-Jurjani, *al-Ta'rifat*, 151; 52.

[78] Shah Wali Allah al-Dihlawi, *Hujjat Allah al-Baligha*, 2 vols. (Beirut: Dar Ihya' al-'Ulum, 1990), 88.

[79] Yazır, *Hak Dini Kur'an Dili*, I:566.

Nursi (d. 1379/1960) associates with the mind and the heart. Nursi states the following in one of his definitions:

> What is meant by the heart is the Divine subtle faculty (*Latifa al-Rabbaniyya*)—not the piece of flesh shaped like a pinecone—the emotions of which are manifested in the conscience and the thoughts of which are reflected in the mind.[80]

According to Nursi, as others have also articulated, the heart is a Divine subtle faculty. It is perpetually the heart that believes in God, knows and loves Him, feels reverence toward Him, shivers and shakes, and is filled with respect for Him; this heart has two important attributes, namely perception and thought. The dimension whereby the heart's emotions, perception, and discernment are manifested is the conscience, while the mirror on which thought and the like are reflected is the intellect. The intellect can also be called the mind.

Here, Nursi considers the mind as a function and operation of the heart. While stating that the heart is the source and site of knowledge, in his view it is essentially the dimension of the heart referred to as the mind that fulfils this function. Thus, there is no difference between the statements "it occurred to me that..." and "I had a feeling that..." In other words, it is always the heart that reasons, thinks, feels and perceives.

Notwithstanding this evaluation, Nursi also considers the mind in its own right and uses the term as such. For example, the mind is the light of life, its radiance, a person's most precious instrument,[81] the most valuable bounty bestowed upon them and the key unlocking God's Divine treasures and store of mercy.[82]

When explaining servanthood, Nursi emphasizes the need for believers to realize this duty through three aspects. In his view, a believer is charged in using their heart for surrender and obedience, their mind for faith and belief in God's unity, their physical being for action and worship.[83] By way of such an approach, by placing the onus of belief on the mind, he draws attention to its value. Acting as a mirror to the heart's ideas, the mind also serves the purpose of knowing God.

---

[80] Nursi, *Signs of Miraculousness*, 86.
[81] Said Nursi, *The Rays*, trans. Şükran Vahide (Istanbul: Sözler Neşriyat, 2007), 24.
[82] Ibid., 225.
[83] Nursi, *Signs of Miraculousness*, 173.

Elsewhere, Nursi touches upon the heart's abandoning its lofty task, together with the mind and the spirit, to participate and aid in the carnal self and base ego's contemptible acts. In such circumstances, these subtle faculties face the possibility of experiencing significant decline and deterioration and turning into base desire and ego. In actual fact, heart, mind and spirit have been given to human beings in order that they may fulfil their noble aims and purpose. When human beings misuse these instruments, squandering them in other places, the faculties—which possess the potential to elevate them to the station of the "perfected human being"—can fulfil the complete opposite function, uniting with the evil-commanding self and bringing the human being to their downfall and ruin.[84]

Considering the mind (which he at times addresses independently) within Nursi's wider classification, is not problematic. This is because it cannot be expected that he refer to the mind as a function of the heart and as the heart's dimension in relation to ideas and thought at each and every mention; this would pose great difficulty in terms of general expression and clarity of meaning. In any case, through his saying "the light of reason comes from the heart; there can be no reason without the heart"[85] in another statement where he associates reason with the heart, Nursi expresses his categorization in another form.

Hilm, Hijr and Nuha

As a final point, the Qur'an also uses the terms hilm, hijr and nuha synonymously with the mind. Hilm, denoting mildness and intellect and with its plural ahlam,[86] is mentioned in the Qur'an as such in the following way: "Do their minds urge them to such (absurd falsehoods), or are they a people rebellious and outrageous?"[87]

A classical Qur'an commentator Razi (d. 606/1209) maintains that the terms hilm and 'aql are synonymous and come to mean "holding the carnal self under control" and he associates a person's being mild in temperament to their self-possession and steadfastness. He also indicates the

---

[84] Said Nursi, *A Guide for the Youth*, trans. Şükran Vahide (Ankara: Ihlas Nur Publications, 2003), 19.

[85] Nursi, *The Words*, 739.

[86] Ibn Manzur, *Lisan al-'arab*, 'h-l-m,' 'h-j-r,' 'n-h-y'; Asım Efendi, *Translation of Al-Qamus*, IV:246.

[87] (52:32)

subtle nuance between *hilm* and the mind. In his view, the word *hilm* also denotes "nocturnal emission." Such discharge from a person signals their reaching puberty and, as a result, their becoming accountable for religious responsibilities. In this respect, God has correlated the mind with carnality and has made the emanation of carnality a sign of the mind's maturity.[88]

As is evident, the Qur'an has used words such as *fuad, lubb, sadr,* and *'aql* to mean heart and has used words such as *hilm, hijr,* and *nuha* in place of the word *'aql*. We can say that the Qur'an mentions all of these within the context of the various functions of the heart. It is also worth mentioning that the Qur'anic representation of the heart—with its multifunctional and just as intricate composition—through the use of different words is significant in terms of showing the importance that Islam places upon it. In such an understanding, heart and reason function as a conduit for gaining insight into the reality of things and how human beings should relate themselves to it. It is in this context that the Arabic linguists have identified *'aql* and *qalb* as being synonymous.[89]

Just as the heart has found extensive room in the Qur'an and the hadith, it has also greatly preoccupied Muslim scholars and has thus played an influential role in the shaping of Islam and especially its spiritual aspect. This, naturally, stems from its dominant position within the human being. Implied in the 'heart' is not just an organ, but on the contrary, a subtlety or essence of the human being that holds command over all the other bodily organs, limbs and faculties. It would not be erroneous to refer to the spiritual dimension of the human being as the heart: as can be gleaned from the definitions, the heart is the reality of the human being. When the heart, which is accepted as the source and center of such elements as intellect, perception, feeling, knowledge and belief, fails to use these faculties, the human being loses their humanity. From this perspective, so long as a person is thus, they are neither God's addressees nor religiously accountable. One of the most important aspects of the heart is its changeability and its being of a disposition that is amenable and susceptible to change. Within this context, the word 'changeability' is suitable for both ascent and decline. That is to say, the heart is able to change in such matters as thought, idea, love, knowledge and belief and a person's

---

[88]   al-Razi, *Mafatih al-Ghayb*, XVIII:221.
[89]   Kalın, "Reason and Rationality in the Qur'an."

alteration in for instance thought, love and belief, becomes another expression of their experiencing a transformation in the heart. It is also useful to recall at this point the heart's being presented for consideration as though it were a living being. In its discussions of it, it is meaningful that the Qur'an describes it as a living entity, attributing to it such qualities as soundness, disease, tenderness and hardness. Despite the heart's being a spiritual organ belonging to the person, its owner in the actual sense is God Himself. From this perspective, a person is unable to hold command, at will, over an organ within them and cannot give form to it as they wish. In such an understanding, the master and shaper of the heart is God. For instance, the heart can lapse or lose its existing state. As this is realized outside of a person's wish and will, the Qur'an teaches Muslims the supplication, "Our Lord, do not let our hearts swerve," and as such instructs them that it is only God who is the true owner of hearts.

PART I

Functions and Characteristics
of the Heart

Functions of the Heart

As can be understood from the definitions provided in the Introduction, the heart, in addition, serves as a source and shelter for "knowledge." From this point on, I will focus on these three aspects and attempt to better understand how the heart serves as both a wellspring and a locus for discernment, feeling and knowledge.

According to Islamic understanding, the most important function of the heart is its task of representing the relationship between human beings and God. In order for it to realize this mission to the utmost degree, the heart has been equipped with many qualities. As mentioned above, the heart possesses such characteristics as reason, understanding and comprehension, and—in the words of the Qur'an—*tadabbur* (contemplation) and *tazakkur* (remembrance). All of these indicate the heart's functions of "understanding and perception."

The Qur'an expresses certain aspects, again in regards to the relationship between human beings and God, directly as functions of the heart. Moreover, in the Qur'an, selected spiritual functions such as love, fear, reverence and humility have also been associated with the heart, albeit indirectly. Hence, it can be said that the heart has an important mission as the center of feeling.

Centre of Insight and Perception

The Qur'an's associating human beings' capacity for understanding and discernment directly with the heart is arguably the natural result of the heart's being a person's focal point. A close study of the Qur'anic verses dealing with the heart reveals that all of the heart's attributes and roles, whether positive or negative, are primarily and directly connected with its capacity to understand and perceive. Correct perception of existence, interpreting it in relation to its aims and purpose, and acting accordingly, can only be possible through the proper functioning of the heart's innate faculties of reasoning, discernment and comprehension.

Just as the Divine scriptures, as a manifestation of God's Attribute of *kalam* (speaking to humanity) are comprehended by the heart, the universe and the entire creation also, as manifestations of God's Attribute of *Qudrah* (power), can be perceived like a book by the heart.[90] Put differently, that which is to understand and comprehend both the Qur'an and the 'book' of the universe, is the heart. The Qur'an, in many of its verses, gives direction in order for these two books to be read and understood. For instance, while stating, "Do they not meditate earnestly on the Qur'an, or are there locks on the hearts?"[91] the Qur'an stresses the need for the heart to ponder upon the Qur'an and strive to understand its meaning. And through the verse, "Do they never travel about the earth, so that they may have hearts with which to reason (and arrive at truth), or ears with which to hear? For indeed, it is not the eyes that have become blind; it is rather the hearts in the breasts that are blind,"[92] the necessity of the heart's reading the book of the universe and contemplating its meaning is explained. If we are to express these meanings through the concept employed in the religious terminology, then the term *basira*, known as the 'eye of the heart,' fulfils the task.

The term *basira* is a word derived from the root *basar*, defined as sight, perception and eye in the dictionaries. It has been defined in general as "the power of a heart illuminated with Divine light to comprehend the reality of both material and immaterial existence."[93] Jurjani asserts that philosophers refer to this power of the heart as *quwwa al-qudsiya* (transcendental power),[94] while Ibn Qayyim (d. 751/1350) defines *basira* as "a light which God deposits in the heart of His servant."[95]

The word *a'ma*, literally meaning blind has been used as the antonym of *basira*. For example, those who fail to take heed of and learn from the disasters befalling former civilizations despite travelling the world, are described as those whose hearts have become blind. That the blindness mentioned here is spiritual is axiomatic. The following incident is nar-

---

90 Chittick, *The Sufi Path of Knowledge*, 212.

91 (47:24)

92 (22:46)

93 al-Jurjani, *al-Ta'rifat*, 46; al-Qashani, *Istilahat*, 64.

94 al-Jurjani, *al-Ta'rifat*, 46.

95 Ibn Qayyim al-Jawziyya, *Madarij al-Salikin*, 3 vols. (Cairo: Dar al-Hadith, 1983), I:139.

rated in many sources as the reason for this revelation of the verse about the subject in question: "When the verse, 'Whoever is blind in this (world), will be blind in the Hereafter,'[96] was revealed, the blind companion of the Prophet 'Abd Allah b. Umm Maktum (d. 15/36) came to the Prophet and said, "O Messenger of God! I am blind in this world, will I be blind in the Hereafter?" Upon this, the verse mentioned earlier[97] was revealed.[98]

According to the Qur'an, inability to use the heart's innate faculty of insight and perception is synonymous with inability to reason. This is because the Qur'an describes those who transgress as those who are unable to use their reason. As such, unbelievers, when they enter the fire, will suffer great remorse and will say: "If only we had listened (to him) or reasoned, we would not (now) be among the companions of the Blaze."[99]

Stating, "Indeed the worst kind of all living creatures in God's sight are the deaf and dumb, who do not reason and understand," the Qur'an also, stresses that those who do not use their intellect and reason are those who, in the eyes of God, are the worst of the living.[100]

The following verse also expresses this same meaning:

> Surely, among the jinn and humankind are many that We have created Hell. They have hearts with which they do not seek the essence of matters to grasp the truth, and they have eyes with which they do not see, and they have ears with which they do not hear. They are like cattle—rather, even more astray. Those are the unmindful and heedless.[101]

Along similar lines, adding that "they are deaf, dumb and blind, and so they have no understanding of (what is said to them)"[102] the Qur'an illustrates that the deniers are those deprived of the ability to see, hear, speak and perceive and, thus, makes reference to the function of the intel-

---

[96] (17:72)

[97] Do they never travel about the earth, so that they may have hearts with which to reason (and arrive at truth), or ears with which to hear? For indeed, it is not the eyes that have become blind; it is rather the hearts in the breasts that are blind (22:46).

[98] Qurtubi, *al-Jami,'* 52.

[99] (67:10)

[100] (8:22)

[101] (7:179)

[102] (2:171)

lect. In view of this, a person's hearing the truth, observing and taking heed of events and the lessons contained in them, and confirming and acknowledging the truth can only be realized through the use of their intellect.

Presenting such expressions used in the Qur'an to his readers in his own distinct way, Hamdi Yazır stresses the issue mentioned in the verse that causes a person's stooping to a level lower than that of animals. He first makes the point that those who reduce themselves to such a degraded level also possess a heart and, therefore, the potential to attain the level of a perfected human being. However, he states that they do not utilize their eyes and ears, as well as their hearts, and remain oblivious to those things that they need to hear and be cognizant of. He emphasizes that these people do not use the inner powers of the mind and of perceptiveness (sensation or feeling) in the way that is required of them. He underscores the fact that while they appear to be human on the outside, they are deprived of the meaning and consciousness distinct to human beings. Because they fail to develop their innate capabilities and, on the contrary, abuse these, they "cannot benefit duly from their primordial nature which is predisposed to improvement and is a candidate for eternal happiness," and consequently "head down a path leading to eternal torment."[103]

As such, the heart holds such a vital place in a person's constitution that, just as it can elevate them to a level surpassing the angels, it can, when not used appropriately, reduce them to a level even lower than that of animals. In other words, it can be said that a person is a person to the extent of their heart and the life of their heart.

Centre of Feeling and Emotion

Emotion is defined as "every type of experience which contains joy and sorrow."[104] An immaterial event or experience that is pleasant is joy, while one that is not, is sorrow. Qualities such as affection, reverence, love, mercy, compassion, happiness, serenity, hope, hopelessness, fear, dread, sadness, sorrow, anxiety, stubbornness, anger, hatred, enmity, revulsion, jealousy

---

[103] Yazır, Hak Dini Kur'an Dili, IV:2337; 38.
[104] Osman Pazarlı, Din Psikolojisi (The Psychology of Religion) (Istanbul: Remzi Kitapevi, 1982), 92.

and vengeance can be provided as examples of emotions. The site from which all these originate is the heart.

Human beings, by virtue of their creation, experience both pleasure and sorrow. Being affected by events in one way or another, being happy or not is within their natural makeup. This being so, this facet shows itself quite strongly in their religious lives also. Emotions can sometimes take control of a person so much that they get swept up in them and act in spite of their intellect and reason. While the Qur'an on the one hand stresses the foundation of belief being love and admiration,[105] on the other hand, through reference to those who idolize their lusts and fancies[106] and the notion that desires cover the heart, it draws attention to the way in which emotion directs a person.

In the verse, "But God has endeared the faith to you (O believers) and made it appealing to your hearts, and He has made unbelief, transgression, and rebellion hateful to you. Those are they who are rightly guided," religious sentiment is associated with affection and is presented as a function of the heart. Hence, it is not possible to separate belief from love and consider them independently of one another. Innate in human beings is the heart's need for deep attachment to another object and it is virtually impossible for this attachment to be realized without love. It is for this reason that the statement, "while those who truly believe are firmer in their love of God"[107] is also decreed. The believers do not take as associates those who take God as an enemy, even if they be those nearest to them, due to their love of God. Hence, from this perspective, it can be said that love is a test of faith. This notion is presented explicitly in the Qur'an:

> You never find a people who truly believe in God and the Last Day loving toward those who oppose God and His Messenger, even if they be their (own) parents, or their children, or their brothers (and sisters), or their clan. Those (are they) in whose hearts God has inscribed faith and has strengthened them with a spirit from Him.[108]

---

[105] (49:7)
[106] (25:43); (45:23)
[107] (2:165)
[108] (58:22)

The love between God and His servants, which rests upon faith, is thus a great Divine bounty. The following Prophetic Tradition is significant in terms of its illustrating the subject in question:

> O Allah! I ask You for Your Love, the love of those who love You, and deeds which will cause me to attain Your Love. O Allah! Make Your Love dearer to me than myself, my family and cold water.[109]

In Islamic understanding, just as loving God is of utmost importance, loving for the sake of God and disliking for the sake of God also possess great significance. It is for this reason that the Qur'an describes all believers as brothers and sisters.[110] The believers thus make the supplication, "O our Lord! Forgive us and our brothers (and sisters) in Religion who have preceded us in faith, and let not our hearts entertain any ill-feeling against any of the believers," in order to stay well away from any kind of illness of the heart marring these feelings of fellowship.[111]

Also underlying this Qur'anic supplication is the notion that hearts are in the hands and at the disposal of God. By saying, "let not our hearts entertain any ill-feeling against any of the believers," the believers express the fact that their hearts are in the control of their Creator. This same thread is also evident in the verse: "And hold fast all together to the rope of God, and never be divided. Remember God's favor upon you: you were once enemies, and He reconciled your hearts so that through His favor, you became like brothers."[112] Accordingly, it is only God who draws together and reconciles hearts. More generally speaking, it is God Himself who bestows all kinds of feeling and emotion upon hearts.

The feelings of mercy and compassion a servant feels towards creation are just as important as the heartfelt love, reverence, and fear that they feel towards their Creator. Loving the created by virtue of the Creator is, in one respect, loving God Himself. The Qur'an indicates the Divine origin of feelings such as mercy and compassion that reside in the heart as follows:

---

[109] Tirmidhi, Da'awat, 72.
[110] (49:10)
[111] (59:10)
[112] (3:103)

...We sent Jesus son of Mary, and granted him the Gospel, and placed in the hearts of those who followed him tenderness and mercy...[113]

The Prophet's responding with, "What can I do for you if God has removed compassion from your heart?" to someone who boasted that he had never played with his children or showed them his love, is important in terms of its indicating that mercy is a Divine blessing.

The following Qur'anic verse also draws attention to the notion that such qualities of heart as mildness and gentleness, as typified by the Prophet, are Divinely bestowed favors.

> It was by a mercy from God that (at the time of the setback), you (O Messenger) were lenient with them (your Companions). Had you been harsh and hard-hearted, they would surely have scattered away from about you.[114]

This verse was revealed in connection with the Battle of Uhud. During this battle, the second of the major battles in the early period of Islam, few of the believers had not yet understood the delicacy of obedience and did not comply with the Prophet's command. For this reason, the battle resulted against the favor of the Muslims. As for the Prophet, he said not a word after the Battle about those who did not obey his orders, and he made no statement that would cause discomfort to either them or the rest of the believers. This verse explains how gentle and gracious the Prophet's behavior was and describes this as a great mercy given to him by God. Had he not been as such, had he reproached those who abandoned their post against his command, held this against them, not shown leniency and been hard-hearted, then the believers would have dispersed from around him. This would have amounted to a great catastrophe.

In brief, it can be said that the heart's constitution being either tender or hard, together with a person's faith preferences for belief or disbelief has a direct bearing on the emotions and feelings created within the heart being either positive or negative. And this is directly related to the Will of God. That virtually all the Qur'anic verses mentioned here, as well as those not mentioned, touch upon the notion that sensation or feel-

---

[113] (57:27)
[114] (3:159)

ing has its source in God, is significant in terms of its illustrating the endless command that God has over the heart.

The Centre of Knowledge

Expressed in Islamic terminology in general through the terms *'ilm* and *ma'rifa*, knowledge has more exactly been understood to mean the relationship between that which knows (subject) and that which is known (object), or the end-result of the action of knowing being represented via a particular mode of expression. In the same way, because it is 'known" the word *ma'lumat* has been used to mean information or knowledge. A knower's encompassing and understanding their topic in all its facets and fields is known as *ihata*, their full comprehension of it *wuquf*, and their steeping themselves in their topic and mastering it *rusukh*. Illustrating the degrees of information or knowledge, these concepts also show that knowledge presents progression and continuity. Similarly, we see another classification with respect to the soundness and reliability of information. The delineation of the term *yaqin* used to express certainty in knowledge into the three categories of *'ilm al-yaqin* (certainty coming from knowledge), *'ayn al-yaqin* (certainty coming from direct observation or seeing) and *haqq al-yaqin* (certainty coming from direct experience), presents this idea in a lucid manner. Moreover, terms such as *zann* (presumption), doubt, suspicion, skepticism and distrust are used in opposition to the word *yaqin* to express the closeness or distance to certainty in knowledge.[115]

There are different views on whether or not the word 'knowledge' adequately reflects the term *'ilm* used in the Qur'an. Toshihiko Izutsu (d. 1415/1993)'s remarks in this regard are of note: The actual meaning of the word *'ilm* is "one's knowing something about something-'knowledge by inference.'" The word carries the same meaning whether in pre-Islamic poetry, or the Qur'an, or in poetry. However, the word's 'relational' meaning changes from system to system. Such change in meaning arises from the source from which it is derived. In the pre-Islamic period, known as the Age of Ignorance (*Jahiliyya*), *'ilm* meant sound knowledge based on personal experience. In this context, the term came to mean the opposite of *zann*, or subjective, and therefore, unreliable thinking. In the pre-

---

[115] Necip Taylan, "Bilgi," in *TDV Encyclopaedia of Islam* (Istanbul: Türkiye Diyanet Foundation, 1992), 157.

Islamic Arabian conception, the source of *'ilm* may have had its origin in tribal tradition. This knowledge was transferred from generation to generation within the tribe and therefore was knowledge with the authority of the tribe behind it. This is not different, in essence, from the first kind. As this knowledge was such that it was confirmed by many people within the tribe throughout the ages and handed down as a 'tribal asset.' In brief, it is possible to thus summarize the definition of *'ilm* for the Arabs in pre-Islamic Arabia: *'ilm* is sound knowledge guaranteed by personal or tribal experience and, therefore, the opposite of erroneous knowledge. As such, there is nothing that changes on the outside.

When the basis for validity of *'ilm* is examined, however, it is possible to see a change in an understanding of the concept in the two systems. That is to say, the source from which *ilm* has been derived has changed. The word *'ilm* in the Qur'an has been placed in the conceptual sphere of Divine revelation and associated with terms other than those it used to be associated with in pre-Islamic Arabia. Now *'ilm* is knowledge derived from none other than God's revelation directly. It is truth in the full sense of the word. So reliable is this source that when other sources are compared with it, they become by nature unreliable and unsound. When examined in this light, the old *'ilm*, considered sound due to its coming from one's personal or tribal experience is relegated to the degree of *zann*. For this reason, the vast majority of the knowledge accepted as reliable during pre-Islamic Arabia is now accepted as innately unreliable and groundless, as mere conjecture. Many Qur'anic verses lucidly depict this significant change. In summary, the word *'ilm*, when used in the Qur'an as a key word, denotes knowledge derived from an absolutely reliable source; this relational meaning of the term has also been transferred to Islamic theology. Here, the Prophetic Traditions (*hadith*) have also been accepted alongside the Qur'an as a true source of knowledge.[116]

A closer analysis of Izutsu's understanding reveals the following:

Alongside pointing to God as the source of knowledge, the Qur'an indicates that the knowledge human beings gain by means of their innate capacities can also be called *'ilm* (knowledge). For instance, in the chapter entitled Yunus (Jonah), knowledge regarding the years and months has been expressed as *'ilm*: "He it is Who has made the sun a radiant, illu-

---

[116] Toshihiko Izutsu, *God and Man in the Qur'an* (Kuala Lumpur: Islamic Book Trust, 2002), 55-60.

minating light, and the moon a light reflected, and has determined for it stations, that you might know the number of the years and to measure (time)."[117] Again, the Qur'an signals that instruments such as the ear, eye and heart have been bestowed as means to gain knowledge: "God brought you forth from the wombs of your mothers when you knew nothing, and endowed you with hearing and eyes and hearts, that you may give thanks."[118] Hence, the knowledge gained by means of these is also *'ilm*.

While the word *ma'rifa* is often used synonymously with *'ilm*, there are important nuances between the two terms. While the subject matter of *ma'rifa* is simple beings (*basit*), *'ilm* is the knowledge of 'composite' beings (*murakkab*). Moreover, *ma'rifa* is the realization of knowing something which is known to exist. In this sense being synonymous with *ma'rifa*, *irfan* is used to refer to knowledge about the being whose handiwork can be perceived, but whose self cannot. For this reason, the word *irfan* has been preferred over the word *'ilm* to refer to knowing God.[119]

Theologians throughout the history of Islamic thought considered the question of the heart's being the source of knowledge together with such concepts as *ilham* (inspiration) and *kashf* (discovery).[120] With regards to the source of knowledge, these scholars who generally do not accept sources other than sound senses, intellect and accurate account, have not accepted inspiration, as they have not considered it to allow for verification via objective criteria. The actual reason for their stance can be said to be preservation of the religion, for they generally do not deny inspiration altogether, but assert that it cannot be binding on others.

---

[117] (10:5)

[118] (16:78)

[119] Taylan, "Bilgi," 158.

[120] The dictionary definition of the term *kashf* includes such meanings as the removal of the veil upon something, the explanation of a matter or its being brought out into the open. In Sufi terminology however, it has been defined as coming to know of meanings and truths from the world of the Unseen—which cannot be perceived through the senses or with reason—by means of *wujud* (finding meaning within it) or *shuhud* (witnessing) (al-Jurjani, *al-Ta'rifat*, 184.). Inspiration on the other hand, a concept derived from the root *lahm* meaning "swallowing something at once," denotes "causing to swallow an object." As a term, however, it generally implies "the knowledge that cannot be gained through deduction being given, at once, to those whose hearts have been purified." (Ibn Manzur, *Lisan al-'arab*, 'l-h-m.')

In Islamic culture, as it is the Sufis who generally deal closely with the heart, it is they who have most defended its being the source of knowledge.[121] The first of these to come to mind are perhaps Ghazali and Ibn 'Arabi. Necip Taylan, elucidating Ghazali's theory of knowledge, has generalized the topic and espoused the following approach which can arguably hold true for all Sufis:

> The Sufis tend toward not the knowledge that is obtained through learning, but the knowledge which is derived from inspiration. For this reason, they do not aspire to read, study written works or research the proofs contained within them. On the contrary, they maintain that the method for acquiring knowledge is struggle with the carnal self, eradicating evil qualities, severing connection with everything and turning to God with one's entire being. When this is realized, God reigns supreme in and possesses the heart of His servant. When God reigns supreme in the heart, mercy descends there with ease (fayd) and light shines in the heart (ishraq), the sadr finds peace, the secret of the unseen is revealed to it (inkishaf), the veil of the heart is lifted with the blessing of mercy and the truths of the Divine mystery begin to shine in the heart. The responsibility falling upon the servant here is to purify the heart at the door of mercy which God Himself will open, preparing for this with a willpower embellished with good intention and then awaiting God's mercy.[122]

Considering the topic from the inverse perspective, Ghazali emphasizes some of the issues that can prevent knowledge from emerging in the heart. In his view, the heart's not seeking knowledge, not knowing that which is sought, pre-established convictions and beliefs in the heart and the accumulation of wickedness and impurities therein prevent the acquisition of knowledge.[123]

In his study on the Ghazali's supreme way to know God, His qualities and His acts—in Ghazali's view the highest objects of humanity's knowledge—Binyamin Abrahamov argues that while some scholars have held that Ghazali preferred the mystical experience as the best way to know God, others maintained that he regarded intellectual endeavors as the most

---

[121] Chittick, *The Sufi Path of Knowledge*, 107.

[122] Necip Taylan, *Ghazali'nin Düşünce Sisteminin Temelleri*, TDV Encyclopaedia of Islam (Istanbul: Marmara Üniversitesi İlahiyat Fakültesi Vakfı (İFAV), 1989), 92; 93.

[123] al-Ghazali, *Ihya,'* III:14.

effective and others, still, combined the two ways, Abrahamov maintains that Ghazali's best means to reach the knowledge of God is intellectual, whether occurring gradually or immediately. He states:

> There is no doubt now that *Iljam al-'awam 'an 'ilm al-kalam* is al-Ghazali's last work. Therefore, the views he expresses in it may reflect either the ultimate development of his thought... An examination of the text of *Iljam* proves that al-Ghazali believes in the superiority of philosophical as the best means to attain belief in God, which is equal to the knowledge of God, even if he admits that this way pertains only to the elect.[124]

According to Ibn 'Arabi, the heart is the center of *irfani* knowledge. He expresses his stance in this fashion: "Our knowledge is neither acquired from word and expression, nor from the lips of human beings, nor from books and pages: on the contrary, our knowledge consists of the manifestations emerging in the heart when one is overcome by *wajd* (ecstasy) and annihilates their existence."[125]

The views of Qur'anic exegetes in their interpretations of the verses dealing with the heart have differed in line with their accepting or rejecting the heart as the source of knowledge. While exegetes with an inclination to *tasawwuf* (Sufism) accept the heart as the wellspring of knowledge, those who emphasize the mind have understood the word *qalb*—mentioned particularly in juxtaposition with such words as *tafakkur* (reflection), *tadabbur* (contemplation), and *tazakkur* (remembrance)—to denote *'aql* and have expounded it as such. In addition, affirmation (*tasdiq*) and qualities pertaining to sensation or feeling have been ascribed to the heart by virtually all Qur'anic exegetes.

The connection that modern thinker Seyyed Hossein Nasr makes between *'aql* and *'ilm* is significant:

> Knowledge or science (*al-'ilm*) in the language of the Qur'an and the *Hadith* means that knowledge which makes man aware of God, of the eternal verities, of the world to come and the return to God... The Intellect, the instrument through which this type of knowledge

---

[124] Binyamin Abrahamov, "Al-Ghazali's Supreme Way to Know God," *Studia Islamica*, no. 77 (1993): 142.

[125] Muhy al-Din Ibn al-'Arabi, *Kitab al-Masa'il* (Damascus: Dar al-Mada, 2004), 113.

is obtained, which is at once the source of revelation and exists micro-cosmically within man, must not be mistaken for reason alone. The *'aql* is at once both *intellectus* or *nous* and *ratio* or reason. It is both the supernal sun that shines within man and the reflection of this sun on the plane of the mind which we call reason... Muslim sages throughout the ages have recognized this two-edged nature of the sword of reason. Some like Ghazali, Jalal al-Din Rumi and Fakr al-Din Razi have emphasized the negative aspect of purely human reason as veil and limitation and its inability to reach the Divine verities. Rumi in fact was very conscious of the difference between reason (*'aql-i juz'i*) and intellect (*'aql-i kulli*) when he said 'It is reason which has destroyed the reputation of the Intellect.' It would sheer folly to ignore these two aspects of reason by equating Islam with ratio-nalism instead of benefiting from the immense treasury of Islamic wisdom wherein this problem is elaborated, especially in the trea-tises of Sufism.[126]

Through these observations, Nasr prefers to view the mind, with its qualities of perception, comprehension and understanding, as a dimen-sion of the heart, rather than as a dry storehouse of information.

As mentioned earlier, the Qur'an states that human beings did not possess any knowledge when they were born, and that they could attain this knowledge through the use of their Divinely bestowed capabilities of hearing, sight and their heart, the vehicles of acquiring knowledge.[127] Again in some verses, those who are unable to use these faculties to attain knowledge are described as those whose hearing and sight are covered and whose hearts are sealed.[128]

Despite the explicit reference to the word *fuad* (denoting heart) in the verses mentioned above and despite the word *'aql* being employed

---

[126] Seyyed Hossein Nasr, *Sufi Essays* (Chicago: ABC International Group, 1999), 54-55.

[127] Verses exemplifying this include: "God brought you forth from the wombs of your mothers when you knew nothing, and endowed you with hearing and eyes and hearts, that you may give thanks" (16:78). "Do not follow that of which you have no knowledge, and refrain from groundless assertions and conjectures. Surely the hearing, the sight, and the heart—each of these is subject to questioning about it" (17:36).

[128] "Those who willfully persist in unbelief, it is alike to them whether you warn them or do not warn them; they will not believe. God has set a seal upon their hearts and on their hearing, and on their eyes is a covering. For them is a mighty punish-ment (in the Hereafter)" (2:6-7), Also see, (4:155); (7:100); (9:87).

not as a noun but as a verb related directly to the heart, we can say that in the history of Islamic thought *'aql* remained on the front burner at the expense of the heart as being the source of knowledge and the heart was virtually understood as just the hub of emotion and feeling.[129] Whereas the Qur'anic verse referred to earlier and whose translation is provided herein openly emphasizes the ability to think and reason as being a function of the heart:

> Do they never travel about the earth, so that they may have hearts with which to reason, or ears with which to hear (God's call)? For indeed, it is not the eyes that have become blind; it is rather the hearts in the breasts that are blind.[130]

Generally known to be functions of the mind, concepts such as *tafaqquh* (penetrating to the essence of a matter), *tadabbur* (understanding meanings completely), *tadhakkur* (grasping the general meanings) and *tafakkur* (reflection) are all associated with the heart in the Qur'anic text. What is more, the impossibility of reasoning and understanding where the heart is sealed or veiled is clearly stated. The single, unique vehicle through which the Divine speech that is revelation is transmitted to human beings is again the heart. The verse, "The Trustworthy Spirit brings it down on your heart, so that you may be one of the warners, in clear Arabic tongue,"[131] lucidly expresses this quality of the heart. Due to all of these reasons, the heart has been presented by scholars as the site in human beings that is held as addressee, which perceives, and is accountable.[132] In short, it can be said that the heart, by virtue of its being the essence of human reality, is the focal point of all human function and purposes.

The Centre of 'Amal

Defined as "work, effort, action and labor," the word *'amal* has been used in the Qur'an to mean "the intentional, purposeful thing which is put forth from a living being." As such, *'amal* is more specific in meaning than *fi'l* (action). This is because any particular intention or *qast* (clear decision)

---

[129] Ergül, *Kur'an ve Sünnette Kalbî Hayat*, 360.

[130] (22:46)

[131] (26:193-195)

[132] al-Jurjani, *al-Ta'rifat*, 178.

is not sought in action. It is for this reason that none of the actions associated with animals have been referred to as *'amal*. *'Amal* is the term that has been designated for the deliberate actions, or deeds, of human beings only, whether good or bad.[133]

That no deed will be futile or left without consequence is a Qur'anic rule. When Luqman advises his son, thus does he teach him this truth: ""My dear son! Whether good or evil, if a deed should have the weight of only a mustard-seed, and though it be kept hidden in a rock, in the heavens or in the earth, God brings it to light (for judgment). Surely God is All-Subtle (penetrating to the most minute dimensions of all things), All-Aware."[134] The verse, "And so, whoever does an atom's weight of good will see it; And whoever does an atom's weight of evil will see it" is another clear case in point.[135]

The word *'amal* in the Qur'an is mentioned in several places alongside the adjective *salih* (righteous). Due to the fact that the righteousness of a deed is directly related to the heart's inclination towards doing that particular thing, the concepts of *salah*, *irada* (will) and *niyya* (intention), and their relationship to the heart, will be examined as sub-headings henceforth.[136]

Salah

The Qur'an, in many of its verses, mentions *iman* (belief) alongside righteous deeds and, in this way, highlights the need for the belief that is to lead a person to success and happiness to be complete with *'amal*.[137]

---

[133] al-Isfahani, *Al-Mufradat*, 348.

[134] (31:16)

[135] (99:7-8)

[136] Frithjof Schuon, "The Quintessential Esoterism of Islam," ed. Jean-Louis Michon and Roger Gaetani (Bloomington, Indiana: World Wisdom, Inc., 2006), 275.

[137] Ergül, *Kur'an ve Sünnette Kalbî Hayat*, 366. The following verses can be provided as examples: "...whoever truly believes in God and the Last Day and does good, righteous deeds, surely their reward is with their Lord, and they will have no fear, nor will they grieve" (2:62). "But as for him who believes and does good, righteous deeds, for him the recompense of the best is due, and we will speak to him an easy word of Our command (we will charge him with easy tasks)" (18:88). See also: (5:69); (34:37); (100:3).

Describing righteous deeds as outwardly manifested *iman*,[138] Izutsu illustrates the extent of this relationship.

The definition of the word *salih* encompasses such meanings as deserving, appropriate, being good and at peace, and a thing's being in its proper place. The word *islah*, which denotes "correcting, reconciling, removing vice" and the word *sulh*, generally translated as peace, are derived from the same root.[139] *Salih* refers to a good person, who is careful in their worship and action, while *islah* refers to both goodness as well as working towards the goodness of others. The goodness in *islah* not purely neutral, but beyond this, the term encompasses the effort exerted towards others being good also. Where it is employed together with *'amal* in the Qur'an, the word *salih* is used as an adjective qualifying the noun.

With reference to the rule, "Things become known through their opposites," it is also useful to briefly mention the antonym of *salah*, namely *fasad*. The word *fasad* denotes "a corrupted, vitiated, perverted, marred, spoiled, deteriorated, or tainted, state; a state of disorder or disturbance, or of destruction, annihilation, consumption, waste, or ruin,"[140] or "a thing's distancing itself, whether in a small or great way, from the condition in which it ought to be."[141] In addition, the Qur'an uses the word *sū,'* meaning "a worldly or incorporeal thing which causes a person grief and sorrow,"[142] as the opposite of righteous deeds.[143]

While it may be possible to have some idea of a deed's being righteous or not through the dictionary definitions of the concepts in question, what is more important are the meanings that these concepts have acquired within Islamic tradition. A broad range of definitions has been provided with regards to righteous action. For instance, righteous deeds are "*fard* (compulsory) deeds" according to Ibn 'Abbas (d. 68/687), and "every kind of good deed" according to Hasan al-Basri (d. 110/728) and Qatada (d. 118/736). Hamdi Yazır's observations are overarching and to the point:

---

[138] Toshihiko Izutsu, *Ethico-Religious Concepts in the Qur'án* (McGill-Queen's Press, 2002).

[139] Mahmud al-Zamakhshari, *Asas al-Balaghat* (Beirut: Dar al-Tanwir, 1984), 257; Ibn Manzur, *Lisan al-'arab*, 's-l-h'; Asım Efendi, *Translation of Al-Qamus*, I:921.

[140] Lane, *An Arabic-English Lexicon*, VI:2396.

[141] al-Isfahani, *Al-Mufradat*, 379.

[142] Ibid., 252.

[143] (4:123, 124); (9:102); (41:46)

Righteous deed is performing good deeds that will earn God's approval in accordance with requirement of belief in the hereafter, in harmony with the proofs, judgments and tidings that God has revealed, and with complete sincerity and good intention.[144]

According to this description, a deed's being righteous or not has been tied to two conditions. The first of these is a deed's being in accordance with Islam and not being outside its boundaries; the other is the pursuit of God's pleasure or approval in the performance of the deed. Since the heart is the locus of perception and knowledge, the realization of these two conditions is directly connected to the heart. Since it is the heart which is to comprehend whether the action that is performed lies within the prescribed religious boundaries or not. We could also refer to this as the intellectual dimension of the heart. Again, in the same vein, a deed's being carried out in accordance with gaining God's approval is directly associated with intention, or "the heart's intent." This, in turn, can be associated with the heart's being the focal point of feeling and perception.

The foremost consideration in a deed's being righteous is *iman* (belief). Expressed differently, it is impossible for a deed to be righteous without belief,[145] as it is the spiritual condition of a person which assigns worth and value to any one of their actions. It is impossible to talk of the "consciousness of carrying out a deed solely to gain the pleasure of God" in a heart which disbelieves. According to Islamic understanding, the deeds of an unbelieving person do not hold any value, even though they be good, religiously speaking. Hence, the Qur'an openly declares the invalidity of the deeds of those who disbelieve and cause dissension. The verse, "Those are the ones whose works have been wasted in both this world and the Hereafter, and they have no helpers"[146] serves as an example of this point. Muslim scholars have stated that even the thought that the deeds of a disbelieving person may be righteous is itself erroneous. Taking into consideration this nuance, it is possible to suggest that calling their actions *'amal* is not even correct. From this perspective, a deed's being righteous or not is directly connected with the heart and belief.

---

[144] Yazır, *Hak Dini Kur'an Dili*, I:274.

[145] The connection between the heart and belief is to be examined in detail.

[146] (3:22) See also: (2:212); (5:53); (7:147).

Irada

Another issue that needs to be examined in explaining the role that the heart plays in *'amal* is that of *irada*, or willpower. The word denotes such meanings as "wanting, desiring, commanding, choosing and to release an animal into a pasture for grazing."[147] Explaining it as "aim, need and the force which arises from the sum of desire," Raghib states that it is a noun in the case of "the carnal self's taking action as a result of its decision to do or not to something." While the term is associated with these meanings when used in relation to human beings, when attributed to God it comes to mean "to rule" or "to judge." This is due to the fact that while the inclination to do or not do any particular thing is relevant when it comes to human beings, it is not possible to speak of inclination or tendency in relation to God.

While in the religious literature issues such as cosmic Divine Will and *irada juz'iyya* (minor human will) are generally elaborated in terms of a person's responsibilities and how they are fulfilled in the face of the infinite nature of the will of God, in psychology they are examined from the perspective of the relationship between a person's mental states and their actions; in philosophy they are considered alongside the problems associated with the more ethical concept of freedom. Nonetheless, it is possible to say that common to all of these approaches is the notion that in the formation of deeds, *irada* needs to exist first.[148]

As elucidated earlier, just as the Qur'an holds the heart as the focal point of God's connection with human beings, it simultaneously defines the heart as the hub of a person's feeling and emotion, perception, understanding and knowledge. Therefore, the heart, then, must be the place where *irada* also, as the wellspring of deeds, is formed. The heart, with respect to its representing the relationship between the human being and God and due to its comprising a person's inner power of perceptiveness, sensation and knowledge, has been likened to a sultan in the surrounds of the body with the other bodily organs and faculties being its soldiers and servants, by such scholars as Tirmidhi, Ghazali and Razi.[149]

---

[147] Ibn Manzur, *Lisan al-'arab*, 'y-r-d'; Asım Efendi, *Translation of Al-Qamus*, I:1149.

[148] Ergül, *Kur'an ve Sünnette Kalbî Hayat*, 362.

[149] Hakim al-Tirmidhi, *Nawadir al-Usul* (Beirut: Dar al-Kutub al-'Ilmiyya, 1992), 94; al-Ghazali, *Ihya,'* III:115-16. Fakhr al-Din al-Razi, *Kitab al-nafs wa al-ruh* (Islamabad: Islamic Research Institute, 1985), 51. Ghazali for instance separates the heart's sol-

The Prophet's stating, "Know that there is a part of flesh in the body. If it is healthy, the body will become healthy; if it is ailing, the body will be ailing. That part is the heart,"[150] has been indicated as evidence for this view. In the same way that the soundness of the heart affects the other organs in a positive manner, its corruptness naturally is also to have a negative impact on the other parts of the body. When *irada* is considered as having been given to human beings to enable them to realize the higher purpose of their humanity, the importance of the heart and its function in this sense emerges even more strongly.

Niyya

Niyya (intention) constitutes another and perhaps the most important expression of the heart's position of dominance over the human being. It is possible to link all of the *'amal* issuing forth from human beings in some way with the heart. So much so that the Qur'an, in describing the behavior and actions not carrying a heart-felt intention, uses the word *laghw*, meaning "disreputable."[151]

Just as the heart possesses a central position in relation to the development of deeds, it is also vested with great importance in relation to their being evaluated and judged. A deed's being righteous or not, its place in

---

diers into two groups: those observed with *basar* (the eye of the body) and those observed with *basira* (the eye of the heart); he includes the hands, feet, eyes, ears and the other organs as those seen with *basar*, and the faculties of *irada*, power and perceptiveness as those seen with *basira*. In his view, the connection between a person's physical-spiritual organs and their heart is akin to the connection between God and the angels. Just as the angels fulfil every Divine command without hesitation, the material and immaterial bodily limbs and organs in much the same way carry out the heart's orders. (al-Ghazali, *Ihya,'* III:115-16.)

[150] Bukhari, Iman, 39; Muslim, Musaqat, 107. The words *salah* and *fasad* mentioned in this *hadith* has been understood to mean the heart's being either spiritually righteous or corrupt and its resultant effect on the deeds performed by the bodily organs, as opposed to the *salah* and *fasad* of the physical body. The drawing of attention at the beginning of the *hadith* to the subject of the religiously permissible and prohibited is aimed at expressing the role of *halal* food on the heart's reform. Ibn Hajar, *Fath al-bari*, I:128.

[151] al-Isfahani, *Al-Mufradat*, 451. The verse expressing this meaning states the following: "God does not take you to task for a slip in your oaths, but He takes you to task for what your hearts have earned (through intention). And God is All-Forgiving, All-Clement" (2:225).

the eyes of God is always directly connected with the heart's intent towards that deed. The concept which represents this input of the heart to deeds is 'intention.'

So close in meaning is 'intention' to *irada*, briefly touched upon under the previous subheading, that it has sometimes been defined in the same way as *irada*. It has otherwise been considered together with the word *ikhlas* (sincerity), or doing something purely for the sake of God.

Egyptian Qur'anic scholar Abdullah Draz's (d. 1377/1958) observations regarding intention are worth mentioning:

> *Niyya* is the name given to *irada*'s focus which is directed to an action that will be, or is being carried out. *Niyya* denotes the virtually unchanging decision, intent and resolve at the commencement of carrying out an action. When this unchanging decision joins action, this being the most favorable state for *niyya*, it is the psychological consciousness which accompanies that action; that is, it is the behavior of *'aql* (reason) that is wakeful and ready in the act that it performs. *Niyya* is required in comprising all these three elements: planning that which is to be done, desiring to do it and being resolved in this desire.[152]

The interconnectedness of *irada* and *niyya* can be seen very clearly in Draz's observations.

The Qur'an emphasizes the two elements which direct a person's deeds, namely *irada* and *niyya*, thus:

> So whoever desires the reward of this world, We give him of it (in the world); and whoever desires the reward of the Hereafter, We give him of it.[153]

The famous words of the Prophet best illustrate the *'amal-niyya* relationship.

> Actions are judged according to intentions. Whatever you intend to do, you get the reward thereof. So, whoever emigrates for God and His Messenger has emigrated for God and His Messenger; whoever

---

[152] M. Abdullah Draz, *The Moral World of the Qur'an* (London: I.B. Tauris, 2008), 224; 25.
[153] (3:145) For similar verses, see: (11:15); (17:18, 19)

emigrates to acquire something worldly or to marry a woman emigrates to what is intended."[154]

Said Nursi also highlights the relationship between the two when he says that gaze and intention can change the constitution of matter. It can transform sin into worship and good deeds into sin. Indeed, intention transforms an ordinary, mundane action into worship and transforms worship which is performed for mere show or outward appearance into sin.[155]

The Qur'an makes frequent mention of sincerity and pure intention, which it presents as needing to be at the heart of worship. In one of these verses it states: "Say: "My Lord enjoins right and justice." Turn toward Him your faces whenever you rise to perform the Prayer, and call upon Him, sincere in your faith in Him and practicing the Religion for His sake. As He initiated you (in existence), so to Him you are returning."[156]

According to one report, a man approaches the Prophet and says, "O Messenger of God, sometimes I am overcome by such states that I perform certain actions for the sake of God; however, at the same time, I wish this state of mine to be seen by the people. What do you command O God's Messenger?" The Prophet does not answer this man and thereafter, the following verse is revealed:

So, whoever is looking forward to meeting his Lord, let him do good, righteous deeds, and let him not associate any partner in the worship of His Lord.[157]

There are many Prophetic Traditions which deal with the importance of intention in relation to the worth of deeds.[158] These Prophetic tradi-

---

[154] Bukhari, Bad al-Wahy, 1; Iman, 41; Muslim, Imara, 155; Abu Dawud, Talaq, 11; Tirmidhi, Fada'il al-Jihad, 16; Ibn Maja, Zuhd, 26. al-'Ayni, *'Umdat al-Qari*, I:30.

[155] Said Nursi, *Mathnawi al-Nuriya*, trans. Huseyin Akarsu (New Jersey: The Light, Inc., 2007).

[156] (7:29) See also: (4:14); (97:5)

[157] (18:110)

[158] The following two Traditions can be cited as examples: "A man came to the Prophet and asked, "O Allah's Apostle! What kind of fighting is in Allah's cause? (I ask this), for some of us fight because of being enraged and angry and some for the sake of his pride and haughtiness." The Prophet raised his head (as the questioner was standing) and said, "He who fights so that Allah's Word (Islam) should be superior, then he fights in Allah's cause." (Bukhari, Knowledge, 45; Jihad, 15; Muslim, Government, 150, 151) Al-Nasa'i reported that a man asked the Prophet, "What

tions demonstrate vividly that whatever the outwardly reflected words and actions of a person, their real value in the eyes of God is shaped according to the condition of their heart.

While the value of a particular deed in God's sight is intention and sincerity in that intention, a person's knowing completely the intention they hold in their heart is a rather difficult matter. That is to say, a person's performing any deed for the sake of God is not something that can easily be realized. This matter has greatly preoccupied such individuals as Ghazali and Muhasibi (d. 243/857)—who played a pivotal role in laying the groundwork for the former's intellectual framework—so much so, that they stressed the need to seek a 'hidden catch' in even the most apparently pure deeds.

Ghazali, for instance, expresses the gravity of the matter by saying, "Despite a person thinking that the most important catalyst is God's pleasure and approval, their hidden carnal desires can sometimes prevail. This is a very subtle, delicate matter and one that is very hard to discern. However cautious and guarded they may be, they can rarely be certain of their sincerity."[159]

Moreover, to be more precise, that which a person harbors in their heart or tries to harbor, the thoughts and ideas that they perpetually strive to keep fresh therein are considered their sincere intention. Perhaps the struggle they wage so as not to lose these represents sincerity, in and of itself. At this point it is useful to add the notion that the earnest intentions that a person cultivates within their heart can always be readily found. While a person may not know for sure the things that cross their heart in the short-term, their heart can possess a rather clear intention in terms of long-term matters. The following Qur'anic verse describing emigration alongside intention exemplifies this notion.

> Whoever emigrates in God's cause will find on the earth enough room for refuge and plentiful resources. He who leaves his home as an

---

is your opinion of one who fights seeking fame and reward?" The Prophet replied, "He receives nothing." The Prophet repeated this three times and then said, "Allah accepts actions that are performed for His sake Alone." (Nasa'i, Jihad, 24) It is quite plausible to suggest that the verb "to fight" in the narration can be replaced with "to worship," "to teach people about God," "to serve His cause," and any other deed that is done for the sake of God.

[159] al-Ghazali, *Ihya,'* IV:295.

emigrant to God and His Messenger, and whom death overtakes (while still on the way), his reward is due and sure with God. Assuredly, God is All Forgiving, All Compassionate.[160]

The Prophet, who associates the important personal, familial, social and economic changes in something so significant as emigration with righteous intention, in another narration heralds the one who dies in their bed with sincere intention, with the station of martyrdom, which is elevated in Islam.[161]

It can also be said that *niyya*, an action of the heart, also possesses the power to enable human beings to transcend their corporeality and, as a result, their finiteness. In actual fact, these can be clearly seen in the Prophetic Traditions just mentioned. According to Islamic understanding, a person will most certainly receive the results of the values that they hold in their heart and reflect, or are unable to reflect, in their day-to-day lives. However much the examples given in the Qur'anic verse and *hadith* are in reference to emigration and martyrdom, it would not be erroneous to generalize this. When one intends to do something that is within the boundaries of Islam, they are treated in the eyes of God as if having done it, even if they were unable to actualize their intention; this is what is meant by a person's transcending their finitude and impotence. The Prophetic Tradition, "A believer's intention is better than their action,"[162] reinforces this notion.

The following *hadith* is also important in elucidating the place, role and importance of intention:

Allah ordered (the appointed angels over you) that the good and the bad deeds be written, and He then showed (the way) how (to write). If somebody intends to do a good deed and he does not do it, then Allah will write for him a full good deed (in his account with Him); and if he intends to do a good deed and actually did it, then Allah will write for him (in his account) with Him (its reward equal) from ten to seven hundred times to many more times: and if somebody intended to do a bad deed and he does not do it, then Allah

---

[160] (4:100)

[161] Tirmidhi, Fada'il al-Jihad, 19; Ibn Maja, Jihad, 15.

[162] Ali al-Muttaqi, *Kanz al-'Ummal*, 19 vols. (Hyderabad: Da'irat al-Ma'arif, 1953), 419-25.

will write a full good deed (in his account) with Him, and if he intended to do it (a bad deed) and actually did it, then Allah will write one bad deed (in his account)."[163]

Hence, the act of goodness that is intended but not fulfilled comes back to a believer as a reward recorded in their book of deeds. The realization of any good deed enables one who performs it to receive at least ten times the reward. As for the person who intends to do evil, they are rewarded when the deed is not fulfilled and receive only a single bad deed in their book of deeds if it is.

As the possessor of an important function with respect to the actualization and worth of any deed, the heart is also in a position whereby it too is directly affected by the result of that deed. While those deeds that are righteous and sincere increase the heart's dynamism and serve as the means of its tranquility and happiness, those that are evil darken and corrode the heart and debilitate it. These issues will be examined in further detail in later stages of this thesis; however, it is important to state that the heart is affected by every kind of deed and is accordingly both positively and negatively impacted. At this point, it is difficult not to concur with Draz's following observations that he makes with reference to Ghazali:

The aim of commands pertaining to morality is not solely to establish justice in the world, but at the same time and in particular to enhance our worth through raising us above worldliness and animal appetites. For instance, the Qur'an maintains that the act of charity strengthens the soul, purifies a person and elevates their worth. According to Ghazali, the same is true for all good deeds. Their foremost aim is to engender change in the attributes of the carnal self. Ghazali says: "Placing the forehead on the ground in prayer has not been demanded as a goal in and of itself; but the reinforcement of the quality of humility in the heart through habit has been aimed at." These views of Ghazali are also significant when it comes to the heart-'amal relationship. If there has been an inclination towards doing something through a consciousness of the heart, this is strengthened through the deed that it produces. As long as one persists in carrying out the deed, this state virtually sustains that inclination and increases it. In contrast, when that inclination is opposed, this opposi-

---

[163] Bukhari, Riqaq, 77.

tion weakens, devastates and sometimes even annihilates it. For example, one who looks at a person with a beautiful countenance naturally inclines towards them. However, this inclination is weak at the beginning. Providing that they continue to look at, speak with and even frequently meet with that person, a powerful inclination they are powerless to resist would emerge. However, if they have taken, from the very beginning, the necessary precautions to stifle the desire in question, this inclination formed in the heart would weaken, due to its being left without sustenance, and consequently wither away. As can be seen, there is a close connection between the heart and the other limbs and organs. For this reason, one is affected by what the other does, the basis of which is the heart. The limbs and organs represent the servants that help the heart strengthen its various attributes.[164] Mawlana Jalal al-Din Rumi (d. 660/1262) too colorfully illustrates this connection, stating, "Hand and foot are plainly at command of the heart, like the staff in the hand of Moses."[165]

Andalusian Muslim scholar Ibn Hazm (d. 456/1064) reinforces the notion of the limbs and deeds supporting intention, illustrating that the work of the limbs is valuable in and of itself, not merely as an outcome of belief in the heart. In her study, entitled "With Heart, Tongue, and Limbs: Ibn Hazm on the Essence of Faith," examining what he believes to be the most essential characteristics that make one a Muslim, Jessica A. Coope argues that these fall into the three specific categories of belief held in the heart, profession of belief with the tongue and pious action of the body:

> Neither belief, profession, nor the two together can constitute *iman*, because works (*a'mal*) are an equally important aspect of *iman*. It is the importance of the work of the limbs, *'amal al-jawarih*, that Ibn Hazm defends most vigorously in the *Kitab al-iman*. By works Ibn Hazm means performance of *a'mal al-birr*, works of piety, including the five pillars of Islam and additional duties such as reciting the Qur'an; he also means abstaining from actions God prohibits.[166]

---

[164] Draz, *The Moral World of the Qur'an*, 242-43. For Ghazali's narrations see: al-Ghazali, *Ihya,'* IV:271.

[165] Jalal al-din Rumi, *The Mathnawi of Jalalu'ddin Rumi: Translation of Books I and II*, trans. R. A Nicholson (Cambridge: E. J. W. Gibb Memorial Trust, 1982), 194.

[166] Jessica A. Coope, "With Heart, Tongue, and Limbs: Ibn Hazm on the Essence of Faith," *Medieval Encounters* 6, no. 1-3 (2000): 108.

In sum, the heart-'*amal* relationship is a multifaceted one. The heart, by means of its attributes such as *irada* and intention, plays a central role in a deed's actualization. Through the *niyya* factor, the heart is the focal point of a deed's being accepted or rejected. Deeds, on the other hand, have a positive or negative influence on the heart. Put differently, '*amal*, after germinating in the heart, develops in the limbs and organs and eventually offers its sweet or bitter fruit to the heart. The heart, in one sense, reaps the fruits of the seed that it sows. '*Amal* is in a constant relationship with the heart, from start to finish. This, in turn, is clear proof of the heart's central and dominant position with respect to '*amal*.[167]

Conclusion

The functions and dynamics of the heart were explored in this chapter. We see here the heart's being the center of such functions as perception, insight, understanding, feeling, knowledge and reason. However, the heart manifests these functions in two ways: the heart perceives, understands, grasps, knows, feels these within its own self; the heart then directs the bodily limbs and organs in accordance with what it understands, perceives and grasps. While the first of these functions is incorporeal and intangible, the second is material. This is the case in both good and evil. The similitude of the heart's being the center of command, with it being the commander and the bodily limbs and organs its troops, is thus rather apt.

---

[167] Ergül, *Kur'an ve Sünnette Kalbî Hayat*, 372.

Characteristics of the Heart

U nder this chapter, the heart's qualities in the light of *hadith* and Qur'anic verses will be discussed. Implied in 'quality' is the heart's being open to every kind of influence. Within this context, its soundness and tenderness on the one hand and its being sealed, locked, diseased and hardened on the other can be provided as examples of positive and negative qualities respectively. The realization of all of these in relation to the heart is an indication of its fluidity and ability to change. As a result, the operative word of this chapter 'Characteristics of the Heart' will be 'changeability.' That its alteration can sometimes occur in the form of a process, or all at once has been considered. When looked at from the Islamic perspective, while the change of the heart towards God is considered as 'development' and 'growth,' other tendencies are deemed 'deviation' and 'lapse.' Accordingly, for instance, while its believing and its tenderness are positive, its unbelief and hardness are considered as being negative qualities. Here, the changeability of the heart, the ambit and measure of this changeability will be examined under separate subheadings.

The Qur'an expresses the development of the heart with the term *hidaya*[168] and employs the words *taqlib*[169], *zaygh*[170] and *sarf*[171] to describe its deviation. Muhammad has also drawn attention to these deviations and swerving of the heart, and expresses the fact that it can be subject to change in an instant with the narration, "The heart is like a feather in a desolate field, which the winds keep turning over and over."[172] He himself is said to have frequently repeated the supplication, "O God, O Converter of hearts! Establish our hearts firmly on Your religion." When

---

[168] (64:11)
[169] (6:109)
[170] (61:5)
[171] (9:127)
[172] Ibn Maja, Muqaddima, 10; Ibn Hanbal, *al-Musnad*, IV:408.

asked why he made this prayer so often, he said, "The heart is between the two Fingers of the All-Merciful; He turns it from state to state and gives it whatever form He wishes."[173] The Prophet's handling the heart with such care and meticulousness, his providing an example of himself when describing its changeability and his praying for its steadfastness has constituted one of the most emphasized matters in Sufism and has been accepted as being laden with meaning. Muslims have interpreted their own Prophet's having supplicated thus as exemplifying the absolute need and difficulty of preserving the heart. Such an approach has also increased the importance of the supplication for the heart not to swerve and deviate. More particularly, the supplication "Guide us to the Straight Path, The Path of those whom You have favored,"[174] taught in the Qur'an's opening chapter and its constant repetition in the Daily Prescribed Prayers has reinforced the value given to the supplication. If following the 'straight path' is necessary so as not to be subjected to the swerving of the heart, praying to God for His not changing the heart has been considered another prerequisite.

Factors Affecting the Heart

There are many factors that influence the heart, which is by nature susceptible to every kind of interplay and change. An attempt will be made to explain these under the subheadings God-Angel, Jinn-Satan and Human Being-Environment.

God-Angel

In Islamic belief, God possesses absolute will and power and encompasses everything.[175] He intervenes between a person and their heart,[176] guides hearts,[177] inscribes faith in hearts,[178] lays veils over some hearts,[179] and sets seal upon them.[180] All of these are the manifestations of God's domi-

---

[173] Tirmidhi, *Sunan,* Qadar, 7; Dawa'at, 89, 124.
[174] (1:6, 7)
[175] (41:54)
[176] (8:24)
[177] (3:8); (9:127)
[178] (58:22)
[179] (6:25); (17:46)
[180] (2:7)

nance over hearts, like His authority over everything else, and hearts being at His disposal. Such is the close connection that the Qur'an establishes between God and the heart.

Falling within the essentials of Islamic belief, the angels are also substantially connected with the human heart. According to the Qur'an, the angels—created of Divine light[181]—were brought into existence before humankind,[182] have wings,[183] glorify God alone by night and day, are tireless[184] and are but God's honored servants.[185] They have duties like bearing the Throne of God,[186] intervening in natural events,[187] asking God's forgiveness for those among His creation,[188] heralding the glad tidings of Paradise[189] and being keepers of the Fire.[190]

The verse that mentions the connection that the angels have with the human heart openly states that Archangel Gabriel brought revelation to Prophet Muhammad's heart.[191] Alongside expressing that the Qur'an was revealed to Muhammad's heart via one of the four greatest angels, as accepted in the Islamic faith, this verse also bears significance with its demonstrating the influence of an angel on the heart of the human being. The view that *ilham*, or inspiration, defined as one of the kinds of Divine revelation in Islamic thought, is also through the agency of angels is one that is accepted in religious understanding. In other words, angels have significant influence in directing human beings to goodness and beauty. The following Prophetic Tradition consolidates this belief:

---

[181] Muslim, Zuhd, 60; Ibn Hanbal, *al-Musnad*, VI:153.
[182] (2:30)
[183] (35:1)
[184] (41:38)
[185] (21:26)
[186] (69:17)
[187] (77:1-5)
[188] (40:7); (42:5)
[189] (41:30)
[190] (74:31); (66:6)
[191] The verse reads: "Say: Whoever is an enemy to Gabriel (should know that) it is he who brings down the Qur'an on your heart by the leave of God, (not of his own accord), confirming (the Divine origin of and the truths still contained in) the Revelations prior to it, and (serving as) guidance and glad tidings for the believers" (2:97).

Satan has some hold over the son of Adam and the angel has some hold over the son of Adam. As for the hold of Satan, it is reminding him of evil and disbelieving the truth. As for the hold of the angel, it is reminding him of goodness and believing the truth. Whoever find the latter, let him know that it is from Allah, so let him praise Allah. Whoever finds the former, let him seek refuge with Allah from the accursed Satan.[192]

As can be gleaned from the *hadith*, the positive inclinations and leanings that a person feels, like goodness, beauty and kindness are planted, or left in the heart of that individual by the angels. As explored earlier, feeling, like willpower and knowledge, is a dimension or profundity of the human heart. This positive feeling or leaning formed in the heart happens by virtue of the influence and agency of the angels, and of course with God's having creating it. Qushayri posits that this enlightenment of the heart occurs through the angels and adds that this does not contradict Islamic discourse.[193] Ghazali has also expressed the notion that out of the random thoughts, promptings and ideas which occur in heart referred to as *khawatir*, those which are conducive to goodness are placed in the heart by the angels.[194]

The Qur'an does not limit the angel-heart relationship to just these, but also adds, for instance, that the angels are sent for the believers to remain firm in time of fear. The verse, "When (in the meantime) your Lord revealed to the angels: "I am certainly with you, so make firm the feet of those who believe, I will cast fear into the hearts of those who disbelieve…"[195] serves to illustrate the certainty of the matter. Thus, in the Battle of Badr, God helped the believers who were much smaller in number than the Meccan polytheists, with "a thousand angels" so as to allow them "to have rest in their hearts."[196]

The angels have various different connections with humanity, and these relations occur between the angel and the human heart. While the heart of the human being is not mentioned in every verse that explains

---

[192] Tirmidhi, Tafsir, 2.
[193] Al Qushayri, *al-Risalah*, 84.
[194] al-Ghazali, *Ihya,'* III:142.
[195] (8:12)
[196] (8:9, 10)

the relationship between angels and human beings,[197] this association ultimately belongs to the heart. From the Islamic perspective, the unique source of this occurrence and any similar ones that are realized in a mysterious manner that human beings cannot feel or understand is the Qur'an and the words of Prophet Muhammad.

Jinn-Satan

The jinn, for whom an entire Qur'anic chapter was revealed and who are mentioned in many verses as being created from fire,[198] were created before humankind,[199] have the ability to move extremely fast,[200] can change shape, multiply, and have the responsibility of servanthood to God, like human beings. That they will also be punished or rewarded, like human beings, is also mentioned.[201] Iblis, who is said to be "of the jinn"[202] and otherwise known as Satan, should be considered from the same perspective. According to the Qur'an, Satan rebels against God and loses completely because of his persistence in this rebellion, is expelled from God's presence, despite this is granted respite until the Day of Judgment and is the greatest enemy of humankind.[203] In order to divert people from the straight path, he frightens them with poverty, makes empty promises, presents those things the carnal self would fancy as attractive, whispers

---

[197] This verse can be provided as an example: "As for those who say, "Our Lord is God," and then follow the Straight Path (in their belief, thought, and actions) without deviation, the angels descend upon them from time to time (in the world, as protecting comrades, and in the Hereafter, with the message): "Do not fear or grieve; but rejoice in the glad tidings of Paradise which you have been promised. We are your well-wishing comrades and helpers in the Hereafter, as we have been in the life of the world. You will have therein all that your souls desire, and you will have therein all that you ask for" (41:29-32). The believers don't have to see the angels when they 'descend upon them.' The angels come to encourage and console them and strengthen their hearts.

[198] The evil spirits are created by fire, which is qualified as *marij* and *samum*. *Marij* is "a smokeless fire," whereas *samum* is interpreted as a fire that can penetrate through the skin of the human body. (For more information see Yazır, *Hak Dini Kur'an Dili*, VII:4669.).

[199] (15:27)

[200] (27:39)

[201] (11:119)

[202] (18:50)

[203] (17:53); (43:62)

evil thoughts, causes humans to forget God... in short, does not stop for even an instant to lead human beings astray, coming upon them from their right and from their left, from in front of them and from behind them and stopping at nothing to inflict harm upon them. Satan wields considerable influence in misguiding human beings from the way of Truth. So much so that, for instance, after his expulsion from Paradise, he led Adam and Eve—who were still in Paradise—to commit the act that caused them to be driven from their abode, making them taste of the forbidden fruit and leading thereafter to their expulsion.[204] The jinn and Satan have the authority of direct influence on the human heart. This influence is clearly stated in the Qur'anic chapter entitled *Naas*.[205]

Consequently, the influence of Satan and those jinn aiding him on the human heart is clearly mentioned in many Qur'anic verses and *hadith*. By planting various thoughts, ideas and baseless misgivings into the heart, they desire that human beings turn away from and grow distant to God. Just as the human heart is open to angelic inspiration, it is also susceptible and exposed to the whisperings and incitement of Satan and others. As previously mentioned above, just as the heart has the capacity for all goodness and beauty, it is also predisposed and prone to evil. In the words of Ghazali, it is like a sea into which the purest, clearest waters flow and the dirtiest, murkiest waters are emptied. It is, at the same time, a target onto which Satan's poisoned arrows are fired. In a sense, Satan is nothing more than a power that increases the weaknesses prone to wickedness in the human being. If perchance a person wants to reject this power, then they are in the position to strengthen and develop the innate inclination to goodness that they carry inside of them.

Human-Environment

The first two subheadings were related to the unseen factors that influence the heart. The issue that will be discussed here pertains to the observable agents. The human being is perpetually influenced by other people and their environment. A social being, the human continues their life within a multifaceted web of interaction. Due to the fact that affecting a person in whichever possible way comes to mean a person's experienc-

---

[204] In relation to Satan, see: (7:11-25); (38:74-83).
[205] (114:1-6)

ing inclination with the heart, it can be said that to influence a person and to wield influence on that person's heart is one and the same thing.

The society in which a person finds themselves, the people that make up that society and elements such as culture, tradition and custom are the factors that influence the person directly. Hence, it is most natural for the human to be influenced by other human beings. It is arguably for this reason that Islamic understanding has it that Divine wisdom requires the Prophets be present in the world as highly influential personalities. They each assumed a place in society as individuals equipped with very unique and exceptional qualities—from their external appearance to the nobility of their lineage, from their power of oration to their charisma and appeal, all the way to their elevated morality—and realized their duty of Prophethood on such a footing. The sole addressees of the Prophets have been the hearts of human beings; it is here that they made their call and they strove to take people from the darkness to the light. Even this alone constitutes a powerful example of a person's interaction with other people.

At this juncture, the importance of eloquence in dealings with human beings is also relevant. A close examination of the Qur'an reveals that God wants from His Prophets to address people in a way that affects their hearts. Prophet Moses asks God to make his brother Aaron—more eloquent in speech than he—a helper to him and his request is accepted.[206] When going to the Pharaoh, God commands them to speak to him with gentle words, decreeing that the result would be more favorable.[207] Prophet Muhammad clearly articulates the power of words with his saying, "Some eloquent speech is as effective as magic."[208]

In addition to these, enjoining believers to "keep the company of the truthful,"[209] the Qur'an indicates another kind of influence, coming from other people and from one's surroundings. Those who keep company with the righteous, even if they are not righteous like them, will eventually end up taking on their hue and become as devoted as they are. This is the case in the negative sense, just as it is in the positive. It is apparent that evil brings with it evil. From this standpoint, Prophet Muhammad's

---

[206] (28:35)
[207] (20:44, 45)
[208] Bukhari, Medicine, 51; Nikah, 47; Muslim, Juma, 47; Tirmidhi, Birr, 79.
[209] (9:119)

likening those who associate themselves with good people to those who befriend sellers of musk, and those who keep company with bad people to those in a blacksmith's shop,[210] is important in terms of reinforcing the idea of such an interchange between people.

Just as the heart's being influenced from its surroundings can occur with respect to the social structure, it can also occur in a wider sense from the environment itself, through physical conditions and the Divinely established natural laws of God. This can be referred to as 'the heart's drawing lesson.' The following verse provides inspiration for this notion:

> Do they never travel about the earth (and view all these scenes with an eye to learn lessons), so that they may have hearts with which to reason (and arrive at truth), or ears with which to hear (God's call)? For indeed, it is not the eyes that have become blind; it is rather the hearts in the breasts that are blind.[211]

This verse openly wants of human beings that they be affected by their surroundings and to take heed from the past by means of examining both the lives of those who lived before and the historical ruins which remain. Travelling the world as much as possible and pondering upon the places that have been visited and the experiences gained therein are presented as a way of one's being conscious of their existence in the world and not repeating mistakes made in the past.

The Qur'an frequently asks its addressees to look at and draw lessons from the skies being raised, the earth being laid, mountains being set therein and the sun, the moon, the wind, the rain and plants. Here, the importance of the aforementioned action of the heart, *tafakkur* (reflection) becomes pronounced once again.

In summary, the human being, in continuing their life, is affected by virtually everything taking place around them. This impact happens in their heart and the person is shaped according to the leanings and inclinations of that heart. As stated before, the sultan of all the physical and spiritual faculties of the body is the heart. The heart influences and is influenced with its all dimensions. Herein, the issue of thoughts and imagination occurring to the heart will be briefly examined.

---

[210] Bukhari, Hunting, 58; Muslim, Birr, 146; Abu Dawud, Adab, 16.
[211] (22:46)

The Heart's Responsibility in View of Thoughts and Imaginings Occurring to It

That many thoughts, feelings and tendencies—beautiful and repugnant, good and wicked—occur to the heart, the center of the thought, emotion, is a matter generally accepted and acknowledged. The question of whether the heart is responsible for all of these and the issue of the heart's purification—famous among Sufis with the term *tasfiyya*—have been frequently deliberated upon. According to Ghazali, this is even a matter that every Muslim is religiously obligated to know.[212]

The word *khatir*, its plural form *khawatir*, comes to mean the passing thought that occurs to the heart involuntarily and the opinion, thought and that which is remembered as though moving within the heart.[213] The issues discussed under the heading 'Factors Affecting the Heart,' namely God, angels, the Jinn, Satan and environment, can be expressed as the source of *khawatir*. Just as these imaginations and thoughts can change from person to person, they can also differ according to the psychological state of each individual.

From the Islamic perspective, the heart's being the locus of willpower and its dominant position in directing a human being's behavior has been perceived as a clear indicator of its accountability for its actions. The verse, "Do not follow that of which you have no knowledge, surely the hearing, the sight, and the heart—each of these is subject to questioning about it"[214] is important in reinforcing this notion. Moreover, verses such as, "God does not take you to task for a slip in your oaths, but He takes you to task for what your hearts have earned (through intention), And God is All-Forgiving, All-Clement"[215] and "There is no blame on you because of the mistakes you may make unintentionally (in naming them), but what your hearts have premeditated (matters greatly). God is All-Forgiving, All-Compassionate"[216] illustrate that the heart is responsible for its voluntary intentions and leanings. Furthermore, the Prophetic Tradi-

---

[212] al-Ghazali, *Ihya,'* I:25.
[213] Al Qushayri, *al-Risalah*, 83; al-Qashani, *Istilahat*, 177.
[214] (17:36)
[215] (2:225)
[216] (33:5)

tion, "Allah has accepted my invocation to forgive what whispers in the hearts of my followers, unless they put it to action or utter it"[217] delineates the boundaries of such responsibility. These sources demonstrate that the passing inclinations and impulses occurring to the heart can each turn into an intention and purpose, and that responsibility begins with these being translated into action.

The thoughts and imaginations that occur to the heart but that do not gain permanence, however, are outside the realm of responsibility. At this juncture, reference to *irada* will be made and the role of this concept in unravelling this issue. It can be argued that even those thoughts and fleeting inclinations which a person brings to their heart through own their willpower, despite not being represented in action, can make a person accountable.

Positive Qualities of the Heart

In analyzing God's disposal over the heart, the heart's guidance, its tranquility, its steadfastness and its purification were examined. Again, under the heading 'The Heart's Turning to God,' its belief in God, its knowledge, love, remembrance and fear of God were discussed. In this section, beyond the heart's relationship with God, some of its states, within a more general framework, will be explored. Its positive qualities such as its soundness and tenderness and its negative qualities like its being sealed, heedless and hardened will be considered.

The Heart's Soundness

The Arabic word *salim*, derived from the root letters s-l-m, means to submit in obedience, to make peace, to accept a judgment, to be free of every kind of visible and hidden danger and illness, as well as slavery.[218] The soundness of the heart, however, has been defined as the heart free of disbelief and wrongdoing, purified from *shirk* and doubt, believing in God, the Hereafter and resurrection after death, clear of every kind of spiritual illness, free of bad character and adorned with virtue,

---

[217] Bukhari, Itk, 6; Muslim, Iman, 201, 202; Tirmidhi, Talaq, 8; Ibn Maja, Talaq, 16.

[218] Ibn Manzur, *Lisan al-'arab*, 's-l-m'; al-Isfahani, *Al-Mufradat*, 239.

and the heart shunning innovation in religion and that which is content with the *sunna*.[219]

The sound heart, from a similar perspective, been interpreted as a heart which is purified from all kind of shortcomings and mischief that contradict human nature,[220] free of disbelief and rebellion,[221] is purged of doubt, *shirk*, and the distraction of wealth and offspring,[222] sincere in its relation to God and His creation,[223] cleared of spiritual calamities and attachment to anything other than God,[224] cleared of spiritual calamities attachment to anything other than God.[225]

Although the word *salim* encompasses all the abovementioned definitions, it completely corresponds to the words *taslimiyya* (submission) and *salam* (peace) also derived from the same root. From this perspective, it can be said that the heart which is submitted to God and which is at peace with religion, is a sound heart. From the inverse standpoint, a heart which entertains doubts about or is displeased with its religion is definitely not deemed to be one that is sound.

The word *salim* is expressed twice in the Qur'an as an adjective in direct relation to the heart. It is rather interesting that both these verses are related to Abraham. According to the Qur'an the most striking aspect pertaining to Abraham's life is his utter submission to God. Even though he is sometimes commanded to do things seemingly contrary to reason,[226] he never hesitates to fulfil the Divine commands. When the Qur'an talks about Abraham, it says that Abraham was never one of the idolaters,[227] recalls his declaring, "I have submitted myself wholly to the Lord of the worlds" when his Lord tells him to submit,[228] explains that he had always

---

[219] al-Razi, *Mafatih al-Ghayb*, XIV:130. Qurtubi, *al-Jami,'* XIII:78. Ibn Kathir, *Tafsir*, VII:20; Alusi, *Ruh al-Ma'ani*, XIX:100.

[220] al-Isfahani, *Al-Mufradat*, 239.

[221] Mahmud al-Zamakhshari, *al-Kashshaf 'an haqa'iq ghawamid al-tanzil wa-'uyun al-aqawil fi wujuh al-ta'wil*, 6 vols. (Riyadh: Maktabat al-'Abikan, 1998), III:118.

[222] Qurtubi, *al-Jami,'* XIII:78.

[223] Ibid., XV:61.

[224] Bursawi, *Ruh al-Bayan*, VII:469.

[225] Yazır, *Hak Dini Kur'an Dili*, VI:4060.

[226] For instance, he is commanded to sacrifice his son Ishmael, and to leave his son and wife in the desolate desert of Mecca.

[227] (2:135)

[228] (2:131)

wanted to be a servant completely submissive to God,[229] that he bequeathed and enjoined this submission to his sons and recommended them to be submissive Muslims,[230] and that he surrendered himself, his son[231] and everything he possessed, to God. Furthermore, the Qur'an states that Abraham turned to God, destroying all the idols that were worshipped at the time,[232] and that he pursued certainty in belief with regard to God's existence, unity, and His endless power.[233]

In the first of the two Qur'anic verses containing the word *salim*, Abraham refers to a characteristic of the Day of Resurrection stating that the only thing that will help Muslims on that day is a "sound heart" (*qalb al-salim*).[234] The second verse declares that Abraham turned to his Creator with a sound and pure heart.[235] While Abraham prays for a sound heart in the first verse, it becomes apparent that his prayer is accepted in the second. Moreover in the first verse, followers of the religion of Islam are not warned by their own Prophet, but by Abraham, who fulfilled his duty of Prophethood to a specific community in former times.

In attempting to define the concept of the sound heart through the example of Abraham, there emerges a heart which is purified of idolatry, utterly submitted to and pleasing to God, that has found rest and one that is overflowing with belief.

Muhammad's supplication serves as confirmation of such an view:

> God, I ask You for steadfastness in my affairs, resolution in guidance, gratitude for Your bounties and acceptable service to You, and a truthful tongue and a sound heart. I seek refuge in You from the evil of what You know. I ask You for the good of what You know, and Your forgiveness for what You already know. Surely You are the Knower of the Unseen.[236]

---

[229] (2:128)

[230] (2:132)

[231] (37:102)

[232] (6:79)

[233] (2:260)

[234] The abovementioned verse is: "And do not disgrace me on the Day when all people will be raised up to life. The Day when neither wealth will be of any use, nor offspring, But only he (will prosper) who comes before God with a sound heart (free of all kinds of unbelief, hypocrisy, and associating partners with God)" (26:87-89).

[235] (37:83, 84)

[236] Tirmidhi, Dawa'at, 23; Nasa'i, Sahw, 61.

The Heart's Tenderness

On the basis of Qur'anic verses discussing the human heart, it can be said that tenderness is both the normal and natural state of the heart. The Qur'an condemns hearts that are hardened and the reasons for such, while on the other hand drawing attention to the sensitivity of heart in the believers while listing their qualities,[237] and also indicates their compassion and mercy.[238] As such, the heart's tenderness is its actual state, whereas its harshness and hardening are aberrations, tied to particular causes. The gentleness and subtlety in a person's behavior is indicative of their heart's being gentle and refined. When the dominance of the heart over other bodily limbs and organs is considered, their states will be realized according to the state of the heart. If the heart is tender and affectionate, then the person who possesses that heart will also be merciful and compassionate. Stating that the hearts of the followers of Jesus were filled with tenderness and mercy,[239] the Qur'an draws attention to this matter and stresses that the believers are also those who are compassionate towards each other. In this context, the Qur'an declares the tender-heartedness of Prophet Muhammad and asserts what a great God-given blessing this particular state of the heart is:

> It was by a mercy from God that (at the time of the setback), you (O Messenger) were lenient with them (your Companions). Had you been *harsh* and hard-hearted, they would surely have scattered away from about you. Then pardon them, pray for their forgiveness, and take counsel with them in the affairs (of public concern); and when you are resolved (on a course of action), put your trust in God. Surely God loves those who put their trust (in Him)."[240]

This verse was revealed in relation to the Battle of Uhud. During this battle, some of the believers were unable to truly comprehend the delicacy of obedience to a command and, because they abandoned their

---

[237] (8:2-3)

[238] (48:29)

[239] The relevant verse is: "Thereafter, We sent, following in their footsteps, others of Our Messengers, and We sent Jesus son of Mary, and granted him the Gospel, and placed in the hearts of those who followed him tenderness and mercy..." (57:27).

[240] (3:159)

posts before they were ordered to, they caused their own defeat and the loss of many lives. In such a situation Prophet Muhammad, as a result of his good character, treated them with gentleness and civility, not holding their actions against them, nor even making single mention of what they had done. Although they deserved to be rebuked, he was not harsh to them. The verse reveals that had he been severe and insensitive, the people would have scattered away from him, and that this would in fact have been the greatest disaster. From this incident, it becomes apparent that patience constitutes one of the dimensions of tenderness of heart.

Stating in addition that hearts can come to rest and soften with the remembrance of God, the Qur'an shows the way to reaching such tenderness of heart.[241] As such, it is possible for a heart that possesses an inherent tenderness, to become even more tender and gain permanence in this state as it remembers God. In addition, the way of turning the hardened heart back to its former, natural state is also indicated. In line with this, alongside functioning to both protect the innate state of the heart and to make it even more tender, remembrance of God is also a means to softening a hardened heart.

Negative Qualities of the Heart

According to Islamic understanding, alongside its positive characteristics, the heart also possesses certain negative ones. These are its hardening, swerving, its being sealed and its being diseased; these will hereafter be examined in the light of Qur'anic verses and *hadith*. These characteristics are especially significant with respect to their showing that the heart is not of such a disposition in essence and by default. The heart is normally not callous, but it can harden and become harsh. There is straightforwardness in its nature, but it is at the same time susceptible to deviation and transgression. Likewise, it can become sealed but by nature it is not. Not every heart is to lose its health and become afflicted with disease. These are anomalies that the heart is subsequently subjected to.

---

[241] (39:23)

Hardening of the Heart

Belonging to the Qur'an, the expression "hardening of the heart" is mentioned in many verses.[242] Here, the interpretation of one of such verses will be examined, with the views of Qur'anic exegetes being presented. The verse containing Divine admonition as well as guidance, reads:

> Has not the time yet come for those who believe that their hearts should soften with humility and submit (to God to strive in His cause) in the face of God's Remembrance (the Qur'an) and what has come down of the truth (the Divine teachings)? And (has not the time yet come) that they should not be like those who were given the Book before? A long time has passed over them (after they received the Book), and so their hearts have hardened; and many among them (have been) transgressors.[243]

The first part of the verse states that hearts would soften through remembrance of God and that with this softening they would be filled with reverence and awe towards Him, as earlier discussed. The second part explains how hearts can harden due to various reasons and that this would result in these hearts and the possessors of these hearts being led astray. In addition to these, the issue of *khashya* (reverence) is also discussed here. That the heart can become filled with fear, tremor and reverence in the event that it preserves its natural state and is nurtured with *dhikr*. Accordingly, reverence is the natural consequence and fruit of remembrance. The negative case of the positive one described above is also true, as the verse demonstrates. Therefore, just as it is not possi-

---

[242] These verses include: "Then, a while after that, your hearts became hardened; they were like rocks, or even harder, for there are rocks from which rivers come gushing; there are some that split and water issues from them; and there are still others that roll down for fear and awe of God. (Whereas your hearts are harder than rocks, and) God is not unaware and unmindful of what you do" (2:74). "If only, when Our trial came upon them, they had invoked Us with humility! But their hearts grew hard, and Satan decked out whatever they were doing as appealing to them" (6:43). "Is he (who derives lessons from God's acts in the universe, and so) whose breast God has expanded to Islam, so that he follows a light from his Lord (is such a one to be likened to one whose heart is closed up to any remembrance of God and, therefore, to Islam)? So woe to those whose hearts are hardened against the remembrance of God (and who learn nothing from His signs and Revelations)! Those are lost in obvious error" (39:22).

[243] (57:16)

ble for the heart which does not remember to be enveloped with *khashya*, it is virtually inevitable that it will become hardened with time and, as a result, deviate completely.

In analyzing this verse, Qur'anic exegetes associate the central issue of this verse with the Companions of Prophet Muhammad. There are two reports regarding the precise time this verse was revealed. According to the first of these, 'Abd Allah b. Mas'ud (d. 32/653) says: "There were only four years between our acceptance of Islam and the revelation of this verse, in which God subtly admonished us." The second narration belongs to 'Abd Allah B. 'Abbas (d. 68/687), known as the Interpreter of the Quran and the Scholar of the Community. He says that this admonition of the Muslims by God happened in the thirteenth year of Islam.[244] These narrations were taken into consideration in interpreting this verse.

When 'Abd Allah b. Mas'ud's narration is taken as a reference, it is possible to draw the following conclusions: In the first years of Islam, in its nascent phase, the Companions were warned and also rebuked with this verse. The time had come for them to undergo a period of purification; however, they had hitherto been unable to reach the level required of them and could not show sufficient effort and exertion to this end. God, therefore, warned them in such a manner and reminded them of their particular standing. That is, they possessed both the favor and responsibility of being friends of God's Messenger. They were in a position of closeness to the Prophet in every circumstance, where they were to embrace him and the message he brought, and to protect him, whatever the cost. By means of the rebuke they received early on, they reassessed their lives and demonstrated that they were worthy of being Companions to the Prophet.

In transmitting interpretations made of this verse, Razi relates the following from A'mash (Sulayman b. Mihran): "When the Companions emigrated from Mecca to Medina, they experienced greater prosperity in their living standards. When some of them went to excess in this matter, they were warned and rebuked with this verse."[245] Moreover, there are those who have said that this verse was revealed when joking among the

---

[244] Ibn Kathir, *Tafsir*, VIII:20.
[245] al-Razi, *Mafatih al-Ghayb*, II:230.

Companions increased.[246] Abu Hayyan says that this humor did not pertain to all the *Sahaba*, but only to those younger in age.[247] Alusi relates the following incident: Once Prophet Muhammad entered the mosque. Some of the Muslims in the mosque were laughing. Muhammad turned his face away from them and said, "Have you received a Divine edict stating that your Lord has forgiven you, that you are laughing so? A verse has been revealed in relation to your laughter." He then recited the verse. The believers then asked what they could do in penance, to which the Prophet replied, "Weep as much as you have laughed."[248]

Just as it can be understood to mean deliberating upon the Qur'anic verses that refer to God and the heart's softening and becoming tender as a result, the issue of the heart's softening through the remembrance of God can also be read to mean that *dhikr* should be performed not in heedlessness, but on the contrary, in reverence and awe and that the result of this would be the softening of the heart.

Mu'tazilite scholar Zamakhshari (d. 538/1144) relates an incident which is also mentioned by Razi: This verse is read in the presence of Abu Bakr (d. 13/635) and a group from Yamama, present at the time, start to sob as they hear the verse. Upon seeing them in this state, says: "We were like that in the beginning, before hearts became hardened."[249]

It is possible to interpret this statement within the context of Abu Bakr's humility. It is difficult to imagine that Abu Bakr, described as "tearful" by his daughter 'A'isha, experienced hardheartedness. With this attitude, he exemplified his humility, seeing others as spiritually higher and closer to God than him, despite being the closest person to Muhammad. Even deeming a sip of cold water to be a form of attachment to the world, he is said to have lived his life at such a level of self-criticism and interrogation that he assessed his not crying while listening to this verse as a sign of a hardened heart. Continuing his words with Hasan al-Basri's interpretation of this verse, Zamakhshari cites his address to the people of his day: "The Companions were rebuked with this verse because they started to read Qur'an less than you. This being the case, you should look

---

[246] Jalal al-Din al-Mahalli and Jalal al-Din al-Suyuti, *Tafsir al-Jalalayn* (Riyadh: Darussalam, n.d.), 539; Wahba Zuhayli, *Tafsir al-Wajiz* (Damascus: Dar al-Fikr, 1991), 540.

[247] Abu Hayyan, *al-Bahr al-Muhit*, 10 vols. (Beirut: Dar al-Fikr, 1992), IX:222.

[248] Alusi, *Ruh al-Ma'ani*, XXVII:179.

[249] al-Zamakhshari, *al-Kashshaf*, VI:48. al-Razi, *Mafatih al-Ghayb*, XXIX:230.

at how much Qur'an you read and the transgression growing within you." Again according to Zamakhshari, this verse demonstrates that hearts need to be enveloped with awe and reverence when reading the Qur'an. As such, he associates this verse with the one which reads, "The true believers are only those who, when God is mentioned, their hearts tremble with awe, and when His Revelations are recited to them, it strengthens them in faith..."[250] and interprets the trembling of the heart herein as *khashya*.[251]

Abu Hayyan (d. 745/1345) interprets the *khashya* in the verse as *ihbat*, which denotes tranquility and submission from the heart. The heart's being filled with reverence towards God is closely connected to its calm and commitment. Abu Hayyan substantiates this view with a Prophetic Tradition relating to *khashya*. Accordingly, Muhammad says, "The first thing that is removed from human beings is the reverence in remembrance of God."[252] This narration has been viewed as important with respect to its drawing attention to the close relationship between *dhikr* and *khashya*. The most salient feature of remembrance is the tongue's being an expression of the 'voice' of the heart. If the heart does not accompany the tongue in the recitation of God's Names, then this is not the required form of remembrance. On the contrary, a person's pushing themselves to recite God's Names with complete respect and mindfulness and their enveloping themselves in tranquility and total submission therein, is the fulfilment of remembrance in the perfect sense. In the event that this is not realized, the hardening, callousness and numbing of the heart with time becomes unavoidable.

In particular examining the last sentence of the verse "many among them (have been) transgressors," Ibn Kathir (d. 703/1373) stresses the nature of the transgression of the People of the Book. As such, the heart's hardening results in transgression and this has resulted in the corruption of their heart. Consequently, they made changes to their sacred scriptures and distorted them by disconnecting the words from their contexts. Because of this, they abandoned those deeds that were commanded of them and committed that which was prohibited. God thus forbids Muslims to fall into the same error and commit such alteration.[253]

---

[250] (8:2)

[251] al-Zamakhshari, *al-Kashshaf*, VI:49-50.

[252] Hayyan, *Bahr al-Muhit*, IX:222.

[253] Ibn Kathir, *Tafsir*, VIII:20.

For Sayyid Qutb (d. 1387/1967), there is affection and encouragement in this verse's reproach. The encouragement here is towards a consciousness and realization of God's greatness and majesty. Beneath this shadow of reproach, believers are enjoined to mention God with deference and are expected to internalize the message of 'truth' that He has sent down with the required reverence, thrill, obedience and submission, and imbue it into their spirituality.[254] Sayyid Qutb's interpretation of this verse, which at first glance seems like a warning and admonishment, is noteworthy and is rather significant in Islamic terms with respect to its stymieing the possibility of doubt and suspicion occurring in the heart in relation to the Companions. In this approach, there is not the inadequacy or failure of the Companions as seen or sensed in some narrations, but on the contrary, a motivation spurring them to even greater aims. The verse does not say, "Why haven't you become...?" but, as it were, declares "Ascend to even greater heights, do not be content with your current state."

The continuation of the verse explains that the People of the Book have taken their sacred scriptures for granted due to the great time passed since their having received them and asserts that they experienced consequent hardening of the heart. This connection can be explained as follows: Human beings possess a nature that with time acclimatizes and becomes accustomed to the conditions in which it finds itself. Just as it can adapt to conditions that seem on the outside to be the worst and most unbearable, it can sometimes develop familiarity towards the remarkable and extraordinary, with time seeing these as quite normal. This appears, in a sense, to be a blessing in order for life not to become insufferable. However, this same issue also has a negative and highly risky dimension, namely blinding a believer towards the blessings in which they find themselves. There are many things that human beings prize greatly that can in time become run of the mill and even lose their worth.

Through this verse and similar ones, first the Companions of Muhammad and then all the other Muslims are urged to look at themselves on the one hand, and are directed to lofty ideals on the other. The Companions, in particular, after living in the Age of Ignorance, had attained the status of being Companions of the Prophet. This was such a status that, alongside great advantages such as being forever remembered with Muhammad, it also brought with it great risk in this world and the Here-

---

[254] Sayyid Qutb, *Fi Zilal al-Qur'an*, 5 vols. (Beirut: Dar al-Shuruq, 1986), V:417.

after in the event that the associated responsibilities were not fulfilled. For this reason, the Divine message envisaged that they needed to be warned if only occasionally and reminded them of the important position they held. Those knowing the Qur'an best according to Islamic understanding, the Companions never experienced the process beginning with lack of *dhikr*, continuing toward hardheartedness and ending in transgression. They did their utmost to fulfil what was expected of them under the guidance and leadership of Muhammad. The Qur'an praised them, describing them as, "The first and foremost (to embrace Islam and excel others in virtue) among the Emigrants and the Helpers, and those who follow them in devotion to doing good, aware that God is seeing them—God is well-pleased with them, and they are well-pleased with Him, and He has prepared for them Gardens throughout which rivers flow, therein to abide forever. That is the supreme triumph,"[255] and held them up as an example for all humanity.

The subsequent verse, "Know that God revives the earth after its death (and He may revive the decaying hearts in the same way), we have indeed made clear the signs and Revelations (to enable such revival, and) that you may reason and understand"[256] is generally interpreted by the Qur'anic exegetes as being directly connected with the main Qur'anic verse in question. Providing a similitude, the verse draws attention to the fact that the earth is resurrected after its death. This is a change in the world that every human being can readily observe. Qur'anic exegetes, in considering the immediate positioning of this easily observable phenomenon after the verse at the center of this discussion, have posited that hardened hearts can soften and become revived through *dhikr* like the revival of the earth in spring. From another standpoint, preventing the heart's hardening from the very beginning and not giving cause for its death has received general acceptance.[257]

The Heart's Swerving and Its Being Sealed

As discussed under the previous subheading, the heart can for various reasons become hardened, despite not being so by nature, and thereby lose the sensitivity and delicacy in its natural endowments in spite of its

---

[255] (9:100)
[256] (57:17)
[257] al-Razi, *Mafatih al-Ghayb*, XXIX:231.

status as a Divine subtle faculty. It is always within the realm of possibility for the heart to deviate from the Straight Path and become closed to God. While there are many Qur'anic verses dealing with these two meanings, the most salient among these are the following two:

(They entreat God:) "Our Lord, do not let our hearts swerve after You have guided us, and bestow upon us mercy from Your Presence. Surely You are the All-Bestowing.[258]

God has set a seal upon their hearts and on their hearing, and on their eyes is a covering. For them is a mighty punishment (in the Hereafter).[259]

The first of these verses refers to the swerving of the heart and mentions that this swerving occurs after being favored with guidance. The term *zaygh*, derived from the root z-y-gh, means "to be inclined" and "to swerve." Although it is possible to translate the first part of the verse wherein this word is mentioned as "Do not let our hearts become inclined away or deviate from guidance," it is also possible to express this meaning with the statement "Do not let our hearts become enslaved to anything that can cause them to incline elsewhere." The Prophet's supplication, "O God! Do not let my heart swerve" has been interpreted as, "Do not direct my heart towards anything but belief."[260] The word *zaygh*, according to Mujahid, means 'doubt,' so the *zaygh* in the heart is dissension.[261]

In describing the situation of a person who has tended to disbelief, the Qur'an uses such words as *hizlan, zaygh, sadd, khatm, tab,' raan, qaswa, waqr* and *kinan*. In much the same way, it uses *tawfiq, rashad, hidaya, tasdid, tasbit* and *ismah* to describe the heart's inclination towards belief. Just as the heart has a capacity for positive faculties like belief and sincerity, benevolence and piety, it also has the potential to harbor negative qualities like disbelief and heedlessness, transgression, discord and arrogance. Only in the heart do traits such as love, inclination, longing, mercy, hatred and enmity emerge and develop. As touched upon above, the *raison d'être* of the heart is to house the positive of these traits and to direct

---

[258] (3:8)

[259] (2:7)

[260] Ibn Manzur, *Lisan al-'arab*, 'z-y-gh.'

[261] Abu Ja'far Muhammad ibn Jarir al-Tabari, *Jami' al-Bayan fi Tafsir al-Qur'an*, 30 vols. (Beirut: Dar al-Ma'rifa, 1986), VI:184.

the others towards goodness and righteousness. Asking for hearts not to swerve in the verse has thus been understood to mean wanting for them not to tend towards disbelief and misguidance and fall into vice.

The inclination of the heart mentioned in the verse has been interpreted in connection with the previous verse, which explains the efforts of some people who try to interpret the verses according to their own whims and fancies in order to cause dissension among the people and mislead them. So as to achieve this, they focus on *mutashabih* verses, or those that are open to various interpretations, and dwell upon these. The common characteristic of these people is the deviousness they harbor in their hearts. In describing the spiritual problem of these people, this verse uses the term *zaygh*, like the main verse at the center of this discussion. The latter constitutes a supplication not to be like these people who are audacious enough to try to change the essence of religion. The entreaty, "Do not let our hearts swerve after You have guided us" is also open to the following reading: "In showing us the way leading to your approval and allowing us to walk therein, do not allow any thought or imagination that can harm Your religion and give rise to its corruption to enter our minds. Do not allow our hearts, through such thoughts, to incline to anything other than You." In other words, this verse has also been interpreted as universal protection against every kind of swerving and transgression of hearts in the general sense and in the broader context. Exegetes in any case have commented on the verse's wider meaning, in addition to its more specific meaning. The heart's swerving and inclination in the verse have been expressed as being in opposition to guidance. As for the opposite of guidance, it is deviation in every sense and meaning that it signifies.[262]

Ibn Kathir interprets the verse as "Do not deviate our hearts from the guidance after You allowed them to acquire it. Do not make us like those who have wickedness in their hearts, those who follow the *Mutashabih* in the Qur'an. Rather, make us remain firmly on Your straight path and true religion." He defines the 'mercy' in the supplication at the end of the verse, "bestow upon us mercy from Your Presence," as the "(Mercy) with which You make our hearts firm, and increase our Faith and certainty."[263]

---

[262] Alusi, *Ruh al-Ma'ani*, III:89.
[263] Ibn Kathir, *Tafsir*, II:13.

'A'isha narrates that the Prophet made the following supplication when waking up at night:

> There is no god but You, glory be to You. O God, I seek Your forgiveness of my sins, and ask for Your mercy. O God! Increase my Knowledge. Do not let my heart swerve after You have guided me. Bestow upon me mercy from Your Presence. You are the All-Bestowing.[264]

Similarly, when 'A'isha asked Muhammad why he frequently repeated the supplication, "God, O Converter of hearts! Establish our hearts firmly on Your religion," she received the response that the All-Merciful could easily turn hearts to whichever direction He willed.[265] In addition to this narration, there is also that related by Anas: "The Prophet used to often say these words, 'O Turner of the hearts, make my heart firm on Your religion.' We said, 'O Allah's Messenger! We believed in you and in what you brought us. Are you afraid for us?' He said, 'Yes, for the hearts are between two of Allah's Fingers, He changes them (as He wills)."[266]

Issues such as the changeable nature of the heart and God's disposal over it in changing it however He wills, are significant in terms of reminding the human being not to rely on themselves. In the Islamic tradition, even the Prophet's concern in relation to this issue, despite being seen to have a faith which is strongest among the believers, and his constant praying for the steadfastness of his heart have been viewed as very meaningful. Thus, perhaps for this reason, in Sufi thought a person's seeing themselves as absolutely secure and assured of avoiding such pitfalls has been viewed as a very dangerous idea. The possibility of one day losing good deeds accrued, and beyond this, the fact that people will not be able to reach salvation through just their own deeds are among the matters most perturbing to Muslims. The Sufi tradition has developed a way of living between fear and hope that it has termed the balance between *khawf* and *raja*. From the vantage point of the Muslim, just as there is no absolute security there is also no absolute despair. On the contrary, remaining at a point between these, sometimes experiencing fear and sometimes having hope has been deemed the soundest path. Stated in the reverse, to

---

[264] Abu Dawud, Adab, 108.

[265] Tirmidhi, Qadar, 7.

[266] Sunan Ibn Maja, Du'a, 3834.

despair of God's mercy totally or to see entry into Paradise as assured is most certainly not the stance and attitude of a believer. Just as it is always possible to lose while on the path to success, it is always just as likely to free oneself from the gutter of failure and attain eternal triumph.[267]

From the Islamic perspective, God is always, so to speak, constructive and positive towards His servants. Whatever they incline towards and wish for, He creates, because He is the Creator of everything, but He does not approve of or sanction disbelief. If human beings know their Lord and praise Him, He is pleased.[268] In this sense, God's turning hearts to any direction that He wills is interpreted not from the perspective of an arbitrary treatment of His servants, but geared towards the human being not seeing themselves as secure from punishment and therefore constantly taking precautions against wrongdoing.

The word *zaygh*, meaning 'to swerve and 'to deviate,' can also be considered within a much broader field of interpretation. As such, the swerving of the heart can be understood not just as the deviation from faith to disbelief, but in addition any kind of negative change. In other words, just as there are many forms of disbelief, belief has within it many different degrees. From the Sufi perspective, while veering from belief to disbelief is considered deviation, experiencing descent in the degrees of belief is deemed to be another form of transgression. The former, of course, is deviation of the deepest and greatest scale, while the latter is not to this same degree. Some Muslims have even deemed a gap between their spiritual stations a deviation. Every believer can experience a kind of divergence and veering at their own personal level. The number of Muslims taking refuge in God from even a momentary spiritual deviation that would take them away from Him, is not small by any means. In a relevant *hadith*, Prophet Muhammad entreats God with the words, "O God! Do not abandon me to myself, even for the blink of an eye!"[269] seeking refuge in God from any kind of shortfall in his own lofty level.

---

[267] Gülen, *Key Concepts in the Practice of Sufism 1*, 38.

[268] This issue is mentioned in In Zumar, (39:7) as: "If you disbelieve in Him (in ingratitude), yet surely God is absolutely independent of you. He is not pleased with ingratitude and unbelief from His servants; whereas if you give thanks (and believe), He is pleased with it from you."

[269] Bukhari, Riqaq, 51.

The second negative quality of the heart indicated in the heading, is its becoming sealed, as explicitly expressed in the second verse mentioned above. In actual fact, the Qur'an does not only define the sealing of the heart, but also refers to the sealing of the ears and eyes. Employing the words *tabb,*' *khatm* and *rayn*[270] for the heart's being sealed, the Qur'an uses *wakr* (deafness)[271] for the sealing of the ears and *ghishawa* (veil)[272] for the eyes.

In discussing the heart's becoming sealed, Mujahid (d. 100/718), one of the prominent interpreters of the successors to the Companions, uses the similitude of the palm of a person's hand. Using the metaphor of the fingers of an open hand being closed in time, one by one with each sin that is committed, he explains that the heart which becomes partially soiled with every sin eventually becomes completely corrupted and thus sealed.[273]

Prominent interpreters Tabari (d. 310/923) and Ibn Kathir clarify the issue of the heart's being sealed with reference to a particular Prophetic Tradition where Muhammad states: "When the believer commits a sin, a black dot will be engraved on his heart. If he repents, refrains and regrets, his heart will be polished again. If he commits more errors, the dots will increase until they cover his heart." This is the seal implied in the Qur'anic statement, "God has set a seal upon their hearts and on their hearing."[274]

Alusi first imparts information pertaining to the heart in the section where he discusses the topic. In his view, the heart is the name of the luminous faculty into which Divine lights descend. The person is, so to speak, 'as human as their heart.' Their avoidance of unlawful things and fulfilment of the religiously ordained are related to the gains of the heart. As the heart is both the essence of spirituality and the target of arrows of wrath as well as of favor, it has been interpreted as *hakim*. It is the object of *jalali* and *jamali* manifestations[275], the origin of spiritual openness

---

[270] (83:14)

[271] (6:25/; (17:46)

[272] (2:7)

[273] al-Tabari, *Jami,*' I:258; Ibn Kathir, *Tafsir*, I:174.

[274] Ibn Kathir, *Tafsir*, I:175.

[275] In the Islamic tradition, God is said to have two kinds of Names: *jalali* and *jamali*, or those pertaining to His beauty and splendor and those pertaining to His wrath

and contraction, the starting point of *mahw* and *sahw*—annihilation in God and spiritual wakefulness or sobriety—and the source of both the morality leading to God's pleasure and approval as well as the base and abject states. It is an organ whose constancy in a particular state and permanence on a particular axis is small. And this is precisely why it is called *qalb*. Its being able to alter its condition is highly probable and when indeed it does happen, very sudden. In this aspect it is very much like a feather being scattered to and fro by the wind in a desolate field. It is the wellspring of all sense and perception in the human being. Both the depravity and righteousness of a person is contingent upon its disease or its soundness. With his statement, "There is a fleshy part in the body. If it is healthy, then the whole of the body is healthy. If it is corrupted, then all the body is corrupted. Beware! That part is heart,"[276] Muhammad draws attention to this close relationship and the role and importance of the heart in one's spiritual health.[277]

The heart that has reached this state no longer wants to hear of truth or righteousness; even if it were to hear, it does not accept that which it hears. The negative perception in their hearts also affects their ears and even if they do hear and listen, they persist in their denial. They spend their lives in this way. Veils emerge over their eyes. They do not read the universe like a book; they fail to see God's Names and signs in its every square inch. They live a life closed to the manifestations of God, to Whom everything points. The veils of oblivion, lust, wickedness, ingratitude and selfishness cover their hearts. They do not exert even the slightest effort to reflect. They are unable to reach the Creator by means of His creation.

Important at this juncture is the fact that the one who seals the hearts is God Himself. What appears at first glance is that God is cause of all these and that human beings are therefore excused of any blame. The matter, however, is altogether different. In assessing this issue, Alusi makes reference to the verse "...God has set a seal on their hearts because of their persistent unbelief, so that, with the exception of few, scarcely do

---

and majesty, respectively. The finest translation of these I have come across is 'severe compassion or compassionate severity.' See, Tariq Knecht, *Journal of a Sufi Odyssey: A True Novel, Book 3* (Tauba Press, 2010).

[276] Bukhari, Faith, 39; Muslim, Musaqat, 107.

[277] Alusi, *Ruh al-Ma'ani*, I:135.

they believe."[278] In line with this, unbelievers are subjected to sealed hearts because of their own evil actions.[279]

It can be argued that the human being will be held responsible for their inclinations, as they are the reason for God's creating them. That is, when the human being turns to sin and wrongdoing with their own will, God in turn creates that sin. In the Islamic understanding, God creates despite "not [being] pleased with ingratitude and unbelief."[280] His creation is not aimless or *ex nihilo*, but one taking shape, so to speak, according to the propensities and dispositions of human beings. It is for this reason that Muslims are deemed accountable for their actions in Islam. As according to a Prophetic expression, sin—resembling a black spot on the heart—remains in the heart if it is not erased through repentance and seeking God's forgiveness. As sin is committed, the blackness on the heart increases and in time takes on such a form that it completely covers the heart like a case, as it were.[281] As explained in the verse, "By no means! But what they themselves have earned has rusted upon their hearts,"[282] this heart has become corroded. This decay has been considered in the same way as its becoming sealed. The cause of this corrosion and sealing is the person themselves, with God being the Creator of that which they will.[283] The sealing mentioned in the verse being attributed

---

[278] (4:155)

[279] Alusi, *Ruh al-Ma'ani*, I:132.

[280] (39:7)

[281] In a *hadith* narrated by Abu Hurayra, Prophet Muhammad says: "When the believer commits sin, a black spot appears on his heart. If he repents and gives up that sin and seeks forgiveness, his heart will be polished. But if (the sin) increases, (the black spot) increases. That is the *raan* which Allah mentions in His Book: 'Nay! But on their hearts is the *raan* (covering of sins and evil deeds) which they used to earn.'" (Ibn Maja, Zuhd, 29; Tirmidhi, Tafsir al-Surat al-Mutaffifin, 1.)

[282] (83:14).

[283] When asked about the wisdom behind the creation of Satan and evil, Nursi responds: "The creation of evil is not evil, the acquisition of (*kasb*) or desire for evil, is evil. For creation and bringing into existence look to all the consequences, whereas such a desire looks to a particular result, since it is a particular relation. For example, there are thousands of consequences of rain falling, and all of them are good. If due to misuse of their wills some people receive harm from the rain, they cannot say that the creation of rain is not mercy or that it is evil. For it is evil for them due to their mischoice and inclinations. Also, there are numerous benefits in the creation of fire and all of them are good. But if some people are harmed by fire due to their misuse of it and their wills, they cannot say that the creation of

to God is arguably not figurative but instead entirely literal. This very point is the secret behind the concept of *tarbiya* or "nurturing process," the word commonly used to define Islamic education.[284] This is the difference, from the religious perspective, between insisting on a sin or not and this is why deeming the permissible to be prohibited and vice versa amounts to disbelief. Certain people remain in disbelief because they have corrupted their original nature, while others remain within the sphere of belief through the second nature they have acquired with their natural faculties and positive habits.

Stressing the same notion, Mawdudi (d. 1400/1979), a near contemporary Muslim scholar from Pakistan, is of the opinion that this is a natural law present in the scheme of things. If a person harbors bias towards a certain subject and constantly nurtures this in their heart, they cannot have any positive attitude towards that matter and cannot reach the truth by means of an objective approach. As he states:

> The Qur'an simply states a law of Nature: if one takes a biased view of something and deliberately nourishes prejudices against it in his mind, he can neither see any virtue in it nor hear anything in its favor nor open his heart to consider it dispassionately. This is the law of Nature and, as it is Allah's law, the act of sealing up of the hearts and the ears and the covering of the eyes has been attributed to Him.[285]

The Heart's Sickness

The heart's sickness is also a Qur'anic expression. When describing the hypocrites—those who outwardly profess belief but who are inwardly disbelievers—the Qur'an says that their hearts are sick.[286] This being the

---

fire is evil; because it was not only created to burn them. Rather, they made a wrong choice and thrust their hands into the fire while cooking the food, and made that servant inimical to themselves." (Nursi, *The Letters*, 59.).

[284] Kabir Helminski, *The Book of Language: Exploring the Spiritual Vocabulary of Islam* (Bristol: The Book Foundation, 2006), 53.

[285] Sayyid Abul A'la Mawdudi, ed. *Tafhim al-Qur'an*, 7 vols. (Istanbul: İnsan Yayınları, 1996), V:32.

[286] The verse in question reads: "In the very center of their hearts is a sickness (that dries up the source of their spiritual life, extinguishes their power of understanding and corrupts their character), and (because of their moral corruption and the tricks they deploy out of envy and malice) God has increased them in sickness. For them is a painful punishment because they habitually lie" (2:10).

case, Islam ascribes another negative meaning to a heart that is sealed and hardened and which experiences swerving and deviation.

Sickness has been defined as transgression of nature because of harmful circumstance. In the medical lexicon it is the opposite of health, or the original condition of wellbeing and freedom from disease or abnormality. Sickness, by virtue of its literal meaning, is evaluated in relation to its effect—it brings agony and pain. It is clear that physical illnesses exhaust the body, dampen everything else to the extent of its severity and bring a person to the point at which they are unable to function. In this sense, one of the consequences of illness is therefore a form of deficiency and deviation from perfection. Just as physical illnesses are like this, spiritual ones are viewed in the same way. Rancor, heedlessness, irregularities in belief, jealousy and other similar spiritual illnesses prevent the heart from functioning normally and healthily and forestall its development. The heart then cannot perform its actual duty and reach its Lord.[287]

The illness of the heart that is mentioned in the verse is afforded not a literal but a figurative meaning by Ibn Mas'ud (32/653), Ibn 'Abbas, Qatada and Mujahid.[288] In other words, the malady of the heart in this verse is not physical, but spiritual. The hearts of the hypocrites are full of various kinds of impurities that deter them from reaching any goodness and beauty, on the contrary reducing them to the lowliest of conditions. Ibn 'Abbas interprets the sickness of the heart to be doubt and hypocrisy. Individuals such as 'Abd al-Rahman b. Zayd (d. 24/644), Rabi' b. Anas (d. 140/757) and Qatada share the same view.[289]

For Hamdi Yazır, such issues as disbelief and doubt assume a secondary place in the heart and such situations are particular to sickness. Touching upon the notion that all children are born with the predisposition to believe in God, he states that this is innate. The capacity of belief in a Creator is not bestowed in order for a person to fall into doubt later on in their lives, but on the contrary to eschew this doubt, find the true path and through developing it, allow belief to form part of their disposition. For this reason, the heart's sickness is not coercive. Those who have brought their hearts to this state are taken ill in such ways because of

---

[287] Yazır, *Hak Dini Kur'an Dili*, I:227.

[288] Alusi, *Ruh al-Ma'ani*, I:150.

[289] al-Tabari, *Jami,'* I:280.

their egos or because they fail to use their willpower. Over time they believe in their suspicions, and this state in turn becomes their disposition and purpose.[290]

In the continuation of the verse in question, it is stated that God increases the sickness of those who have such disease of heart. Exegetes who have attempted to understand this section of the verse have evaluated it in light of certain verses in the Qur'anic chapter entitled *Tawba*. While these verses explain that the revelation increases the belief of believers, they also assert that those in whose hearts is a sickness belittle God's revelation and add denial to their denial.[291]

The heart's sickness is the expression of the corrupted view of the hypocrites towards affirmation of the Prophet and the Divinely inspired message that he conveyed, as present in their religious doctrine. They approached the Prophet with suspicion and wholeheartedly surrendered neither to *shirk* nor to the Prophet. Their hearts have in effect been dragged to and fro.[292] The Qur'an points to their particular psychology with the verse, "That is because they declared faith but thereafter (inwardly) disbelieved, so a seal has been set on their hearts so that they do not grasp the truth (and cannot recover the ability to reach it)."[293]

The operative word in such a discussion is arguably *irada*, or willpower. Those who are subjected to spiritual illnesses have come to this point as a result of their willpower and individual inclination. As Ali Ünal vividly illustrates:

---

[290] Yazır, *Hak Dini Kur'an Dili*, I:227.

[291] The verses in question are: "Whenever a surah is sent down, there are some among them (the hypocrites) who say: "Which of you has this strengthened in his faith?" As for those who believe, it does strengthen them in faith, and they rejoice in its being sent down and in the glad tidings (they receive thereby). But as for those in whose hearts there is a sickness (that dries up the source of their spiritual life, extinguishes their power of understanding, and corrupts their character), it increases them in foulness added to their foulness, and they die while they are unbelievers" (9:124, 125).

[292] al-Tabari, *Jami,'* I:280. This verse depicts this position of the hypocrites: "Vacillating between (the believers) and (the unbelievers), neither with these, nor with those. Whoever God leads astray, for him you can never find a sound way (to follow)" (4:143).

[293] (63:3)

A person gets his or her just deserts in recompense for his or her inclinations, thoughts and actions. A person wills and acts, and God creates. Creating human deeds means giving "external" existence or reality to human will and human actions. The Qur'ānic statements cited above mean that, in response to people using their will-power in a certain direction and acting in that direction, God has given "external" or "visible, material" existence to their intentions, choices and actions.[294]

Moreover, the idea that when these people want to free themselves from this negative predicament God still leaves them therein with His own will is totally contrary to Islamic belief. On the contrary, God informs that He will judge human beings, first and foremost, with mercy.[295] From this perspective, there is nothing saying that their condition will continue in such a manner. The ones who reform themselves can be freed of these kinds of illnesses and continue their lives like other believers.

Conclusion

In this chapter, the heart's characteristics continue to be elucidated. That which differentiates this chapter from the previous ones is its looking at the external, immaterial factors influencing the heart. These include, God, the angel, the jinn and Satan. Despite its clearly defined nature and functions, as was previously defined, the heart possesses an extraordinary susceptibility to external factors. Furthermore, the heart's positive and negative qualities, in light of the Qur'an and the *hadith*, have been described in depth. These positive and negative outcomes emerge as a result of the external influences described herein. Thus, the heart can become ill when sound and harden while tender. These are all the result of external influences.

---

[294] Ali Ünal, *The Qur'an with Annotated Interpretation in Modern English* (New Jersey: Tughra Books, 2008), 63.

[295] Bukhari, Tawhid 15, 22, 28, 55, Bad'u'l-Khalq, 1; Muslim, Tawba, 14.

Heart in the God-Human Relationship

This chapter constitutes the backbone of this thesis. In the previous three chapters the heart's nature and functions were expressed from different perspectives, while here the most important mission of the heart in Islamic thinking, that is its relationship with its Creator—God, will be discussed.

What I aim to stress here is that from the Islamic standpoint, like everything else, the heart is also under God's control and command. It is "between the two Fingers of the All-Merciful; He turns it from state to state and gives it whatever form He wishes."[296] At the same time, as mentioned earlier, the heart possesses such dynamics as *irada*, *qast* and *niyya*. As such, and in this respect it is both free and accountable for its actions in the eyes of God.

This issue will be examined under the subheadings "Divine disposal of the heart" and "The heart's turning to God" respectively.

Divine Disposal of the Heart

The God-Human relationship has continued its presence and dynamism since human beings first emerged on the field of existence. The first human on earth, also being known in Islam as the first Prophet, is the most explicit indicator of this. It is said that the chief mission and duty of the Messengers and scriptures sent by God is oriented towards shaping this relationship. At the fore of this connection is the matter of a person's belief in

---

[296] Tirmidhi, Qadar, 7; Da'awat, 89, 124. There are also verses clearly expounding this matter. These two can be provided as examples: "Just as they did not believe in it before, and We confound their hearts and eyes, and leave them blindly wandering in their rebellion." (6:110) "(They entreat God:) "Our Lord, do not let our hearts swerve after You have guided us, and bestow upon us mercy from Your Presence. Surely You are the All-Bestowing." (3:8)

their Creator, described in the language of the Prophets as 'calling to faith' in the Qur'an.[297]

Whatever the form and nature of the association between God and human beings, that which renders this contact and communication possible is the heart. It is arguably for this reason that—as mentioned under the conceptual framework heading—the heart has been called the Divine subtle faculty. One of Nursi's definitions of the heart that will be described in detail later in the thesis, is that of the heart being an "Intermediate Realm" or *barzakh* between the Corporeal or Visible Realm (*'Âlam Shahada*) and the Unseen Realm (*'Âlam Ghayb*), the relevance and significance of which is great in terms of explaining the God-human relationship.

Rumi also emphasizes the heart and presents it to purview from his own unique standpoint and with his particular style. One of his most striking interpretations with respect to the heart is his likening it to an 'interpreter.' In the couplet in which he states, "The heart acts as an interpreter between the *'arif* and the *ma'ruf*, or the knower and the known,"[298] the heart is a translator between the human being, who is in the position of knowing/becoming acquainted with God, Who is in the position of the One Who is Known. The word 'interpreter' is rather accurate and evocative. Accordingly, the heart is like a mediator for the purpose of knowing the Creator and understanding His purpose and will. The human being is obliged to use their heart in order to procure all of these with respect to God. The heart thus contains such capacity and facility geared towards gaining knowledge of God.

One of the underlying tenets of the Sufi system of thought is the heart's being a 'mirror.' Mawlana too uses this trope and likens the heart to a mirror which reflects the realm of the unseen. Love of the world and carnal desires blur and tarnish this mirror, while cleansing it of these impurities serves as a means for it to fulfil its actual mission.[299] A heart that is

---

[297] One of these verses is as follows: "Our Lord! Indeed We have heard a caller calling to faith, saying: 'Believe in your Lord!' so we did believe. Our Lord, forgive us, then, our sins, and blot out from us our evil deeds, and take us to You in death in the company of the truly godly and virtuous." (3:193) See also: (7:59, 65, 73); (11:50); (16:32)

[298] Mawlana Jalal al-Din Rumi, *Diwan-ı Kabir*, vol. 6 (Istanbul: Remzi Kitabevi, 1958), 2722.

[299] Rumi states the following: "When the mirror of your heart becomes clear and pure, you will behold images (which are) outside of (the world of) water and earth."

oriented to the world and preoccupied with it becomes soiled and in this way is unable to realize its *raison d'être*. A purified heart entrusted to the protection of God will be able to see and read the Names of God manifested ubiquitously and will be able to know and become closely acquainted with the Creator, the Owner of those Names. Rumi vividly depicts this point in the following way:

> You will behold both the image and the image-Maker, both the carpet of (spiritual) empire and the carpet-Spreader.[300]

With these interpretations, Rumi presents the notion that the transition from the Name to the Essence is realized through the agency of the heart. In this way, by means of gazing upon the handiwork of the Creator, the heart possesses the ability to seek and find the Great Artisan. Rumi also likens the heart to a 'city.' By means of this approach, and in the same vein, he again connects its actualizing its mission to its being kept free from impurity and blemish.[301]

God's knowing the heart, His intervening between a person and their heart, His expanding and contracting the *sadr*, leaving it in heedlessness, causing it to harden and sending the heart astray are among the topics that will be addressed in this section.

Knowing the Heart

Al-'Alim, one of the Divine Attributes meaning the All-Knowing, is an expression of God's knowing everything hidden and out in the open, all that has happened and is to happen and His encompassing everything, all time and space with His knowledge. One of the verses depicting this is the following:

See: Ibrahim W. Garnard and A. G. Rawan Farhadi, *The Quatrains of Rumi: Ruba 'iyat-i Jalaluddin Muhammad Balkhi-Rumi* (New York: Sophia Perennis, 2008). Book II/70. Rumi touches upon this issue again with this couplet: "...polish it...So that the forms of hidden (things) may appear in it, (and so that) the reflections of the virgins of Paradise and the angels may leap into it." Garnard and Farhadi, *The Quatrains of Rumi*. Book IV/2470.

[300] Rumi, *The Mathnawi of Jalalu'ddin Rumi*. Book II/70.

[301] The relevant section reads: "Don't stir (the heart) up so that the water may become clear and (so that) you may see the moon and stars circling in it. Because man is like the water of a river; if it becomes muddy, you can't see its bottom." Garnard and Farhadi, *The Quatrains of Rumi*. Book IV/2480.

He it is Who has created the heavens and the earth in truth. Whenever He says, "Be!" it is. His word is the truth. And His is the Sovereignty on the day when the Trumpet is blown, the Knower of the Unseen and the witnessed. He is the All-Wise, the All-Aware.[302]

'ilm, one of the most oft-mentioned concepts used in the Qur'an, in its various forms, refers to the complete comprehension and grasp of something.[303] Since God is the Creator of everything that takes its place on the stage of existence, there is nothing more natural than His knowing His creation, as is axiomatic in this verse: "Is it conceivable that One Who creates should not know? He is the All-Subtle, the All-Aware."[304] Some of the verses which refer to God, the All-Knowing, Who especially knows the heart are as follows:

God knows (O people) whatever is in your hearts. God is indeed All-Knowing, All-Clement.[305]

God was assuredly well-pleased with the believers when they swore allegiance to you under the tree. He knew what was in their hearts (of sincere intention and loyalty to God's cause) and, therefore, He sent down (the gift of) inner peace and reassurance on them, and rewarded them with a near victory.[306]

God knows the treacheries of the eyes and all that the bosoms conceal.[307]

Whether you keep concealed what you intend to say or speak it out loud, He surely has full knowledge of all that lies in the bosoms.[308]

Emphasis on the heart's being within Divine knowledge is geared towards a person's constantly reviewing themselves, spiritually as well as materially, and living in a controlled and careful manner. The Prophet's declaring, "Assuredly, God does not consider your bodies, nor your

---

[302] (6:73) See the following related verses: (13:9); (23:92); (39:46)
[303] al-Isfahani, *Al-Mufradat*, 343. al-Jurjani, *al-Ta'rifat*, 155.
[304] (67:14)
[305] (33:51)
[306] (48:18)
[307] (40:19)
[308] (67:13)

appearances. Rather, He considers your hearts," serves to consolidate this concept.[309]

It is arguably with reference to this Prophetic Tradition that the heart's being called *nazargâh-i İlahî* (the focus of God's sight) has become famous in Sufi tradition. Considered from this perspective, the reasons behind deeds—their 'backdrop' so to speak—come to the fore more so than their exterior and assume greater importance. As elaborated in the section on the functions of the heart, the factor that determines the worth of deeds in the eyes of God is the clear decision and inclination of the heart with respect to doing that deed. God's knowing hearts prevents a believing heart from leaning towards anything other than Him. A heart at such a level of consciousness holds a position of dominance over a person's body and keeps its 'servants,' the other limbs, organs and faculties, away from error and transgression.

Another point important at this juncture is that of God's taking the heart as 'a measure' and accepting it as "a criterion" in his treatment of a servant. An examination of the Qur'anic verse dealing with this issue and a discussion of the reason behind its revelation are significant. The verse in question states:

> O (most illustrious) Prophet! Say to the captives in your hands: "If God knows any good in your hearts, He will grant you something better than what has been taken from you, and He will forgive you." God is All-Forgiving, All-Compassionate.[310]

The verse is significant in terms of its articulating the notion that goodness does not go to waste. God, who does not overlook any good done by His servants,[311] even when that goodness first emerges in the heart as an intention, weighs it terms of its aspects looking to the world and the Hereafter. An incident reinforcing this notion transpired during the time of the Prophet.[312]

---

[309] Muslim, Birr, 33; Ibn Maja, Zuhd, 9.

[310] (8:70)

[311] Refer to relevant verses: (9:120); (11:115); (12:90)

[312] According to the report narrated by 'Abd Allah b. 'Abbas, the reason behind the revelation of this verse relates to his father, 'Abbas: During the Battle of Badr, Prophet Muhammad's uncle 'Abbas was among those held captive. He had with him six hundred dirhams of gold. He had taken this with him in order to feed the polytheists of Mecca. This was because he was one of the ten people who took on the

As stated in the verse, if God finds goodness in hearts, He bestows upon human beings beautiful things in relation to this world, and forgives them in relation to the Hereafter. It can be understood from this verse and its commentary that 'Abbas held in his heart goodness, good intention and the capacity for belief and sincerity such that God granted him guidance by virtue of these. This notion is not applicable to 'Abbas only, but for all those who believe. It follows that whoever holds in their heart those attitudes and feelings of which God will approve, they will receive its return in this world and the next in a manner in which they will be pleased.

A final point to be examined in relation to God's knowing hearts pertains to *taqwa*. Derived from the Arabic root letters w-q-y, the word *taqwa* means "to protect oneself well" and "to be cautious." In the religious terminology, it refers to "the struggle to protect oneself from Divine punishment in the Hereafter by means of obedience to God's commands and avoidance of the religiously forbidden."

In Islamic understanding *taqwa* has come to represent the exclusive formula for increasing one's worth in the Creator's sight. This is clearly highlighted in the Qur'anic verse which states: "Surely the noblest, most

---

responsibility of providing food and rations for the Qurayshi forces participating in the battle. However, he was taken prisoner before his turn to feed the troops had come. The gold pieces that he brought with him fell into the hands of the Muslims when he was taken prisoner. Abbas told the Prophet that he had in fact already accepted Islam but that he was forced to participate in the battle. The Prophet said, "If what you are claiming is true, then God will compensate you. As for your outward appearance, it was against us." When 'Abbas wanted the gold taken from him during the battle to count towards his ransom, the Prophet refused. He demanded that 'Abbas also ransom his two cousins Nawfal and 'Aqil, as well as an ally. 'Abbas claimed that he did not have the money, whereupon the Prophet said: "What about the wealth that you and Umm al-Fadl buried, and you said to her, 'If I am killed in this battle, then this money that I buried is for my children al-Fadl, 'Abdullah and Quthm. 'Abbas, in complete astonishment, asked how the Prophet had known this when only he and his wife knew of this. When Prophet Muhammad responded that His Lord informed him, 'Abbas declared his belief in his Prophethood. It is later narrated that 'Abbas, indicating the meaning of this verse, said the following: "After I became Muslim, God gave me twenty servants in place of the twenty ounces I lost. Moreover, God favored me with Zamzam. If they were to offer me all of Mecca's wealth in its place, I would reject it. And I hope for God's forgiveness." Yazır, *Hak Dini Kur'an Dili*, IV:2436-37.

honorable of you in God's sight is the one best in piety, righteousness, and reverence for God."[313]

Taqwa has a very close connection with the heart. Through pointing to his heart and repeating several times "*Taqwa* is here," the Prophet indicates clearly and emphatically this relationship. The Qur'an also leaves no doubt as to the existence of this relationship: "Keep from disobedience to God in reverence for Him and piety. Surely God has full knowledge of what lies hidden in the bosoms."[314]

As such, God is fully aware of everything that hearts conceal within them. He is aware of the degree of their soundness, where they stand in terms of belief and the extent to which they are oriented towards His pleasure and approval. Moreover, as Ghazali appropriately points out, a person cannot even be aware of their own heart most of the time and understand it completely. This is perhaps the reasoning behind the verse cautioning human beings thus: "So do not hold yourselves pure (sinless; it is vain self-justification). He knows best him who keeps from disobedience to God in reverence for Him and piety (*taqwa*)."[315]

In a verse where the Qur'an mentions the heart in juxtaposition with *taqwa*, hearts' being tested with *taqwa* is mentioned. The verses at the beginning of the chapter entitled *Hujurat* were revealed in relation to the association between the Companions and the Prophet. The verses command believers to have utmost respect and reverence for God's Messenger, even so far as being careful of the tone of their voice while in his presence. Furthermore, they connect obedience to this command with *taqwa*, or the piety of hearts:

> O you who believe! Do not raise your voices above the voice of the Prophet, nor speak loudly when addressing him, as you would speak loudly to one another, lest your good deeds go in vain without your perceiving it.
>
> Those who lower their voices in the presence of God's Messenger, those are they whose hearts God has tested and proven for piety

---

[313] (49:13)

[314] Muslim, Birr, 32, 33; Tirmidhi, Birr, 18.

[315] (53:32)

and reverence for Him. For them there is forgiveness (to bring unforeseen rewards) and a tremendous reward.[316]

The Prophet holds such an apparently esteemed and elevated position in God's sight that any disrespect shown towards him amounts to blasphemy and is enough to nullify all good deeds. This is due to the fact that disrespect towards him is considered as being directed towards God who sent him with the mission of Prophethood. But such an ordinance does not apply to any other individual.

As a result, those who are able to adopt the manner and attitude that is required of them even to the point of adjusting the level of their voices in the presence of the Messenger are those believers who have demonstrated the presence of *taqwa* in their hearts and have passed the test. In other words, they are those individuals whose hearts God has assessed for piety. As mentioned in the Qur'anic chapter entitled *Fath* (The Victory)[317], God, demanding piety (*taqwa*) from believers, familiarized them with it through various trials and tribulations in the arena of lived experience, and revealed to them their *taqwa* through such experience. The recompense for such believers is God's favoring them with His forgiveness and their receiving great reward in the Hereafter.

Consequently, God is with the human being no matter where they are[318] and it is not possible for them to conceal anything whatsoever from Him. He knows all that hearts possess, whether good or bad, little or great, what they are nourished with, what they themselves nourish— in short, everything about them. God's being with the human being in every time and place has been viewed as directing them to constant precaution and watchfulness in way of acquiring those qualities that will earn God's approval and pleasure.

---

[316] (49:2-3)

[317] The verse in question states: "When those who disbelieved harbored in their hearts fierce zealotry, the zealotry particular to the Age of Ignorance, God sent down His (gift of) inner peace and reassurance on His Messenger and on the believers, and bound them to the Word of faith, piety, and reverence for God. They were most worthy of it and entitled to it. And God has full knowledge of everything" (48:26).

[318] The verse which describes God being present everywhere, in all time and space via His knowledge and power reads as follows: "And He is with you, wherever you may be. And God sees well all that you do" (57:4). Also see: (58:7); (10:61).

Intervening between a Person and Their Heart

The Qur'an makes explicit mention of God's intervening between an individual and their heart. The verse in question reads:

> O you who believe! Respond to God and to the Messenger when the Messenger calls you to that which gives you life; and know well that surely God "intervenes" between a person and his heart (to cause his heart to swerve); and that He it is to Whom you will be gathered.[319]

There have been myriad approaches to and commentaries of this verse which at a cursory glance seems rather difficult to grasp. A summary of these interpretations will be provided below.

According to an approach preferred by exegetes Baydawi (d. 684/ 1286) and Alusi (d. 1269/1853),[320] this statement constitutes another distinct way of expressing God's closeness to His servants. That is to say, God is very close to His servant. So close is this proximity that He even 'comes between' a person and that which forms their essence—their heart. Through this interpretation, the verse parallels the verse which declares that God is nearer to human beings than their jugular vein.[321] Accordingly, the meaning implied in the verse is thus: So close is God to you, that He knows the hearts of yours that even you, more often than not, do not know. He is aware of every kind of idea and emotion that your hearts contain, and knows the nature and essence of their inclination, supplication and reciprocation to Him.

Raghib al-Isfahani's preferred interpretation is that God comes in between an individual and the desires and inclinations that their heart contains. In Tahir b. Ashur (d. 1392/1960)'s view, implied with the "person" in the verse is a "person's deeds and those things at their disposal." God intervenes between the proclivities of their heart and that which is to occur as a result of those proclivities, not allowing these to be realized. Stating that God intervenes "between a man's desires and the outward action that may result from those desires, indicating that God can turn man away from what his heart urges him to do," Muhammad Asad

---

[319] (8:24)

[320] Nasr al-Din Baydawi, *Anwar al-Tanzil wa Asrar al-Ta'wil*, 2 vols. (Istanbul: Şirket-i Sahafiye-i Osmaniye, 1884), 380; Alusi, *Ruh al-Ma'ani*, IX:191.

[321] (50:16)

(d. 1414/1992) concurs with this view.[322] In other words, when God so wills, He prevents his servants carrying out their desires and it is only God-consciousness that can prevent human beings from being misled by sinful desires.

As for Hamdi Yazır, he considers the issue vis-à-vis the first part of the verse and, after evaluating the available commentaries he presents his own in the following manner:

> God indeed intervenes between a person and their heart. He is closer to them than their heart and is closer to their heart than they themselves are. He knows their state better than their heart and knows the state of their heart better than they do, and takes closer command and possession of it. So effectual is His might that he does not only intervene between a person and others, but even comes between a person and their own heart. He intervenes between the "I" who thinks and the "I" who is thought of, and separates these two selves from one another.[323]

It is useful at this point, to examine the difference between Divine will and that which human beings possess. While Divine, or Universal, will is infinite, human beings have been given a partial, particular will and they have been left with such in a world of trial and examination. When considered from the Islamic perspective it becomes apparent that a person gives direction to their material and spiritual life, first and foremost their belief in or denial of God, through their own will and inclination. The verse, "And say: "The truth from your Lord (has come in this Qur'an)." Then, whoever wills (to believe), let him believe; and whoever wills (to disbelieve), let him disbelieve,"[324] clearly emphasizes a person's freedom in this regard. A person does as they so choose, but subsequently faces the consequences. The Qur'anic expression "You cannot will unless God wills"[325] pertains to everything consequently returning back to God. That is to say, He knows what everyone desires and will desire. For Him, there is no difference between what has happened and what will happen. No one can go beyond His will and judgment; because He knows how

---

[322] Muhammad Asad, *Message of the Qur'an* (Gibraltar: Dar Al-Andalus, 1980), 325.
[323] Yazır, *Hak Dini Kur'an Dili*, IV:2385-87.
[324] (18:29)
[325] (76:31); (81:29)

human beings will use their freewill, He has ascribed the matter back to Himself.

If we are to express this in more general terms, God has informed human beings that He leads astray those who follow their whims and fancies, the disbelievers, oppressors, and the transgressors of all bounds (of sense and decency), and in contrast guides those who turn to Him. According to the Qur'an, human beings, with their will, reason, perception, emotion (each being a dimension of the heart as elucidated earlier) have been made an addressee and those things that they are able to do—not those that are beyond their power—have been demanded of them. In this respect, a person is responsible and accountable for their actions; they will either reap the rewards of their good deeds or face the penalties of their evil. That the failure to consider such issues holistically would lead one to drawing erroneous conclusions is self-evident. It is important that such expressions to be made hereafter be evaluated in light of this.

Expanding and Contacting the *Sadr*

That the word *sadr*, in the Qur'anic language, comes to mean the site of the heart and represents one of the meanings pertaining to it was mentioned earlier. For this reason, it is possible to say that the expansion and contraction of *sadr* denotes the heart's expansion and contraction.

The expansion of *sadr* is appears in the Qur'an as *sharh al-sadr* five times, while its contraction appears as *diyq al-sadr* six times. Under this heading, an elucidation of these terms will be followed by what has been discussed in the literature in relation to them.

Sharh denotes cutting opening, splitting, expanding the flesh and explaining a vague or inexplicit expression. According to Raghib, the *sharh* of *sadr* means "the chest's opening and expansion by means of Divine light and serenity." The word *diyq*, however, means contraction, tightening and feeling asphyxiated. When the term is associated with *sadr*, it indicates such meanings as inner suffering, stress, grief, sorrow and sadness.[326] The Qur'an's associating these two words not with the heart but with that which constitutes the heart's locale is significant.

While the first thing that comes to mind with the mention of the expansion of *sadr* in the religious literature is *sadr*'s opening up to belief and

---

[326] al-Isfahani, *Al-Mufradat*, 300.

Islam and its being favored with guidance, the Qur'an in actual fact mentions that *sadr* can open and expand towards denial and disbelief also. Attracting attention to this point, is the fact that *sharh al-sadr* which is guidance-oriented is associated directly via God, while the opening of *sadr* towards disbelief and denial is most frequently associated with human beings. The following two verses can be offered as examples:

> Thus, whomever God wills to guide, He expands his breast to Islam, and whomever He wills to lead astray, He causes his breast to become tight and constricted, as if he were climbing towards the heaven. Thus, God lays ignominy upon those who do not believe (despite many signs and evidences).[327]

> Whoever disbelieves in God after having believed—not him who is under duress, while his heart is firm in and content with faith, but the one who willingly opens up his heart to unbelief—upon them falls God's anger (His condemnation of them), and for them is a mighty punishment.[328]

In the first of these verses, the expansion and contraction of *sadr* has been attributed to God, while in the second verse, association has been made to the human being, on the premise that the disbelievers have themselves first opened their 'bosom' or heart to denial.

In relation to this, Tirmidhi states that when hearts expand towards the Truth they contract towards falsehood and when they open to unbelief, they narrow and contract to the Truth.[329]

Hamdi Yazır's observations also are worth mentioning. He observes:

> For whomsoever God wills guidance and whomsoever He wants to bring to Himself, He opens their heart to Islam. Such is the capacity that He gives to their carnal self, in order for them to accept the Truth and calls to the truth, that their bosom expands with belief and obedience and their heart attains peace and happiness. It is known that the broadness of the chest indicates power, breath and perseverance. The opening of the chest and its taking deep breaths necessitates the relief of the heart. The chest's finding relief in this

---

[327] (6:125)

[328] (16:106)

[329] al-Tirmidhi, *Bayan al-Farq*, 42, 43.

way has to do with power, perseverance and happiness and relief. The chest's opening to Islam here connotes the ego's being given the capacity of readiness to accept the truth and its being purified of barriers and opposition therein. Therefore, when the Prophet was asked regarding the expanding of the bosom, he replied that it is, "A Divine light which God plants in the heart of a believer and with it the heart is soothed and opened." Upon this, his Companions asked whether there was a sign through which it can be identified and were told, "Yes, it is inclining towards the abode of eternity, distancing oneself from the abode of delusion (the world) and preparing for death before it comes." Thus is the light that God gives to the heart of a person whose guidance He wills, and the heart of such a person finds complete happiness with faith and Islam and, as a result, expands. This heart is neither wearied by fulfilling the obligations that come with acceptance of the truth nor is encumbered by these, but on the contrary experiences joy and jubilation.

Whosoever God wills to lead astray, He tightens and presses their chest and weighs it down. Such is the strain that they feel that, to them, it is as though the climb is directly towards the sky, not just up a steep slope. However impossible the burden and struggle of climbing towards the sky seems to them, that is precisely how difficult it is for them to accept the truth and abide by it. When Islam and righteousness is made mention of, they feel suffocated and experience great distress. They seek expansion, not in righteousness and peace, but in wrongdoing and ruin.[330]

We have, hitherto, considered the expansion and contraction of *sadr* from the perspective of faith and disbelief. In addition to this, there can also be expansion and contraction in the hearts of believers for different reasons. For this reason, making mention of the contraction of the Prophet's *sadr* and in order to put ease in his heart, the Qur'an states: "Endure patiently; your endurance is only for God's sake and by His help; and do not grieve for them (because of their attitude toward your mission), nor be distressed because of what they scheme."[331] Again in relation to Prophet Muhammad, one of the interpretations of the verse "Have We not expand-

---

[330] Yazır, *Hak Dini Kur'an Dili*, I:125.
[331] (16:127)

ed for you your breast" is "Did we not deliver you from various tribulations and sorrows."[332]

The experiences of Prophet Moses, as mentioned in the Qur'anic text, serve to consolidate this approach. He once entreated God saying, "My Lord! I fear that they will deny me, And my breast will be constricted, and my tongue will not be free..."[333] and when given the mission of going to the Pharaoh prayed, "Loosen a knot from my tongue (to make my speech more fluent)."[334] It becomes possible in this context, therefore, to interpret the expansion of *sadr* as relief from difficulty, the cessation of anxiety and unease as well as the prevalence of steadiness and tranquility in the heart.

The contraction and openness of the heart that even the Prophets experience is of course something that can be expected to surface in average human beings also. The different kinds of expansion and contraction that the hearts of believers undergo are directly connected with the manifestations of God's Attributes of *Qabid* (The Constrictor) and *Basit* (The Reliever). Contemporary Muslim scholar and thinker Fethullah Gülen says the following with respect to *qabd* and *bast*:

> Literally meaning being caught, being in straits or distressed, and being grasped by hand, Sufis use *qabd* to mean that the link between an individual and the source of his or her spiritual gifts and radiance has been severed for a certain period. This causes distress and makes one suffer from spiritual obstruction and blockage. On the other hand, *bast* can be described as openness, expansion, development, relief, and being freed from spiritual blockage, and as developing inwardly or spiritually to the point that the seeker becomes a means of mercy and embraces all things or beings in existence.[335]

The Qur'an refers to the truths of belief with the word *nur* (Divine light) and in contrast describes ascribing partners with God, denial and every kind of disbelief as *zulumat*, or darkness.

---

[332] (94:1)
[333] (26:12-13)
[334] (20:27)
[335] M. Fethullah Gülen, *Key Concepts in the Practice of Sufism 1*, trans. Ali Unal (Fairfax, Virginia: The Fountain, 1999), 167.

God is the confidant and guardian of those who believe (to Whom they can entrust their affairs, and on Whom they can rely), bringing them out from all kinds of (intellectual, spiritual, social, economic and political) darkness into the light, and keeping them firm therein. And those who disbelieve, their confidants and guardians are the *tāghūt*; bringing them out from the light into all kinds of darkness. Those are companions of the Fire; and they will abide therein.[336]

The light which disperses darkness, opens and penetrates it referred to in the verse can be understood as the expansion of *sadr*. Again in the same way, cleaving the grief, sadness and sorrow emerging in the heart for various reasons and relieving and freeing the heart of them, as well as removing the veils of sin covering the heart can also be described as *sharh al-sadr*.

On the other hand, the claim that the heart, created with the potential to know and believe in God, would choke up and contract due to denial and deviation would not be unjustified. It is not too difficult to predict the difficulties that such spiritual 'maladies' would engender in the heart. Therefore, understanding the difficulties and such tightening of the heart within the meaning framework of *diyq al-sadr* appears not to be implausible.

Guiding the Heart

In Islamic tradition, the words *hidaya* (guidance) and its opposite *dalala* (transgression or misguidance) are among concepts that are most frequently used. An analysis of the Qur'an reveals clearly the association between guidance and the heart. In Islamic understanding, the heart is not only the site of faith and guidance but also constitutes the locale of misguidance and disbelief. The heart's being guided simultaneously means a person's being kept on the path of guidance. In other words, guidance is not a momentary matter but is instead a process. In the section below, the concept of guidance in particular and its close connection with the heart will be examined.

Derived from the letters h-d-y, the term *hidaya* is an infinitive noun meaning "guiding with mercy and compassion to that which is sought."[337] Just as this guidance, which is generally realized to allow a being to attain

---

[336] (2:257)
[337] al-Isfahani, *Al-Mufradat*, 538.

a purpose that is good and beneficial, can be realized by merely showing the road leading to the goal, it can also be realized by taking one to that road and even by carrying one to the ultimate goal.

In Islamic theology absolute guidance has only been attributed to God. One of the Divine Attributes, *Hadi*, according to Ibn Athir, refers to God's opening the eye of the hearts of His servants, showing them the roads to His knowledge, *ma'rifa*, and His instructing all those He creates in everything that they need to know for the continuance of their lives. Ibn Sayyida states that the word *hidaya*, being the opposite of misguidance, means reliability or *rashad*. Associating the concept with the nature and essence of guidance in lieu of the person who is to be guided, Abu Ishaq sees *hidaya* as the name of the true path itself to which God invites and calls. Expanding the semantic repertoire of *hidaya*, Qatada states that the term also comes to mean "declaring and expounding."[338]

Examination of the Qur'anic verses wherein *hidaya* is explained reveals that some of the verses explicitly mention both the words *hidaya* and *qalb*, while others directly associate the former with the latter. Some of the verses explaining the close association between guidance and the heart will be considered at this point.

Stating that, "No affliction befalls except by God's leave. Whoever believes in God (truly and sincerely), He guides his heart (to true knowledge of His eternal Will, and how He acts with regard to the life of His creatures, and so leads him to humble submission to Him, and to peace and serenity). God has full knowledge of all things,"[339] the Qur'an draws a direct parallel between belief and guidance. It is possible to extract from this expression the meaning that a person who searches for truth in an objective way will be guided; the true path will be shown to them. The verse draws attention to the fact that no tribulation would befall a person without the permission of God. All things that a person faces, including those trials and difficulties, are from God, realized through His will and at His command. This belief is of particular importance in terms of a believer's remaining firm on the path of guidance: when a person with a believing heart suffers misfortune, they seek the help of the Lord in whom they believe, remain righteous in thought and remember that the difficul-

---

[338] Ibn Manzur, *Lisan al-'arab*, 'h-d-y.'
[339] (64:11)

ty they face can only transpire with God's permission and that they too will one day return to Him. They believe that their misfortune holds within it much wisdom, goodness and benefit. They design their behavior on the conviction that such tribulations bring reward in both this world and the world hereafter. They refrain from wrong feeling, thought and action. All of these constitute the stance that a believing person takes when confronted by adversity and hardship and is the manifestation of God's having guided them thus.

As such, the concept of guidance in this verse is not merely that of guiding from the darkness of disbelief to the light of belief, but also implies the notion of not 'losing' guidance when one had already been guided and, in contrast, confronting events under its direction. That such verses simultaneously play the role of a control mechanism in the lives of Muslims is apparent. The notion that these not only provide hope and glad tidings, but also prevent believers taking on mistaken attitudes and ideas are among the themes most emphasized.

Another verse in the same vein mentions that belief is beautified and adorned in hearts. What is more, that God has made denial, disbelief and rebellion repugnant to believers is also mentioned and that all of these are Divine favors and bounties is underlined. The verse in question states:

> ... But God has endeared the faith to you (O believers) and made it appealing to your hearts, and He has made unbelief, transgression, and rebellion hateful to you. Those are they who are rightly guided (in belief, thought, and action), As a grace from God and a favor. God is All-Knowing, All-Wise.[340]

This verse asserts that the beginning and completion of all deeds and actions belong to God and these are carried out with His permission, and also calls attention to His infinite will. Just as is the case with every other matter, this is also applicable in relation to a pivotal issue such as *hidaya*, which concerns a person's corporeal world and their life hereafter.

At this juncture, it is useful to point out that in Islamic understanding, human beings are enjoined to exert effort with their particular or partial willpower in the way of attaining guidance. Those who are able to show such performance are also considered to have, in effect, asked God

---

[340] (64:7-8)

to guide them. But all these considerations do not imply that a person guides himself or herself; God's universal will is never overlooked. That *hidaya* belongs purely and solely to God is mentioned explicitly in the Qur'an. For this reason, being guided in the Islamic understanding, or in other words being far from every kind of transgression or deviation, is associated with God more than with human beings. In brief, both reaching *hidaya* and living a life maintaining it belongs to God alone.

A final verse that will be used as an illustration of the topic in question is at the same time a supplication that the Qur'an teaches to Muslims:

(They entreat God:) "Our Lord, do not let our hearts swerve after You have guided us, and bestow upon us mercy from Your Presence. Surely You are the All-Bestowing.[341]

As is evident, that the true owner of hearts is God is again expressed, from a different perspective. Steadfastness after belief's having entered the heart and weaving one's life with the threads of guidance is only possible with Divine assistance. A believer, alongside doing what is necessary with their willpower for their faith not to be taken away from them, is dependent upon God for their hearts not to swerve after having believed and not to be subjected to deviation. That this need is expressed via supplication and entreaty to God in the aforementioned verse is of significance and warrants attention.

Of equal weight and meaning to the Qur'anic supplication just mentioned is that which is included in the opening chapter of the Qur'an entitled *Fatiha*, which Muslims recite several times daily in every ritual Prayer, is the entreaty "Guide us to the Straight Path."[342]

As mentioned earlier, it is God who creates and maintains, incessantly, *hidaya*. There is, however, the aspect which looks to human beings and this is the performance that they exert by way of ensuring its continuation. Stating, "...Surely God leads astray whomever He wills, and guides to Himself all who turn (to Him whole-heartedly)..."[343] the Qur'an places emphasis on a servant's willpower and effort. As the word mentioned in the original Arabic text is *inaba*, it is useful to elaborate on this further.

---

[341] (3:8)
[342] (1:6)
[343] (13:27)

Denoting heartfelt turning to God, *inaba* is a degree deeper and more comprehensive than *tawba*, or repentance. While in *tawba* there is generally a turning to God due to wrongdoing or transgression, *inaba* entails a questioning of one's connection to God without there being a need for such a lapse. In Sufi terminology, turning to God has been examined in three categories; these are *tawba*, *inaba* and *awba* respectively.[344]

Describing *inaba* as "Turning to the Truth (God) in submission," Elmalılı states that its actual meaning is "being on guard for goodness." A prerequisite of *hidaya* is a partial or particular willpower, which in itself implies transcending the desire and will of the carnal soul, turning to God's will and utmost surrender to Him. Every person has been given a set period of time, albeit unique to all, and opportunity to choose guidance for themselves. Choosing guidance or transgression in this set period, known as life, is left up to the servant. Those who use their preference in the way of *inaba* will be upon the path of guidance, while deviation will become an inevitable habit of those who do not obey God.[345]

As is implied in these statements, such a turning to God is again realized with the heart, as *inaba* is an action of the heart. Also implied is the notion that the first action, or the first leaning belongs to the servant. This is deemed to be Divinely ordained. Accordingly, one who is able to perform this initial turning and inclination is to receive the rewards of such action. Just as no goodness is wasted, God is to recompense this effort also. A famous *hadith qudsi*, or Divine *Hadith*, symbolically and vividly expresses this very issue:

> If My servant comes one span nearer to Me, I go one cubit nearer to him; and if he comes one cubit nearer to Me, I go a distance of two outstretched arms nearer to him; and if he comes to Me walking, I go to him running.[346]

In such an understanding, *hidaya* is a vehicle whereby God enables human beings to realize the purpose of their creation, as a manifestation

---

[344] 'Abd al-Karim Al Qushayri, *al-Risalah al-Qushayri fi al-'Ilm al-Tasawwuf* (Beirut: Dar al-Kitab al-'Arabi, 2005), 259.

[345] The life span given to each human being is described in the Qur'an as follows: "Did We not grant you a life long enough for whoever would reflect and be mindful to reflect and be mindful?" (35:37)

[346] Bukhari, *Tawhid*, 502; Muslim, *Dhikr*, 2; Tirmidhi, Da'awat, 142.

of His mercy and compassion towards His creation. So long as human beings utilize their willpower in the way of turning to God, they effectively attract God's guidance. In the face of His servant turning away from Him and His signs, and virtually closing off all doors leading to *hidaya*, He who calls His servants to His paradise[347] and states His disapproval with their denial[348] leaves them in heedlessness—this being a natural result of the test.

Giving Inner Peace and Reassurance to the Heart

The verse, "Those who have believed (and become established in belief), and whose hearts find rest and contentment in remembrance of, and whole-hearted devotion to, God. Be aware that it is in the remembrance of, and whole-hearted devotion to, God that hearts find rest and contentment"[349] will be examined in this section. This verse is in close correlation to the last section of the previous verse. This previous verse finishes with mention of God's guiding "to Himself all who turn (to Him whole-heartedly)."[350] The key words employed in this verse are *hidaya* and *inaba*. These two concepts, examined previously, can be considered to be chief arguments and instruments leading to and serving the purpose of the goal described by the *mutasawwifun* (the Sufis) as the heart's finding rest through the remembrance of God. A brief explanation of these concepts is therefore of critical significance to the topic at hand.

Before proceeding to the issue in question, these two concepts can be briefly redefined at this point, from a different perspective. As cited above, *inaba* means turning to God in penitence.[351] It is another dimension of *tawba*, or turning to God. In its broadest sense, *inaba*, or sincere penitence denotes turning to and 'returning to' God in repentance.[352] It illustrates a further dimension of *tawba*, which denotes seeking concur-

---

[347] "And God invites to the Abode of Peace (where they will enjoy perfect bliss, peace, and safety) and He guides whomever He wills to a Straight Path. For those who do good, aware that God is seeing them, is the best (of the rewards that God has promised for good deeds), and still more. Neither stain nor ignominy will cover their faces. They are the companions of Paradise; they will abide therein." (10:25-26)

[348] "...He is not pleased with ingratitude and unbelief from His servants" (39:7).

[349] (13:28)

[350] (13:27)

[351] Ibn Manzur, *Lisan al-'arab*, 'n-e-b.'

[352] Ibid.

rence with the truth after transgression and seeking forgiveness from God for sin and wrongdoing. Sincere penitence also implies acting with caution and vigilance with the aim of preserving the spiritual states and stations that one has been favored with.

Hidaya, on the other hand, implies accompanying that which will lead to the desired destination with grace and delicacy. The 'delicacy' in guidance mentioned here implies the opposite of harshness and force, being kindness and tenderness. As for grace, it is subtlety and refinement. When viewed from the Qur'anic perspective, it is easy to see that *hidaya* is guidance only towards goodness. Hence, direction or showing the way for the purpose of theft is most certainly not guidance.[353] In these verses, the state of those turning in such a way and attaining guidance is explained as that belonging to believers whose hearts found peace and contentment with the remembrance of God.

As can be seen, the principal terms that are stressed in these verses are sincere penitence and guidance, followed by *dhikr* (remembrance of God) and *itmi'nan* (tranquility), which will be elucidated later. There is a virtuous circle linking these key terms. One who turns to God in contrition though faith and remembrance is privileged with God's guidance; God grants serenity and repose to the heart of His servant. If a servant turns to God in sincere penitence and remembrance, God reciprocates by way of guidance and making easy the path to living a life that earns His approval. He also bestows tranquility and happiness upon their heart. It is possible to summarize the same notion as follows: sincere penitence from the servant leads to guidance from God; remembrance from the servant leads to tranquility from God. As can be gleaned from this explanation, it is first necessary for the servant to take a step, or exert some effort in order for God to respond to their entreaty and reward them in abundance. In Sufi terms, this is God's responding to a servant's favoring Him, with the bestowal of His favor. The recompense for turning to God is hence guidance, while that of remembrance of Him via the heart is peace and serenity. Thus, in this sense, the heart is the site at which a believer directly meets with their Lord.

The key terms warranting attention in the verse, "Be aware that it is in the remembrance of, and whole-hearted devotion to, God that hearts

---

[353] Yazır, *Hak Dini Kur'an Dili,* I:121.

find rest and contentment" can be summarized as *qalb*, *dhikr* and *itmi'nan* (tranquility). The observations and commentaries of Qur'anic exegetes who have interpreted this verse will be presented chronologically. In addition to the rich commentary of this verse in the classical *tafsir* tradition, I will offer my own interpretation and reading, where appropriate.

The concept of tranquility is that which is at the fore of the issues stressed in the verse. The majority of Qur'anic exegetes, offering a linguistic analysis of the word itself, define *tuma'nina* or *itmi'nan* (tranquility) as the heart's finding rest and becoming calm after turbulence and turmoil. When expanding on this heart's state of restfulness, they repeatedly emphasize 'experiential knowledge of God,' or *ma'rifa*, and a 'life of intense worship.'[354] Hanbalite scholar Ibn al-Jawzi, in a more mystical interpretation, states that *tuma'nina* denotes love of God, establishing a relationship of nearness to Him and the realization of peacefulness with God, through the elimination of all doubt.[355]

The second important concept, *dhikr Allah*, in its most general sense, refers to remembrance of God, recitation of His Names and invoking Him. However much the first meaning coming to mind is the Qur'an, as purported by classical exegetes, its scope is much broader and more encompassing. From the performance of the five Daily Prayers and mentioning God's Names, to attending gatherings where His Name is invoked, calling upon Him in supplication and recognizing God's signs and actions in the universe through reflection, one is able to discern the extent to which the meaning of remembrance is broadened.[356]

---

[354] al-Isfahani, *Al-Mufradat*, 't-m-n.'

[355] Ibn al-Jawzi Abu al-Faraj 'Abd al-Rahman ibn 'Ali, *Zad al-Masir Fi 'Ilm Al-Tafsir*, 8 vols. (Beirut: Dar al-Kutub al-'Ilmiyya, 1414 [1994]), IV:250.

[356] Al-Zamakhshari (d. 538/1143), one of the most prominent scholars of the *tafsir* tradition, connects the tranquility of the heart with the Qur'an. He states that the Qur'anic verses dealing with reward and punishment engender tranquility and quietude in the heart of a believer. In a similar vein, Abu al-Su'ud (d. 982/1574) states that hearts can only find rest with the Qur'an and makes reference to verses where the Qur'an is expressed as the word *dhikr* (Reminder) such as: "And this one, too, is a Reminder full of blessings which We are sending down" (21:50); "Indeed it is We, We Who send down the Reminder in parts, and it is indeed We Who are its Guardian" (15:19); and "Those who disbelieve in this Reminder when it comes to them (are among those who will be thrown into the Fire). For it is surely a glorious, unconquerable Book. Falsehood can never have access to it, whether from before it or from behind it" (41:41-42).

Exegetes' interpretations of the verse in question have necessitated the simultaneous consideration of several themes. Two points possess special significance in terms of the overall discussion: remembrance of God and its effect on the heart. As will become clear through the understandings and analyses presented below, implicit in the remembrance of God is that it is a duty that needs to be performed with the heart, as opposed to the tongue. Through openly expressing this aspect, the verse conveys the fact that it is the heart that finds rest through remembrance. A close reading reveals that the use of the word 'heart' instead of the terms 'human being' or 'tongue' in the verse, is directed at giving emphasis to the notion that it is the very heart itself, which carries out remembrance of God.

Through his emphasis on the heart and its field of influence Fakhr al-Din al-Razi, one of the leading representatives of Sunni *tafsir* tradition, mentions that existents (*al-mawjudat*) are comprised of three categories: namely, those which influence but which themselves are not influenced; those which are constantly influenced, but which do not have the capacity to yield influence; and those beings which are both influential and open to influence. The first of these is God, the Possessor of Absolute Influence, Who is exempt from any fault, defect, or imperfection. The second are those who are amenable to assuming a different disposition, such that when they are subjected to influence, they have no alternative but to accept. The third are spiritual beings. Razi, regarding the heart as one of these spiritual beings, explains its impressionability as follows:

> When the spiritual being of the heart turns to consideration of the world of forms, it finds itself in anguish and commotion. However, when it turns to consideration of God Almighty it is favored with Divine light. Peace and tranquility then descends upon a person; this is hearts finding rest with the remembrance of God.[357]

Muhy al-Din Ibn al-'Arabi, in interpreting this verse, gives prominence to the concept of *dhikr Allah*, and through painting a more elaborate tableau, attempts to broaden the term's gamut of meaning:

> There are many degrees of recitation. The recitation of the carnal self (*nafs*) is by means of the tongue and thinking about provisions

---

[357] al-Razi, *Mafatih al-Ghayb*, XIX:50.

granted; the heart's recitation is by means of reflecting on God's Attributes; recitation of a secret is through entreaty; recitation of the soul is through sight. The carnal self and the heart are plagued by distress and anguish due to the effect of worldly concerns. When God's Names are recited the carnal self is steadied and doubts come to an end.[358]

Through this approach Ibn 'Arabi forms a cogent connection and association between *ma'rifa* and remembrance of God. In his view, the heart's absolute invocation and constant remembrance of God is contingent upon recognizing and knowing Him through His Names, Attributes and actions. In other words, the likelihood of a heart that is not aware of and which does not recognize God of duly remembering and invoking Him is next to nothing. Ibn 'Arabi's explanations are not confined to those mentioned above. By drawing attention to the existence in a person's spiritual life of the carnal self (*nafs*) and the soul as part of the Divine Essence,[359] together with the heart, he posits that all of these faculties have a kind of remembrance, which is particular to them. In order for a person to engage in a deeper level of thinking, known in the religious terminology as *tafakkur* (reflection), it is necessary that they use their intellect. Consequently, notwithstanding the extent to which hearts find rest and reach contentment through the remembrance of God, it is essential that the remembrance of the *nafs*, the intellect, the soul and, in Ibn 'Arabi's terms the *sirr*, or secret, are brought into play together with the heart in order for this to be fully realized. By means of these observations, Ibn 'Arabi essentially gives added depth to the approach to *dhikr Allah* and, by appealing to reason he introduces new horizons regarding the verse's meaning.

Moving a step beyond these explanations Ibn 'Arabi makes reference to the remembrance of the *sirr* in addition to willpower, perception and intellect as deeper aspects of the heart, and associates this with supplication. *Sirr*—whose essence is not fully known—is defined as the heart's dimension capable of knowing God and discovering secrets pertaining to

---

[358] Muhy al-Din Ibn al-'Arabi, *Tafsir al-Qur'an al-Karim*, 2 vols. (Beirut: Dar al-Andalus, 1981), 642.

[359] The Qur'an presents this notion stating, "...and I breathed into him out of My Spirit..." (15:29); (38:72).

Him, and a spiritual faculty deposited in the heart as a Divine trust.[360] According to him, if a believer wholeheartedly turns to God and entreats and beseeches Him, the Divine trust-secret of their heart is performing remembrance of the Creator.

In interpreting the verse in discussion, Alusi, both a Sufi scholar and Qur'anic exegete, on the other hand repeatedly directs attention to the heart's perception and awareness. In his view, when the heart tends towards consideration of creation, it experiences anguish and turbulence and finds itself in the midst of intense inclination that has the capacity to overpower it. However, as it turns toward contemplation of God, Divine light emerges and the heart achieves repose and becomes content. Whenever it attains anything, it desires to restore itself to something more valuable and esteemed. For the happiness of the heart in the world is contingent upon its possession of the finest of everything. The heart finds rest, settles and is contented when it reaches experiential and illuminative knowledge of God. This is because there is nothing beyond God. According to him, this beloved is none other than God. When God's light enters a heart, it transforms it into a state that is eternal, pure and luminous. Because, in Alusi's view, when the heart is imbued with God's light it reaches the state where it no longer accepts change. And this is the very cause of its tranquility. Because believers remember God, God places in their hearts a light which frees them of such states as turmoil, tribulation and loneliness.

Furthermore, Alusi states that some have understood remembrance to mean contemplation of the signs of God's Oneness. Engaging in deep and systematic thought about God's existence and unity, exchanging views and ideas on the essentials of belief have also been considered as part of the domain of remembrance.

Alusi's description of the word *dhikr* mentioned in the verse is quite extensive. In a different interpretation, he states that another meaning implied in the remembrance of God is intimate awareness of Him, establishing a connection with Him and turning completely to Him. There is a very clear and direct reference here to the concept of *wali/awliya* (friends of God). In this manner, when the friends of God, the believers, remem-

---

[360] M. Fethullah Gülen, *Key Concepts in the Practice of Sufism 2*, trans. Ali Unal (Somerset, New Jersey: The Light, Inc, 2004), 66.

ber God and recite His Names they feel a nearness to Him in their hearts.[361] Through taking such an approach, Alusi converges with Ibn 'Arabi, thereby stressing the close connection between remembrance and *ma'rifa*.

Alusi also states that this verse indicates that the hearts of those who do not believe in God can never attain absolute rest. Believers are favored with tranquility of heart by means of their recollection of God's mercy and compassion. The great reverence and fear they feel towards God engenders in them a serenity and stillness of heart. This meaning is present in the verse, "Then, their skins and their hearts come to rest in the Remembrance of God (the Qur'an)."[362] Moreover, there is a strong correlation between the aforementioned verse and the verse, "...when God is mentioned, their hearts tremble with awe."[363] As such, when God's Name is invoked in the presence of believers, just as when they remember Him, they feel a quiver in their hearts due to His greatness and might. These tremors constitute a sort of serenity and contentment of heart.[364]

When the topic at hand is examined in relation to the Qur'an it quickly becomes apparent that a believer, when God is mentioned in their presence, does not and cannot remain neutral. This point bears special significance, as a believer is enjoined to be an 'active' participant not just when they themselves recite the Qur'an, but when its verses are recited in their presence, participating in the worship that is the reciting of the sacred text realized by someone else. Also relevant at this juncture is the notion in Islamic jurisprudence that reciting the Qur'an is classed as *sunna*, or recommended, while listening to it falls within the *fard*, or mandatory, category. Listening with utmost attention and without speaking when the Qur'an is being recited is a Qur'anic injunction.[365] When the fact that God's Name is frequently made mention of in the Qur'an is considered, the meaning of the 'active participation' we speak of is going to be more readily understood.

---

[361] Alusi associates this idea with the verse: "When God as One (and only God) is mentioned, the hearts of those who do not believe in the Hereafter recoil in aversion; but when those (whom they worship) apart from Him are mentioned, they are surely gladdened" (39:45).

[362] (39:23)

[363] (8:2)

[364] Alusi, *Ruh al-Ma'ani*, VII:150.

[365] (7:204)

Continuing to further expand the verse's meaning, Alusi posits that the love and reverence toward Prophet Muhammad and his Companions is also a means to the heart's attaining a state of peace and calm. His interpretation has strong grounding in the Islamic tradition: When the verse, "Be aware that it is in the remembrance of, and whole-hearted devotion to, God that hearts find rest and contentment" was revealed, Prophet Muhammad asked his Companions if they knew the meaning of this. When his Companions replied that "God and His Messenger know best," the Prophet stated that, "They are those who love God, His Messenger and my Companions." This statement of the Prophet has been interpreted by exegetes as describing the condition of those who remember God.[366]

As can be seen, Alusi does not simply confine love to love of God, leaving it to just a celestial connection. Through bringing to the fore a different manifestation of love that is the worldly dimension, he expands its corporeal dimension on the basis of Qur'anic verses and Prophetic Traditions, and then puts forward the argument that the meeting point of both these kinds of love is the heart. The believers whose hearts find rest in the remembrance of God are at the same time those who love God, his Messenger and the Companions. In other words, the hearts of such individuals can only attain quietude when they remember God and invoke His Name. Akin to a person finding peace and happiness in the recollection of someone they love, a person's connection with their Lord reveals the same idea. When the believers—who love God, the Prophet who has earned God's love, and the Companions of that same Prophet—remember God, they feel their hearts brimming with peace, calmness and happiness. Such is the close relationship between these two qualities.

Ismail Haqqi Bursawi (d. 1137/1725), one of the great Sufi guides and writers author of the famous four volume commentary on the Qur'an *Ruh al-Bayan*, deals with the heart in three different categories and, while making this division, buttresses his view with the Qur'anic verses he cites for each separate category. In his view, the first kind of heart is the heart of those who disbelieve and spend their lives pursuing this world and their worldly desires. The second kind of heart is the 'forgetful heart' of those believers who cannot save themselves from sin and wrongdoing. These hearts attain repose with the remembrance of God. That consti-

---

366 Alusi, *Ruh al-Ma'ani*, VII:149.

tuting the third category is the heart overflowing with belief in Divine unity, being the hearts of the Prophets and friends of God. They are only contented with God and His Attributes.

If the topic is to be approached from the inverse perspective, the heart's not finding peace and repose will, as stated by Burhan al-Din Buqa'i (d. 885/1480), bring that heart to a lifeless state. Remembrance of God holds a pivotal position with regards to the heart's not losing its liveliness. As many exegetes have pointed out, the utilization of the verbal phrase *tatma-innu* (find rest and contentment) expresses continuity. That is, the heart is in need of constant nurture, and remembrance of God serves an essential role herein.[367]

The last Qur'anic exegete whose views on the topic will be examined here is Elmalılı Muhammad Hamdi Yazır. Starting from its specific, narrowly defined meaning, Yazır interprets the remembrance of God mentioned in this verse as the Qur'an itself. This is due to the fact that the Qur'an has been referred to in some verses with the word *dhikr*.[368] He refers to some of these verses in order to substantiate the argument that the remembrance mentioned in the verse in discussion is the Qur'an itself.[369] Yazır thereafter focuses on the general meaning of remembrance, and proceeds to describe the journey to reunion with God, which can be expressed as the process of heart's attaining tranquility, as follows:

> As the center of a person's spiritual life, the heart will find rest and contentment by no other means than through the recitation of God's Names and remembrance and invocation of Him. Through remembrance, hearts attain serenity and find rest, inner pain and anguish

---

[367] Bursawi, *Ruh al-Bayan*, III:139.

[368] "And this one (the Qur'an), too, is a Reminder full of blessings which We are sending down, Will you then reject it" (21:50); "Indeed it is We, We Who send down the Reminder in parts, and it is We Who are its Guardian" (15:9); and "Those who disbelieve in this Reminder (the Qur'an) when it comes to them (are among those who will be thrown into the Fire). For it is surely a glorious, unconquerable Book. Falsehood can never have access to it, whether from before it or from behind it (whether by arguments and attitudes based on modern philosophies, or by attacks from the past based on earlier Scriptures)" (41:41-42).

[369] Some of these verses have been provided in the footnote above. As can be seen, the central criterion that Qur'anic exegetes—in interpreting the verse in question—have given prominence to is that 'The Qur'an needs to be interpreted with the Qur'an itself." They then expressed their own views and interpretations.

subsides and is remedied. This is because the beginning and end of all things is at God's disposal. The entire chain of causes begins with God and ends with Him. Since God is the One Most Great above and beyond limit and measure, there is nothing beyond Him, whether in outer creation, or in the conscience. Consequently, the heart is in no need of seeking anything else. When God is invoked, thoughts reach their last point, reason and intellect come to a halt, and all feeling, and fear and hope arrive at their final station. Whichever worldly provision hearts tend to other than Him, whichever aspiration is realized, they cannot settle for any of these because there exists that which is greater and loftier, and transcends anything worldly. The heart in search of peace and calmness battles with pain and anguish. The only thing that will give it this peace and tranquility is remembrance and invocation of God. It is only God Almighty who can remove the heart's inner turmoil and agitation and placate it.[370]

The influence of his predecessors can be clearly seen in Yazır's commentary. But he does, however, attempt to broaden the subject with theological and psychological analysis. Yazır's interpretation of hearts finding rest with remembrance is noteworthy in this context. He highlights the fact that this can be realized via two distinct ways. The first is God creating the act of remembrance directly in the human heart: this is 'active guidance.' That is, the human being who is favored with guidance invokes, remembers and recites the Divine Names with all their faculties and with their heart. The second is a person's becoming unified with the Qur'an and responding to its calls for reflection via engaging in systematic and profound thinking about Qur'anic truths and the 'book' of the universe. The hearts of those who are deprived of such remembrance and recitation, as indicated, are unable to achieve true serenity and tranquility of heart.[371]

There is a very close connection between the human being and the world. Just as this connection can be a necessary one in relation to a person's continuing their life in the world, it can also be considered as a connection relating to their wants and desires. By means of this second facet, the world perpetually addresses a person's emotions and constantly provokes them. If one is to consider the modern era in which we live, the

---

[370] Yazır, *Hak Dini Kur'an Dili*, VIII:5815-16.
[371] Ibid., V:146.

continually changing currents in technology and fashion serve to increasingly stimulate a person's whims and fancies. In the face of the diversity that such changing technology and fashion presents, human beings fluster desperately in the eddy of dissatisfaction and restlessness. This is because worldly desires and cravings repeatedly undergo change and renewal. Possessions become outmoded and obsolete. Buried under such a psychological negativity, the modern-day individual's being freed from this is contingent not upon their worldly and physical contentment, but on their contentment of heart and spirit. This in turn, as propounded by the abovementioned scholars and thinkers, is possible only through hearts finding God. Accordingly, there is nothing beyond Him. Virtually all exegetes, the aforementioned ones included, have evaluated this psychological state of human beings and the greatness of God in unison, and have interpreted this verse in such a manner.

Making Hearts Steadfast

Alongside its close connection with the previous topic, the Qur'an's reference to this question is another reason why its analysis is relevant.

Accordingly, if the belief system that the Qur'an presents finds its place in the heart, that heart in turn finds serenity and stability. Moreover, those things experienced within the course of life necessarily engender diverse feelings and effects in the hearts of believers. This is especially important when it comes to hearts feeling some form of support in events appearing outwardly unfavorable and therefore their not being weighed down by them. It is at this point where God provides assistance to those hearts in need of His help that can be represented with the terms *thabat* (steadfastness), *sakina* (serenity) and *inaya* (providence).

A Qur'anic verse in the chapter entitled Fath, or The Victory, mentions two places in which a *sakina*, or serenity descended upon the believers:

> He it is Who sent down His (gift of) inner peace and reassurance into the hearts of the believers, so that they might add faith to their faith. To God belong the hosts of the heavens and the earth; and God is All-Knowing, All-Wise.[372]

---

[372] (48:4)

God was assuredly well-pleased with the believers when they swore allegiance to you under the tree. He knew what was in their hearts (of sincere intention and loyalty to God's cause) and, therefore, He sent down (the gift of) inner peace and reassurance on them...[373]

Two matters, in particular, are noteworthy in relation to these two verses. The first of these is the Treaty of Hudaybiya mentioned, as the reason for the revelation of these verses, while the second is God Himself mentioning the reason behind His sending down inner peace and reassurance to believers. These will be examined respectively.

The Treaty of Hudaybiya took place in the sixth year after the Hijra, or Emigration from the city of Mecca to Medina. Prophet Muhammad saw a dream in which he was circumambulating the Ka'ba. He related this dream to his Companions and gave them the glad tidings that they were to visit the Ka'ba. A group of 1400 Companions set off with the intention of performing the minor pilgrimage. Upon hearing that the Muslims had left for Mecca, the Meccan polytheists decided not to allow them into the city. With this not being enough for them, they dispatched a force of 200 men. When Muhammad received news of these developments, he changed his route. The Muslims had not taken arms along with them, as they had no intention of engaging in conflict. The Prophet later turned not towards Mecca but in the direction of Hudaybiya and the Muslims redirected their journey and eventually camped there. Muhammad continually sent envoys to Mecca. When the envoys sent previously were unsuccessful in their attempts, the Prophet sent 'Uthman (d. 36/656) who was well connected and respected in Mecca. However, his efforts, too, were unsuccessful. The Meccans deemed a debasement and refused to allow the Muslims into Mecca, whatever the cost. They told 'Uthman that he himself, however, could visit the Ka'ba and perform his worship there as he wished. His responding in the negative incensed the Meccans. They therefore refused to let 'Uthman go, imprisoning him for several days. This reached Hudaybiya in the form of news that "Uthman was martyred. Accordingly, there was nothing left to do but to advance upon the Quraysh. As appeared from the outside, the Meccans were not only uninterested in a peaceful resolution, but on top of that had killed the Prophet's ambassador. Prophet Muhammad gathered his Companions. He took

---

[373] (48:18)

an oath from them that they would hold together and fight to the death. This is known as the "Pledge of Ridwan." Passing this test of commitment, the Companions were praised in the Qur'an.

Hearing the news of this oath, the Meccans were overcome by fear. Muhammad's resolve caused them great anxiety. They immediately released 'Uthman and sent 'Amr bin Suhayl to Hudaybiya for the purpose of reaching an agreement. Negotiations began for peace. Consequently, an agreement that on the surface was against the interests of the Muslims was reached. After nineteen days in Hudaybiya, the Muslims set off on their return to Medina. On the way back, the verses, "We have surely granted you a manifest victory (which is a door to further victories), That God may forgive you (O Messenger) your lapses of the past and those to follow, and complete His favor on you, and guide you (to steadfastness) on a straight path (leading to God's being pleased with You and eternal happiness); And that God may help you to a glorious, mighty achievement,"[374] the beginning verses of the chapter entitled The Victory were revealed.[375]

A brief examination of these verses is important in terms of allowing a better contextual understanding. As according to these verses, Muhammad and his Companions had circumvented such a dangerous and risky event by means of the tranquility that had been given to them, placed in their hearts by God. In line with such an understanding, those who do not possess such steadfastness of heart are driven to instability due to such feelings as fear, anxiety, and insecurity. The single element ensuring the attainment of steadfastness is the emergence of a complete sense of security and trust in the heart. This, however, belongs to God, the converter of hearts. Those who believe in God and in the truths that He has revealed have held fast to them, as to a rope, and have been brought to the path leading to God.[376]

---

[374] Fath, (48:1-3)

[375] Ibn Sa'd, *al-Tabaqat al-Kubra*, 8 vols. (Beirut: Dar Sadir, 1960), II:95, 96.

[376] (2:256); (3:101) The Qur'an also makes mention of God sending down inner peace and reassurance to the hearts of others also. For instance, to the Companions of the Cave (18:14), the mother of Moses (28:10), and the Qur'an's stating "They have indeed sought to tempt you (O Messenger) away from what We have revealed to you so that you may fabricate something else against Us. And then (had you done so), they would have taken you as a trusted friend" (17:73-74) and "All that We relate to you of the exemplary narrative of (the lives of some of the earlier) Messengers is in order that whereby We make firm your heart" (11:120) indi-

It is noteworthy that in the first of the verses cited at the beginning, by means of the statement "so that they might add faith to their faith..." the Qur'an reveals the purpose behind this serenity descending upon believers' hearts. The wisdom and Divine purpose behind difficulties experienced may not be immediately recognized and understood. The visible face of events can sometimes appear unfavorable. Not immediately rushing to remonstrance and criticism, but instead waiting for the result of events is thus more appropriate. However, this is no easy feat. As such, not every believer but only those who reach *yaqin*, or certainty in their faith can overcome difficulty with Divine help and support. In line with such an understanding, God has revealed through this verse that He enhances the faith of believers when they are faced with trial and tribulation so that they do not alter their standing as believers.

At this point, it is useful to briefly examine another action pertaining to the heart—the concept of *yaqin*. *Yaqin*, or certainty, essentially means having a strong, firm belief or conviction. It refers to soundness in faith in and a conviction of the truth expressed in all the essentials of belief such that even any possibility to the contrary is not entertained. Derived from the same root, the words *iqan*, *istiqan* and *tayaqqun* have the same meaning and are the terms used to describe a correct view of all things and events and constant and certain belief free from any kind of doubt and question. It is the heart's resolve in a certain matter and knowledge entailing the discernment or penetration of the realms beyond this material one.[377]

It is, at the same time, a knowledge that cannot be changed or corrupted. Those things which can be seen with the eyes, personally experienced, conveyed through narration, and whose existence and verity can be established, amount to certainty. For example, those areas in the disciplines of physics, chemistry, mathematics, and logic which have moved beyond theory and whose truth have been verified in practice are all included in the concept of certainty. By way of example, through implementing the sciences and the laws discovered therein, human beings have managed to construct the airplane and helicopter.

---

cates the inner peace and reassurance sent down to the heart of the Messenger himself.

[377] Ibn Manzur, *Lisan al-'arab*, 'i-q-n.'

In describing certainty, Abu 'Abd Allah al-Antaqi explains that even the smallest amount of it illuminates the heart, removes all doubt and fills it with gratitude and fear of God. A heart favored with certainty begins to see all created things—living and non-living—with insight and starts to witness things beyond their manifestations in the visible, corporeal realm. Such a heart reaches a degree whereby it as though sees the truths expressed in the essentials of belief such as the Hereafter, paradise, hellfire and the angels. Abu 'Uthman al-Hiri (d. 298/910) succinctly describes certainty as "careful attention to provisions for tomorrow." According to this definition, certainty derives from knowing full well the world and the Hereafter. The word 'tomorrow' is used in the Qur'an to refer to the Hereafter. "O you who believe! Keep from disobedience to God in reverence for Him and piety, and let every person consider what he has forwarded for the morrow. Keep from disobedience to God in reverence for Him and piety. Surely God is fully aware of all that you do."[378] However, in his description of certainty, Hiri employs the word 'tomorrow' in reference to the future in this world and describes the state of a person's not feeling great anxiety and perturbation in terms of their life in this world as certainty. A person who deeply believes in the essentials of faith, sees the fleetingness of this world and consequently the beauty of the Hereafter and paradise and directs their heart to eternity. Beyond all of these, in line with such a view, the desire to gain God's approval and pleasure and see Him extinguishes the charm and attraction of the world. A believer who possesses certainty thus weaves their life in this world with their desire and enthusiasm to attain eternal happiness in the Hereafter. They virtually live their lives in this world for the world to come. This state and circumstance means that one esteems both the visible and the incorporeal realms in accordance with their import and worth. In this respect, believers who possess certainty can be referred to as those who do not attach much importance to the affairs of the world in their hearts. As for Sahl b. 'Abd Allah (d. 200/815) who states that "it is forbidden for a heart that has savored the smell of certainty to attain inner peace and tranquility with anything other than God," there is a very close association between certainty and serenity. As such, it is not possible for a believer who possesses certainty to be content with and attain tranquility and reassurance with anything other than God. A believer at this

---

[378] (59:18)

level, only finds inner peace with God, by remembering and worshipping Him, and by struggling and serving in His way. Nothing else can provide such a believer with this relief and inner tranquility.[379]

Dhu al-Nun al-Misri (d.245/860)'s descriptions of certainty are quite original. In his view, "certainty suggests severing short-lived worldly ambitions and hopes, while short-lived hopes suggest renunciation." Renunciation bequeaths wisdom, while wisdom bequeaths consideration of possible consequences and ramifications. In line with such a definition, certainty results in one's directing their attention away from the world and towards death and life thereafter. A person who possesses certainty thus comes to mean one who strives seriously for their afterlife. Again, according to Dhu al-Nun, three things are signs are of certainty: "Directing one's attention to God in every case, turning only to Him and seeking help only from Him." As can be gleaned from his approach, certainty and belief in the oneness and unity of God are interconnected. Living a life of attachment to God and consideration of those things that earn His favor constitute certainty itself. A person's turning to God with their heart and their maintaining this orientation without cessation can each be viewed as indicators of certainty.[380]

Certainty has been delineated into the three categories of certainty coming from knowledge, certainty coming from direct observation or seeing and certainty coming from direct experience. The most oft-repeated similitudes used as examples of these three categories are honey and fire. Telling people about honey is certainty through knowledge, showing them the honey is certainty through direct observation and allowing them to taste of that honey is certainty through direct experience. Again, in the same way, having as much knowledge about fire as is explained by someone else constitutes the first category, seeing fire itself is the second, and personally entering the fire and burning therein is the third.

At this point, it is useful to examine a particular semantic explanation relevant to this issue. As is known, the word *mu'min* in Arabic comes to mean 'a believer,' while iman (belief), derived from the root letters a-m-n is an infinitive (*masdar*) in the form *if'al*. In Arabic, infinitives derived in this form are used both in the active and in the passive voice. For this

---

[379] al-Makki, *Qut al-Qulub*, I:236.
[380] Ibid., I:237.

reason, the Arabic word for *belief* refers to both "giving security" and "making secure," as well as "being secure," "relying upon," and "attaining safety and peace."[381] In addition to these, the word has another dimension of meaning, especially important with regards to the topic at hand. The meaning in question is "to reassure, and make safe." As will be remembered, one of God's Names in the Islamic tradition is Al-Mu'min and comes to mean "the source of safety and security and He who grants security to those seeking refuge in Him." When a believer relies on and trusts in their Lord, He takes them under His protection, reassures them and admits them into an atmosphere of safety and security. He is, at every moment, with His servant and at their aid, fulfilling their every need. As such, all of these can be evaluated as God's bestowing steadfastness, constancy and inner peace and reassurance upon the heart of a believer.

Cleansing the Heart

The last topic to be explored in this part is the notion of God's cleansing and purifying hearts. Just as the Qur'an employs the word *rij'sa*, meaning filth, to refer to such deviations of the heart as disbelief, attributing partners with God and hypocrisy,[382] it also defines deviation in action, referred to as sins, with the same word.[383] On the other hand, the Qur'an also makes mention of the exoneration of the carnal self, the purification of the soul and the cleansing of the heart, the third of which will be examined henceforth. The Qur'an, in several verses, mentions purification in juxtaposition with the heart. The first of the two verses that will be examined states the following:

> Whoever God has willed to put to a trial (to prove his nature, and has failed in this trial), you have no power in anything on his behalf against God. Such are those whose hearts (because of their rushing

---

[381] al-Isfahani, *Al-Mufradat*, 25, 26; Ibn Manzur, *Lisan al-'arab*, 'a-m-n.' Asım Efendi, *Translation of Al-Qamus*, IV:548.

[382] The verse serving as an example reads: "Thus, God lays ignominy upon those who do not believe (despite many signs and evidences)." (6:125) See also: (9:28, 95)

[383] "O you who believe! Intoxicants, games of chance, sacrifices to (anything serving the function of) idols (and at places consecrated for offerings to any other than God), and (the pagan practice of) divination by arrows (and similar practices) are a loathsome evil of Satan's doing; so turn wholly away from it, so that you may prosper (in both worlds)" (5:90).

in unbelief) God does not will to purify. For them is disgrace in the world, and in the Hereafter a tremendous punishment.[384]

The verse was revealed in relation to certain Jewish learned men. They were telling their coreligionists to accept Muhammad's teachings if it suited them, otherwise to outright reject them. The verse simultaneously refers to their words and attitudes. It also indicates, from the outset, that belief is realized with the heart.[385] In this respect, from the point of view of belief, what the tongue utters is of no consequence without the approval, sanction and confirmation of the heart.

The second verse to be examined under this heading is the following:

> Then, after grief, He sent down peace and security for you: a slumber overtook some of you; and some, being concerned (merely) about themselves, were entertaining false notions about God—notions of (the pre-Islamic) Ignorance—and saying: "Do we have any part in the authority (in the decision-making)?" Say (to them, O Messenger): "The authority rests with God exclusively." Indeed, they concealed within themselves what they would not reveal to you, and were saying (among themselves): "If only we had had a part in the authority (in the decision-making), we would not have been killed here." Say (O Messenger): "Even if you had been in your houses, those for whom killing had been ordained would indeed have gone forth to the places where they were to lie (in death)." (All of this happened as it did) so that He may test what (thoughts, intentions, and inclinations) is in your bosoms, and purify and prove what is (the faith) in your hearts. God has full knowledge of what lies hidden in the bosoms.[386]

This verse was revealed in relation to the Battle of Uhud, the second major battle in Islamic history. This battle had turned against the Muslims. The believers underwent a severe trial. Sixty-nine of the Companions of Muhammad were killed, and many others injured. While the beginning of the verse highlights the Divine will behind these events, the end of the verse serves as a reminder that everything is in the hands of God and

---

[384] (5:41)

[385] As the topic of belief will be explored in more detail later, this has been omitted for the time being.

[386] (3:154)

that this reality should never be forgotten, and informs believers of the reason why such an end was ordained for them. Accordingly, the believers experienced all this trial and tribulation not because God did not help them but, on the contrary, with much wisdom and for their benefit, especially to assess the sincerity or hypocrisy that they held in their hearts and to purge and purify them of the hidden things, misgivings and doubts they held therein.

The following observations can be made with regard to the association between these experiences of the Companions and the purification of their hearts: Human beings possess hearts that are susceptible to many influences, both positive and negative.[387] The carnal self and Satan are perpetually preoccupied with the human being and work constantly against their interests. The defeat at the Battle of Uhud was an ideal opportunity for the ego and Satan to inflict harm on the Muslims, with regards to both their beliefs and their actions. Hence, the first part of the verse reveals the psychology of the Muslims at the time. God tests the faith of the believers by means of differing conditions and situations. Their defeat in this battle was significant in terms of measuring their belief and illustrating the importance and necessity of remaining steadfast, whatever the conditions may be.

This meaning can be expanded further: Human beings are constantly tested in the world on the basis of belief, first and foremost, and then action. In addition to these, wealth and poverty, life and death are each means of trial and examination. By means of stating, "We will certainly test you with something of fear and hunger, and loss of wealth and lives and fruits (earnings); but give glad tidings to the persevering and patient," the Qur'an[388] indicates that the road leading to an understanding of the realities of existence as well as success passes through patience. The Qur'an informs human beings that they should not think that they would be left to their own devices after they have affirmed their belief, but that they would most certainly be tested on the sincerity of their words and affirmations.[389] The verse, "...

---

[387] Julian Baldick, *The Essence of Sufism* (Edison, NJ: Chartwell Books Inc., 2004), 20.

[388] (2:155)

[389] The relevant verse is as follows: "Do people reckon that they will be left (to themselves at ease) on their mere saying, "We believe," and will not be put to a test?" (29:2) See also: Qiyamah, (75:36); (23:115).

We try you through the bad and the good things (of life) by way of testing,"[390] also explicitly expresses this notion.

The words *ibtila* and *fitna*, generally used interchangeably in Arabic, are used in the lexicon to describe "putting a person through various trials to know fully or to reveal the aspects that are unknown," "retrieving mud or soil from the bottom of a well," and "softening and peeling leather."[391] The concept of *fitna* also comes to mean "putting gold in fire to separate it from foreign matter and purify it."[392] Such words as wealth and children being described in the Qur'an as *fitna* can also be considered as geared towards the purification of a human being. Hence it can be said that gratitude and thankfulness for the favors one has received and enduring the undesirable with patience fulfils a very important function with regards to a cleansing of the heart. Believers who are able to achieve these thus demonstrate the sincerity in their hearts, or in other words become those whose hearts have been purified and cleansed by God.

As topics evoked by the cleansing of the heart such as the heart's soundness and its submission will be examined separately, they will not be elucidated here.

The Heart's Turning to God

It is the heart which actualizes spiritual inclination. The heart has very important functions like reasoning and understanding, perception and comprehension, and discernment and feeling. The heart uses these functions to incline to God. It is the heart which carries out such actions as belief in God, submission to Him, knowing Him, loving Him, fearing Him and mentioning Him, which are each to be discussed under separate subheadings.

The Heart's Belief in God

The heart's belief in God presents itself as its most important mission. The prominent scholars of the Islamic tradition ascribe the issue of faith to the heart, and have called heart the locus of faith. It is possible to mention many verses that can be referenced to their view. Moreover, the Qur'an heavily criticizes those who verbally express their faith, but deny it by

---

[390] (21:35)
[391] al-Isfahani, *Al-Mufradat*, 61.
[392] Ibid., 372.

heart.[393] Analysis of the Qur'anic verses describing the unity of the heart and faith reveal that when the Qur'an mentions belief, it naturally does not allude to this connection and mention these two concepts together in each and every instance. So, not every verse that describes belief contains the word *qalb*. However, it is always present in the meaning and context.

Although much has been said about the meaning of belief as a term, the summary of such is that belief constitutes the confirmation or affirmation of the heart. The Sunni majority, first and foremost, and virtually all the different schools of thought have associated belief with the heart and have seen it as an action of the heart. Only the two marginal sects known as Murji'a and Karramiya, have understood belief to be verbal admission. The inaccuracy of this view is suggested by the verses of Qur'an, wherein it is explicitly stated that those who deny by heart but declare their belief with their tongue are not true believers.[394] This verse, which also indicates that belief is directly associated with the heart, underlines the affirmation by heart behind outer appearance:

> Some of the dwellers of the desert say: "We believe." Say (to them): "You have not believed. Rather, (you should) say, 'We have submitted (to the rule of Islam),' for faith has not yet entered into your hearts.[395]

Here, the mentioning, in juxtaposition, of the expression *aslamna*, which means "we have submitted," and the expression *amanna*, meaning "we believe," presents the question of the relationship between the terms belief and Islam (in terms of one of the latter's literal meanings being surrender) and the nuances between them. Although the difference between these words is apparent in terms of their literal meanings, there are diverging opinions about the meanings that they construct when used together. While some scholars have argued that the meanings that these terms signify are analogous, others have pointed out the differences between them.[396] In the famous Prophetic Tradition, known also as the Jibril *hadith*[397], the Prophet was asked regarding the terms belief and Islam sep-

---

[393] (5:41)

[394] (2:08); (5:41); (63:01)

[395] (49:14)

[396] For detailed information see Yazır, *Hak Dini Kur'an Dili*, VI:4482; Izutsu, *God and Man in the Qur'an*, 50-55.

[397] Bukhari, Faith, 37; Muslim, Faith, 1.

arately, and the answers he gave were different. Accordingly, while belief constitutes the facet of the matter which pertains to the heart, and means to believe in and affirm God and all that which He enjoins human beings to believe in, and to be spiritually content in this, Islam can be summarized as submission in the direction of that which the heart confirms, and carrying out what is required in terms of deed and action.

It thus becomes possible to express the difference between belief and Islam with the words 'theory' and 'practice.' Faith is the belief in a person's heart, and Islam is the reflection of this affirmation in the heart, in everyday life. The theoretic faith finds its expression in everyday life. Human beings who have perfected belief in their hearts reflect this is their actual lives. Relevant Qur'anic verses explain this notion as such:

> The true believers are only those who, when God is mentioned, their hearts tremble with awe, and when His Revelations are recited to them, it strengthens them in faith, and they put their trust in their Lord. They establish the Prayer in conformity with its conditions, and out of whatever We have provided for them (of wealth, knowledge, power, etc.), they spend (to provide sustenance for the needy, and in God's cause, purely for the good pleasure of God, and without placing others under obligation.) Those (illustrious ones) are they who are truly believers.[398]

As can be seen, in these verses, belief and Islam are mentioned together. Islam is described as the material manifestation of belief and examples are provided on its reflection in everyday life. The close connection between belief and deeds illustrated in these verses can also be seen in many other Qur'anic verses. The Qur'an on several occasions mentions faith together with good deeds.[399] In fact, the word *iman* (belief) in the verse "God will never let your faith go to waste"[400] is described by some of the scholars as the ritual Daily Prayers.[401] This Prophetic Tradition points out the possible characterization of deeds as belief:

> There are over 70 branches of faith. The highest is to bear witness that 'There is no god but Allah and Muhammad is the Messenger of

---

[398] (8:2-4)
[399] For sample verses, see: (2:62); (5:169); (18:88); (19:60)
[400] (2:143)
[401] Ibn Kathir, *Tafsir*, I:278. Yazır, *Hak Dini Kur'an Dili*, I:526.

Allah.' The lowest is the removal of harm from the road. Modesty is also of faith.[402]

In this Nabawi expression, theory and practice are mentioned together, with the implication being presented that if there is no practice, there is also no theory. For instance, at the end of the *hadith* is mentioned that modesty is a complementary part of belief, so much so that it immediately evokes the idea that similarly, if there is no shame, then there is also no belief. On the basis of this and similar statements, sects like the Mu'tazilites and Kharijites have accepted deeds as an indispensable part of belief. Nevertheless, this approach has not been accepted by scholars of the traditional view; the *ahl al-Sunna* (mainstream) scholars have separated belief and action, and have entertained no doubt as to the status of those who have belief but no action as *mu'minun* (believers). Likewise, stating that in certain situations of necessity belief can be concealed in the heart, the Qur'an has separated belief from action.[403] In some circumstances, it may be necessary to display nothing in terms of deeds. Claiming that those who have been subjected to such circumstances are no longer believers would not be Qur'anic in approach. As alluded to in the Jibril *hadith* mentioned earlier, when Muhammad is asked about the nature of belief, his stating that "is to believe in Allah, His angels, (the) meeting with Him, His Apostles, and to believe in Resurrection," and at another time mentioning that "those who have had faith equal to the weight of a grain of mustard seed to be taken out from Hell,"[404] indicates the need for approaching belief and deeds separately.[405]

In addition to this, it is stated that although those who give up performing deeds when there is no pressure and obstacle to their doing so will be evaluated as believers in God's presence, they would not be deemed as such in the eyes of the people. For this reason, it has been viewed as necessary for believers to show their spirituality outwardly and belief has been described as "the affirmation of the heart" together with "the

---

[402] Muslim, Faith, 58; for similar narration, see: Bukhari, Faith, 3.

[403] (16:106); (40:28)

[404] For related *hadiths*, see Bukhari, Faith, 33; Muslim, Faith, 52, 302, Abu Dawud, Salat, 36, Tirmidhi, Hell, 9.

[405] For further information, see Ahmet Saim Kılavuz, *İman Küfür Sınırı* (Istanbul: Marifet Yayınları, 1997), 32-41.

confirmation of the tongue." In this context, deeds have been interpreted as the requirement of a perfect belief.

From a different vantage point, the following issues also warrant attention with regards to belief: to affirm, by heart, God and those things in which He wants human beings to believe in, to work steadily on the acquired belief in order to free it from imitation and elevate it to verification, to protect it from all kind of harm and to exemplify it in day-to-day life through good deeds. The first and the last points have been elucidated in quite some detail. The two points that will be touched upon here relating to belief itself encompass consolidating as well as protecting it.

In such an understanding, belief assumes the position of being the heart's state of reaching complete security and tranquility. For this reason, when such matters like suspicion and assumption emerge in the heart, there can be a slackening of trust and confidence towards the realities that the heart affirms. The heart can curtail or completely lose its belief over time. Virtually every Muslim scholar discussing the topic of belief has pointed out the changeability of belief and has drawn attention to its associated risks.

At this juncture, the sustenance and protection of the heart bear special significance. To be well acquainted with the essentials of belief and the heart's constant preoccupation with these emerge as the most important factors by way of nurturing the heart. Its being brought to a position of certainty and constancy and this being perpetually maintained, constitute an important dimension of belief. As such, the subject of *ma'rifa*, which can be defined as the heart's spiritually knowing God, comprises the second part of this section. The question of the heart's becoming blackened by means of wrongdoing and deviation will be touched upon separately.

The Heart's Knowledge of God

The concept of *ma'rifat Allah* is the meaning of the term *ma'rifa*—denoting "full knowledge and perception of something via contemplation and complete understanding of its signs"—becoming the adjectival clause to the Name of God,[406] and comes to mean experiential knowledge of God. Although it is not directly ascribed to the heart in the Qur'an, it is a con-

---

[406]   al-Isfahani, *Al-Mufradat*, 331.

cept well known in Islamic religious literature and especially in Sufi terminology for expressing the heart's function of knowing God. After touching upon the heart's belief in God, its knowing the God in which it believes and its turning to Him will be examined under this heading; the topics *mahabbat Allah* or love of God, and *makhafat Allah*, fear of God, as the two natural fruits of knowledge of God, will also be elaborated.

The Qur'an clearly defines the *raison d'être* of human beings as "to (know and) worship" God exclusively."[407] Therefore, in order to realize this purpose, it is necessary to know the Being that is worshipped. Ibn Jurayj (d. 150/767) interprets the expression "worship Me" in the verse "I have not created the jinn and humankind but to worship Me"[408] as "to know Me"[409]. *Ma'rifa* serves a very important mission in Sufi terminology with regard to enabling a person to reach the station of *al-insan al-kamil*, or the perfected human being. Before citing and analyzing the definitions of knowledge of God, it is necessary to stress again the consensus in *ma'rifa* being an action of the heart that possesses such capacities as reason, understanding, perceiving and feeling.

One of the Sufis of the early period, Dhu al-Nun al-Misri describes the fact of knowing as "the human being's attaining the mystery by using the most luminous lights that are granted to them."[410] The expression, "the most luminous lights that are granted to them," arguably refers to such dimensions of the heart as willpower, the power of perceptiveness, consciousness, secret, arcanum and super arcanum, which can be expressed as the heart and its profundities.[411] Implied in 'mystery,' denoting the unknown, the hidden and mysterious, is God Himself.

---

[407] (51:56)

[408] (51:56)

[409] Ibn Kathir, *Tafsir*, VII:401. At first it is stated that this comment belonged to Ibn 'Abbas. ('Ali al-Qari, *al-Mawdu'at al-Kubra* (Beirut1986), 269.)

[410] Hujwiri comments on this approach saying, "Gnosis is in reality God's providential communication of the spiritual light to our inmost hearts," i.e., until God, in His providence, illuminates the heart of Man and keeps it from contamination, so that all created things have not even the worth of a mustard-seed in his heart." {Ali B. Uthman al-Hujwiri, *The Kashf al-Mahjub (The Revelation of the Veiled) An Early Persian Treatise on Sufism*, trans. Reynold A. Nicholson (Cambridge: Gibb Memorial Trust, 2000).}

[411] These terms are discussed in detail in the section, "Fethullah Gülen and Heart."

Interpreting *ma'rifa* again at another instance, Dhu al-Nun describes the state of the person who possesses *ma'rifa* as that of loneliness, even when in the company of others.[412] Although this approach has become famous with Rumi's statement "To be with God while among the people," it first found expression with Dhu al-Nun.

It can be concluded from this description that the person who knows God is the one who knows the fact that He sees and hears everything and is present everywhere with His knowledge and power. Moreover, the person who carries this knowledge of the Divine in their heart, in whatever space and time they may be, realizes and perceives with their heart that they are forever in His company and under His control. In this sense, the loneliness of human beings in this world is a sacred loneliness, in the sense of their being with God and not sharing company with anyone but Him.

On another occasion, Dhu al-Nun is asked about the ultimate fate of a person endowed with experiential knowledge, and he responds saying, "To become as he (*sic*) was, where he was, before he came into being."[413] Dhu al-Nun's response is reminiscent of the pure and innocent state of the human being in the realm of the spirits, namely *alast bazmi* of the human in a spiritual world. Accordingly, God asked all the spirits, "Am I not your Lord?" They said in full submission and obedience: "Yes, we do bear witness."[414] Later draped in the garments that were their bodies, the spirits were sent to the world. Carnal, vain desires began exerting pressure on those spirits and in time they became more and more estranged from their initial pure state. Some proceeded to distance themselves from God, while others waged a struggle to allow their spirit to triumph over their carnality. According to Dhu al-Nun, the only means that will allow the human being to return to the state of "before he came into being," or their initial, pure state is experiential knowledge of God. Hearts that know God will enable their spirits to dominate their bodies to the extent to which they know, and in such a manner allow themselves to return to their former state.

---

[412] Ibid.

[413] Abu Bakr Muhammad ibn Ibrahim Kalabadhi, ed. *al-Ta'arruf li-madhhab ahl al-tasawwuf* (Beirut: Dar al-Kutub al-'Ilmiyya,1993), 108.

[414] (7:172)

Highlighting the outward appearance of those people who possess experiential knowledge Yahya b. Mu'adh (d. 258/872) points out that because their hearts are continuously preoccupied with God, they are indifferent to and uninterested in worldly affairs.[415] According to Muhammad ibn Fadl (d. 319/931), "*ma'rifa* is the heart's life with God."[416] On the other hand, author of the famous *Kitab al-Luma'* (The Book of Flashes), Abu Nasr as-Sarraj (d. 378/988) contributes a different dimension to the issue with his relating 'Abd ar-Rahman al-Farisi's statement that, "experiential knowledge reached perfection 'when multiplicity becomes unity, and when the (various) spiritual states and resting places are equalized, and when the appearance of distinctiveness has vanished.'"[417] This approach can also be expressed as the possessor of experiential knowledge's observing just how active the secret hand of God is, even in their own works and deeds, and their reaching the point where they see nothing but His manifestations and expressions. Moreover, he also argues that unless the awe of God is totally dominant in the heart, God cannot be known experientially. As such, mindfulness of God and love of Him cannot be possible without "experiencing His graciousness in your heart, heedless of what He had in mind for you before He created you."[418]

As is evident in the descriptions analyzed above, experiential knowledge of God has been directly associated with the heart and is presented as being under its dominion or disposal. Some scholars elaborating on this point have discussed the avenues to attaining experiential knowledge of God. For instance, one of the most influential early medieval Muslim spiritual writers Abu Talib al-Makki (d. 386/1006), stresses the importance of "hearing, sight and heart" in order to acquire experiential knowledge of God, and states that these are the roots of knowledge and grace that God bestows on humankind. Using these three faculties properly is of great importance with regard to being a possessor of experiential knowledge.[419] That which led him to draw such a conclusion is arguably the verses, "God brought you forth from the wombs of your mothers when you knew noth-

---

[415] Abu Nasr 'Abd Allah ibn 'Ali Sarraj, *Kitab al-luma' fi'l tasawwuf*, ed. Reynold A. Nicholson (London: Luzac & Co, 1914).

[416] Al Qushayri, *al-Risalah*, 295.

[417] Sarraj, *Kitab al-luma,'* 89.

[418] Ibid.

[419] al-Makki, *Qut al-Qulub*, I:237.

ing, and (in order that you might be perfected through learning) endowed you with hearing and eyes and hearts, that you may give thanks (from the heart, and in speech and in action, by fulfilling His commandments)."[420]

At this juncture, it is useful to point out the noteworthy style these verses and ones expressing similar meanings retain. When listing the capacities of human beings of hearing, sight and perception, they express the ability of hearing as singular and infinitive, while "eyes and hearts" are plural and take noun forms. Those interpreting this manner associate it with the notion that reality is single and unchangeable. For instance, it is said that a truth can be heard by everyone but every individual reaches a different understanding and perception by means of their eyes and heart. There is a connection established between humans' inability to find the truth and their being unable to use these instruments properly. Expressed differently, God has given ears, eyes and hearts to human beings in order that they find Him. By means of hearing and listening, looking and seeing, and evaluating that which is heard and seen, they can reach God. Failure to use these abilities brings with it liability and responsibility. Stating, "Do not follow that of which you have no knowledge (whether it is good or bad), and refrain from groundless assertions and conjectures. Surely the hearing, the sight, and the heart—each of these is subject to questioning about it (you are answerable, and will be called to account, for each of these on the Day of Judgment),"[421] the Qur'an affirms that human beings will be held to account for these.

A final point worthy of mention from Abu Talib al-Makki is the meaning that he ascribes to the word *'ilm* (knowledge). He argues that this word referred to in Prophetic Traditions has been understood to mean "knowledge of God, that... leads to God, and that returns one to Him" and stresses that all these are very closely related to the knowledge of faith and certitude and experiential knowledge, what he terms collectively "the knowl-

---

[420] (16:78). In another verse the same issue is held in a different perspective: "We had, assuredly, given them such power and prosperity (on the earth) that We have not given to you (O Quraysh), and We had appointed for them (the faculty of) hearing, and eyes, and hearts (all the means of perception, outward and inward). But neither their ears, nor their eyes, nor their hearts, availed them anything, as they obstinately rejected God's signs and Revelations, and what they used to mock overwhelmed them." (46/26).

[421] (17:36)

edge of hearts."[422] Al-Makki describes the way in which he interprets the phrase *ahl al-dhikr* (the people of recollection) in the verse "...and if you (O people) do not know, then ask the people of expert knowledge (those who have knowledge of the Divine Revelations)"[423] as follows:

> They are the people ever-mindful of God and the people of the Divine transcendent unity and of understanding from God. They have not acquired this knowledge through the study of books, nor received it from one another by word of mouth. They were people of action and elegant deeds of devotion, so that when one of them was entirely dedicated to, and occupied with, God, he sought to labor in the service of the Master through deeds of the heart. They were with Him in seclusion before Him, remembering nothing but Him and occupying themselves with Him alone.[424]

As we can understand from this statement, Al-Makki interprets the people of recollection as those who have esoteric and spiritual knowledge, as opposed to exoteric knowledge. Here, he refers to the Gnostics who not only have this knowledge but also know how to shape this knowledge as experiential knowledge in their hearts, and conduct their lives with this consciousness. These people focus everything in their lives to the approval and pleasure of God and keep themselves busy with useful knowledge and good deeds that will strengthen their bond with their Lord. Even if they are present among the people, they search for togetherness with God.

As al-Makki cites, when Abu Muhammad is asked about those who are truly learned, he mentions "Those who prefer the next world to this, and God to themselves."[425] This answer points out that the learned person is not just a bearer of knowledge but rather expresses that it is through knowledge that reality is reached and which brings a person to the level of those who are truly learned. Knowledge is the guide and deeds are its followers; they depend on knowledge. Knowledge that does not breed

---

[422] al-Makki, *Qut al-Qulub*, I:240.
[423] (16:43); (21:7)
[424] al-Makki, *Qut al-Qulub*, I:127.
[425] Ibid., I:152.

deeds and action is useless. Dhu al-Nun says, "Sit with those whose qualities speak to you, not with those whose tongues talk at you."[426]

Moreover the essence of *dhikr* has also been considered "knowledge of God," while the acquisition of the essence of knowledge only being possible through forgetting all other than God. These approaches lead one to the conclusion that real knowledge is experiential knowledge of God. Stating, "While we were with God's Messenger we came to know the faith before we came to know the Qur'an," Jundab b. 'Abd Allah sheds light on approaches and prioritizes certain kinds of knowledge over others. Another Companion of Prophet Muhammad, 'Abd Allah b. Rawaha is famous for his call to other Companions: "Come, let us be believers for an hour." So they would sit with him, and he would recall for them the knowledge of God and of the Divine transcendent unity and of the hereafter. Often, Prophet Muhammad came to them while they were together with 'Abd Allah and they would fall silent. He sat with them and instructed them to continue what they had been doing, saying, "In this I have instructed you, and to this I have called you."[427]

Abu Ali ad-Daqqaq (d. 405/1014) also relates experiential knowledge with awe, and states that the person who increases in experiential knowledge of God also increases in their awe of Him. He makes the same connection between experiential knowledge and inner peace, and says that solemnity and tranquility increase at the rate of *ma'rifa*.[428]

It is possible to draw the following conclusion from the definitions relayed above. Knowledge of God is like an elixir. It lends its color to every place in which it is present and likens it to itself. The state of every believer possessing it changes and becomes beautified. They are enveloped with high moral norms. They live upright lives. Their awe and tranquility increase. They become exceptionally reverent to God, and possess an atmosphere commanding the respect of those around them. Because they live as though they see God, their every action reminds others of Him.

'Ali b. 'Uthman Hujwiri (d. 465/1072) describes experiential knowledge of God as being of two kinds: one relating to principles and the other to practice. As can be gauged from their names, "knowledge-based *ma'rifa*"

---

[426] Abu Talib Muhammad ibn 'Ali Makki, ed. *Qut al-qulub fi mu'amalat al-mahbub wa wf tariq al-murid ila maqam al-tawhid*, 2 vols. (Beirut: Dar Sadir,1995), I:202.

[427] Ibid., I:287-88.

[428] Al Qushayri, *al-Risalah*, 291.

is to have theoretic knowledge of God while "active *ma'rifa*" is the manifestation of the close connection with God in daily life.

Hujwiri describes *ma'rifa* as, "the life of the heart through God, and the innermost being's refusal to attend to anything but God,"[429] and draws attention to the relation between God and the heart thus:

> God fashioned the body and entrusted its life to the soul; He fashioned the heart and entrusted its life to Himself.[430]

Hujwiri draws attention to a very important dimension of experiential knowledge seeing it as virtually a guarantee in belief in God. According to him, a believer that possesses experiential knowledge of God is assured keeping their relation with God, to the extent that they retain this quality. This is because severance of this relationship results in the severance of *ma'rifa*.[431]

Author of one of the seminal Sufi treatises on Sufism Abu'l-Qasim al-Qushayri (d. 465/1072), who describes *ma'rifa* as knowing God—whose Essence is unknown—by His Names and Attributes,[432] elaborates on the terms *'ilm* (knowledge) and *irfan* (personal and accurate knowledge of the Divine) and states while some scholars view *ma'rifa* as synonymous with *'ilm* and every *ma'rifa* as knowledge, in the *tasawwufi* context, *ma'rifa* is "a characteristic of an individual who is intimately familiar with God through His Names and Attributes." He then goes on to emphasize the manifestations of this characteristic on everyday life. Qushayri draws a relationship of inverse proportion between the carnal self and *ma'rifa*, and posits that the latter is commensurate with the degree to which a person parts company with the carnal self. He concludes that all the descriptions of the scholars discussing *ma'rifa* are shaped in this way.[433]

Some of the issues that Qushayri draws attention to in relation to the manifestations of experiential knowledge on a person are noteworthy: The actions of the possessor of *ma'rifa* towards God are entirely authentic. They purge their character of baseness and vulgarity. The tempting beauty of the world cannot affect them. They await God's pleasure and

---

[429] al-Hujwiri, *Kashf al-Mahjub*, 203.
[430] Ibid., 204.
[431] Ibid.
[432] Al Qushayri, *al-Risalah*, 290.
[433] Ibid.

approval and they retreat spiritually from the world. They are liberated from the mumblings of the carnal self. They purge their heart from all imaginings and thoughts evoking anything other than God and do not cease their struggle for purification even for an instant. They incessantly carry on the most secret of intimate conversations with God. When reaching such a degree, they are sure from moment to moment of returning to God and orient themselves to Him. Such a person is known as one endowed with experiential knowledge.[434]

Ghazali of course also discusses experiential knowledge, quoting preceding scholars' ideas, and putting forth his own interpretations and approach. The connection he makes between the concept of *ma'rifa* and *amana* (trust) can be provided as a case in point of unique perspective and insight that he offers in relation to experiential knowledge. Ghazali understands the concept of *amana*, stated in the Qur'an to be offered to humankind, as the term "*ma'rifa*."[435] According to Ghazali, the most unique feature distinguishing human beings from the rest of creation and that which renders them capable of undertaking the Divine exalted charge is their potential to know God experientially. That is why humankind undertook this trust when the rest of creation declined to bear it. If humankind is conscious of their responsibility and acts accordingly, then they are able to be those who know God intimately.

It is God's endless mercy that He has placed within the human being a mechanism enabling them to know Him and reach Him by means of its use. The name of this mechanism is *qalb*. The notion of mechanisms, or 'spiritual centers' given to human beings for differing purposes is elementary in Sufi psychology, which as Schimmel (d. 1423/2003) asserts, is based on Qur'anic principles. She presents the *nafs*, *qalb* and spirit tripartition as the "foundation of later, more complicated systems."[436] Schimmel states that while some Sufis have followed this tripartition, others have insert-

---

[434] Ibid.

[435] The verse in question is: "We offered the Trust to the heavens, and the earth, and the mountains, but they shrank from bearing it, and were afraid of it (fearful of being unable to fulfill its responsibility), but man has undertaken it; he is indeed prone to doing great wrong and misjudging, and acting out of sheer ignorance." (33:72)

[436] Schimmel, *Mystical Dimensions of Islam*, 191.

ed and introduced other elements between *nafs* and *qalb*. "Each of these spiritual centers has its own functions," she maintains.[437]

Those who use their hearts to find their Lord will attain happiness in two abodes again with His favor. It is God Who bestows the heart, makes Himself felt therein and Who rewards those who use their hearts. When Dhu al-Nun was asked, "By what means did you come to experiential knowledge of your Lord?" he replied, "I know my Lord closely through my Lord, and were it not for Him, I would have no experiential knowledge of Him."[438] Kalabadhi (d. 380/990) also reinforces the same notion stating that God is the one who discloses Himself to human beings through Himself and shows them ways to reach Him.[439] In consideration of all the above, it is inevitable that when a person fails to fulfil this trust, or in other words when they fail to use their potential to know God, they will in the end become tyrannical and ignorant.

Fethullah Gülen, one of the contemporary scholars that will be described in detail in a separate section, also examines the concept of *ma'rifa*. Some of the meanings that he attributes to the term "*ma'rifa*" are: A "special knowledge" acquired by "using one's conscience and inquiring into one's inner world,"[440] to know God "beyond all conceptions of modality," "according to travelers on the path of God, it is the station where knowing is united with the one who knows, where knowing becomes second nature, and where each state reveals what or who is known," and "the appearance and development of knowledge of God in one's conscience, or knowing God by one's conscience."[441]

As a result, it is possible to conclude that it is the heart which fulfils the duty of knowing God in the human being. In other words, the heart has been created with the aptitude and potential of realizing this function. *Ma'rifa*, another dimension of the heart's turning to God, has many outcomes and benefits. Among these are two in particular that increase and develop as *ma'rifa* develops in a believer's heart. These are love of God and fear of God. It may not be erroneous to suggest that these three terms are parts and natural consequences of each other. That is to say,

---

[437] Ibid., 192.
[438] Al Qushayri, *al-Risalah*, 293.
[439] Kalabadhi, ed. *al-Ta'arruf li-madhhab ahl al-tasawwuf*, 78.
[440] Gülen, *Key Concepts in the Practice of Sufism 2*, 135.
[441] Gülen, *Key Concepts in the Practice of Sufism 1*, 146.

the heart knows God by means of using its own faculties like perception and understanding, and discernment and feeling. It learns of Him through His Names and Attributes and also feels His presence in a way that is indescribable in physical terms and such that only a person receiving this favor can perceive. This knowing brings along with it the love of God. Namely, that heart which is aware of God at the same time begins to love God also. The more it loves, the more it wants to know Him. As such, a virtuous cycle emerges. However, knowing God and increasing in knowledge of God do not just produce love of God. Because the being that is to be known is none other than God, *khawf*, or fear of God accompanies this love. In other words, *ma'rifa* produces both love of God and fear of God. One who knows God both loves and fears Him.

These two natural outcomes of *ma'rifa* will hereafter be examined. It is important to state at this point that Qur'anic verses and Prophetic Traditions will be employed as reference points in delineating the general framework, noteworthy views will be presented, and the approaches of Said Nursi and Fethullah Gülen will be elucidated at length.

The Heart's Love of God

The word love is a term oft-mentioned in virtually every religion and culture and which perpetually maintains its relevance and weight. In the Islamic culture also, *mahabba* (love) constitutes one of the underlying topics of disciplines such as Sufism, literature and philosophy. There are many among Sufis and philosophers who deem *mahabba* to be sole goal and purpose of creation,[442] with "the Sufi Path [being] intrinsically trans-

---

[442] Nursi holds the same view. He states: "Love is the very leaven of the universe. It is through love that all beings are in motion. It is from love that the laws of attraction, affinity, and ecstasy present in all beings spring." (Nursi, *The Words*, 652.) Moreover, in his view, when a thing is created, the principle characteristics being formed first in that thing's essence are the various degrees of love: "Contained all together in the obedience and conformity of contingent beings to the pre-eternal command of "Be!" proceeding from the Pre-Eternal will are inclination, need, desire, and attraction, which are also manifestations of Divine will." (Nursi, *The Words*, 549.) According to Nursi, the scope of *mahabba* is expansive enough to encompass all living beings. This is because God has created human beings with an encompassing nature. For this reason, the *mahabba* in their nature is of the expansiveness and greatness to embrace the whole universe: "Since man is the most comprehensive fruit of the universe, a love that will conquer the universe has been included in his heart, the seed of that fruit." (Said Nursi, *The Letters*, trans. Şükran

formative and... permeated with and predicated upon love for God."[443] As discussed several times previously, it can be said that one of the most particular manifestations of the heart, with functions such as reason, comprehension and feeling, is *mahabba*.[444] Accordingly, it is indispensable to direct and satisfy feelings appropriately in order for the attainment of happiness for the human being. The most essential spiritual feelings that need to be found in the human being are those directed toward God. In this sense, love of God is one of the topics most stressed by the religion of Islam.

In describing love of God, the Qur'an uses the words *mahabba* and *mawadda*. The former lexically means purity and whiteness, to rise and to emerge, constancy and resolve, essence, seed, and to protect and maintain.[445] On the other hand, the latter is derived from *al-wudd*, which means "to love, to want something to happen." One of the ninety-nine Names of God in the Islamic tradition is *Al-Wadud*, meaning "the One who is best-loved" and "the One who loves the one that turns to Him (All-Loving)."[446]

The synonymous words *mahabba* and *mawadda* have been defined by Muslim scholars of the classical period as "the inclination of human nature towards that which gives pleasure,"[447] "to ask for that which appears to be beneficial, preferring the beloved over everything else in one's possession, following the beloved in every situation and leaving nothing but the beloved in the heart."[448] Scholars examining the reasons of love have generally referred to such issues as "advantage, benefit, fancy, and appreciation." According to them, just as love can emerge through the perceptions of the five sensory organs, the beauty that the mind takes pleasure in can also be a source of love. In addition, things such as acts of good-

Vahide (Phoenix: Nur Publishers, 2008), 367.) The significance of this statement emerges in terms of its demonstrating Nursi's understanding and expression of love as an action of the heart.

[443] John A. Napora, "Love and Lover Transformed: The Sufi Path to God," in *Metanexus Conference on Works of Love* (Philadelphia2003).

[444] Chittick, *The Sufi Path of Knowledge*, 108, 48, 93.

[445] al-Jawziyya, *Madarij al-Salikin*, III:10.

[446] (11:90); (85:14)

[447] After stating that *mahabba* emerges by means of knowledge and perception, Ghazali posits that everything that gives pleasure or comfort is loved by the perceiver. (al-Ghazali, *Ihya,'* IV:296.)

[448] al-Jawziyya, *Madarij al-Salikin*, III:11, 17.

ness and protection from harm have also been mentioned among the reasons for the emergence of *mahabba* in the human heart.[449]

In discussing the reasons for love, Said Nursi, mentions 'perfection,' 'beauty' and 'virtue,' and states that these are 'loved for themselves.'[450] He expresses that God is the One who has all these three qualifications in the absolute sense and because of this, He is the One who deserves to be loved best.

Contemporary scholar Fethullah Gülen defines *mahabba* and its profundity in this way:

> *Mahabba* means fondness, tender and kind feelings, inclination, and love. Love that affects and invades one's feelings is called passion; love that is so deep and irresistible that it burns for union is called fervor and enthusiasm.[451]

Love should not be interpreted as the manifestation of merely a single function of the heart. It presents itself as the result of almost all its functions, such as intellect, comprehension and feeling. The heart's inclination towards a thing is like a step taken towards love. Thereafter, as the dose of this inclination increases, a gravitational force that can be defined as need, desire and inclination takes root in the heart and results in *mahabba*.

The word *mahabba* is interpreted in two ways: The love of the servant for God and God's love for his servant. Explaining these two facets of *mahabba*, the Qur'an, in an oft-repeated verse, says: "...A people whom He loves and who love Him."[452] The love of God for His servants has been interpreted as His willing goodness for them in the world and in the Hereafter, while the love of the servants for God is taken to mean their complete obedience to God and their avoiding rebellion and deviation. When

---

[449] al-'Ayni, *'Umdat al-Qari*, I:144.

[450] Nursi, *The Words*, 599.

[451] Gülen, *Key Concepts in the Practice of Sufism 1*, 149.

[452] (5:54). The entire verse reads:" O you who believe! Whoever of you turns away from his Religion, (know that) in time, God will raise up a people whom He loves, and who love Him, most humble towards the believers, dignified and commanding in the face of the unbelievers, striving (continuously and in solidarity) in God's cause, and fearing not the censure of any who censure. That is God's grace and bounty, which He grants to whom He wills. God is All-Embracing (with His profound grace), All-Knowing."

love is attributed to God it has been understood as benevolence; when attributed to human beings, however, it is read as obedience, submissiveness and unconditional surrender.

A directly related verse states:

> Yet there are among humankind those who (devoid of good sense and unable to reason) take to themselves objects of worship as rivals to God, loving them with a love like that which is the due of God only—while those who truly believe are firmer in their love of God.[453]

This verse is striking in the sense that it clearly identifies to whom love, one of the most special qualities pertaining to human beings, should be most directed. While the verse asserts that the ability to love should be used for God, it also draws attention to the fact that it can be misused also. Accordingly, if a person associates somebody other than God as partners with Him, or if they show greater affection to those other than God, then this means that such a person uses this ability—bestowed on them in order for them to love God—elsewhere and thus misuses it.

In another related verse, love of the Prophet is mentioned alongside love of God and the desire to strive in their cause, with the possibility of other love or desire getting in the way of these being prohibited in a rather admonitory tone.[454] Parents, children, one's spouse, friends, wealth and property coming before God and His Messenger and striving in their way, pose a very dangerous situation for a believer. They have thus been enjoined to avoid every kind of attachment and relationship at odds with love for God and His Messenger and which are obstacles to the fulfilment of religious obligations.

In examining the heart's love of God, the love of God for His servants will be touched on first, followed by the key question at hand—servants' love of God; in this way, the two dimensions of *mahabba* will be presented.

---

[453] (2:165)

[454] The relevant verse is: "Say: "If your fathers, and your children, and your brothers and sisters, and your spouses, and your kindred and clan, and the wealth you have acquired, and the commerce you fear may slacken, and the dwellings that you love to live in, are dearer to you than God and His Messenger and striving in His cause, then wait until God brings about His decree. God does not guide the transgressing people (who prefer worldly things to Him, His Messenger and striving in His cause, to truth and true happiness in both the world and the Hereafter)" (9:24).

God's Love for His Servants

As it is stated in the abovementioned Qur'anic verse from the chapter entitled al-Ma'edah, God loves His servants. In many verses, God attributes love to Himself.[455] Before proceeding to an examination of relevant Qur'anic verses and *hadith*, it is useful to consider 'what' God's love for a person or thing actually entails. Generally Muslim scholars do not approve of the idea that God's love for His servants can be identified with the love that human beings possess, and its being reduced to longing and yearning. For everything pertaining to God the *Subhan* (All Glorified)[456] is considered in terms of His Majesty and His being the Eternally Besought of All[457]. Qualities such as yearning or longing, belonging to human beings have been accepted as irrelevant and inappropriate for God. Muslim scholars have generally understood Divine love to be diverse and particular blessings bestowed upon servants. The issue of God's love for His servants, moreover, has also been viewed from the perspective of His approving of their deeds and rewarding them as a result, as well as His praising them.[458] Qushayri, for instance, says that God's love is more particular than mercy. In his view, God's causing his servants to perform good deeds, and his numerous blessings to them are His mercy; His making His closeness felt to them and honoring them with many elevated states constitute His love. According to another category, God's general blessings show His mercy, while His specific favors are manifes-

---

[455] The following verses are cases in point: "Surely God loves the God-revering, pious" (3:76). "God loves the patient and steadfast" (3:146). "God loves (such) people who are devoted to doing good, aware that God is seeing them" (3:134, 148). "Surely God loves those who turn to Him in sincere repentance (of past sins and errors), and He loves those who cleanse themselves" (2:22). "God surely loves those who fight in His cause in ranks as though they were a firm and solid structure" (61:4). In addition to the things that He Loves, there are also some other issues that God dislikes. Example verses for these are: "Surely God does not love disorder and corruption" (2:205). "God does not love the wrongdoers" (3:57, 140). "God does not love those who are conceited and boastful" (4:36). "God does not love anyone proud and boastful" (57:23).

[456] *Subhan* is one of the Names of God, expressing that He is free of all fault, defect, deficiency and weakness.

[457] *Samad* is one of the Names of God which expresses God's self-sufficiency; this entails God's not needing anything, but everything's being in need of Him.

[458] al-Jawziyya, *Madarij al-Salikin*, III:18.

tations of His love.[459] As such, God's mercy is a wide circle while His love is akin to a smaller one placed therein. In other words everyone honored with God's love is at the same time favored with His mercy. However, this does not mean that every individual attracting His mercy will also attain His love. As evident in Qushayri's example, every believer can perform good deeds and receive rewards, but not everyone can acquire proximity to God, or *qurbiya,* and wake to the different and very unique sensations and perceptions as a result of this connection. In order for this to happen, beyond God's mercy, there also needs to be His love towards the servant.

The issue of God's love for His servants also features rather frequently in the *hadith.* But there are two *hadith* in particular which are used and examined as reference in virtually every discussion. The narrator of both these two traditions is Abu Hurayra (d. 58/677). The first is one characterized as also a Divine (*qudsi*) *hadith.* In this *hadith* God is reported to have said:

> I will declare war against him who shows hostility to a pious worshipper of mine. And the most beloved things with which My slave comes nearer to Me, is what I have enjoined upon him; and My slave keeps on coming closer to Me through performing Nawafil (praying or doing extra deeds besides what is obligatory) till I love him, so I become his sense of hearing with which he hears, and his sense of sight with which he sees, and his hand with which he grips, and his leg with which he walks; and if he asks Me, I will give him, and if he asks My protection, I will protect him.[460]

In another tradition Prophet Muhammad says:

> When God loves His servant, He calls Gabriel: "O Gabriel! I love one of my servants namely...I want you love him also." Then Gabriel loves him and calls to the other angels in Heaven: "God loves the servant..., and then you love him too." Hereupon all the angels in Heaven love him. Right after that, a kind reception for him accrued in the world."[461]

---

[459] Al Qushayri, *al-Risalah,* 296, 97.

[460] Bukhari, Riqaq, 38.

[461] Bukhari, Adab, 41; Muslim, Birr, 157. Some of the *hadiths* that express love for God are: The good deed most loved by God is the one that committed less but contin-

As can be seen, these *hadith* clearly demonstrate the notion of servants being loved by God. The former expresses the path leading to the love of God. As such, the servant attains an elevated station by means of obedience to the Creator, passing a threshold, so to speak, and becoming loved by Him. The religiously ordained obligatory worship together with the supererogatory constitutes an important means of reaching this station. A servant being favored thus is now under the special protection and watch of the Creator. Akin to the person who is extremely compassionate towards their beloved and their doting on them, God perpetually directs his servant towards goodness, enables them to perform good deeds and make the right decisions, and never misleads them. He protects those who seek refuge in Him and does not allow harm to come to them. As mentioned at the beginning of the Prophetic Tradition, it is stated that when a friend of God has enmity shown towards them, God Himself declares war on the aggressors, and this corresponds completely with the last part of the *hadith*.

The second *hadith* asserts that a believer who is loved by God will not only be loved by Him but also by all the angels, first and foremost by Archangel Gabriel. In the latter part of the *hadith*, that such a person loved by God and His angels will be loved by human beings also is expressed, with a love towards this person being planted by God in their hearts.

Nursi's view in relation to the topic also warrants closer attention. In explaining the love of God for His servants, his point of departure is the Names of God. He examines the manifestations of these Names and then proceeds to a discussion of God's love towards His creation. Nursi considers God's love for humanity, as the highest of His creation, from a distinct perspective. He holds the reference point of this evaluation to be God's endless perfection and beauty. According to Islamic belief, God has created the whole universe with endless beauty and perfection. There is neither defect nor deficiency in the universe and this shows the Creator's

---

ued constantly. (Bukhari, Faith, 32; Muslim, Musafirun, 215-218) When God's Apostle was asked the most loved good deed by God, he replied "good manners towards parents." Then he was asked again, and he gave the same reply. At last, when he was asked for the third time he said, "holy battle for the Straight Path." (Bukhari, Mawaqit al-Salah, 5; Adab, 1) Whoever loves and wants to reach God, God loves to reach him, in return. On the contrary, whoever sees reaching God as terrible, then God doesn't love and want to reach him, as well. (Bukhari, Riqaq, 41; Muslim, Dhikr, 14-17)

limitless perfection and beauty. At the same time, God loves His Own beauty and perfection. Just as a human being takes pleasure in their beauty, God loves His beauty and perfection in a way befitting Him. All of God's 'beautiful Names' are gleams and reflections of these qualities. Accordingly, God loves His art, so to speak, His power to create. All created things are again the manifestations and the indications of these Names. As a result, then, He loves creation, which is the manifestation of these Names, and every beauty and goodness that emerges therein. As is evident, Nursi expresses God's love of creation by means of five degrees. Firstly, God loves his beauty and perfection, then the gleams and manifestations of His beauty, His creation, created beings, which can be referred to as the practical reflection of His art and finally, the beauty of that creation.[462]

With views along the lines of Nursi's thought, Gülen also states that God's love for His creation is an expression of His love for Himself. God's loving creation and humanity—the most honored among creation—is due to His love for His own life, knowledge, will, power and other Names and Attributes.[463] This is because all creation is a result of the reflection and manifestation of God's Names.

In addition to the abovementioned, it is also useful to briefly touch on the ways leading to God's love. The Prophetic Tradition asserting that religiously obligatory and supererogatory worship causes one to earn God's love was presented above. Two further points will be mentioned at this juncture. The first of these is the role that Prophet Muhammad plays in attaining God's love. Stating, "If you indeed love God, then follow me, so

---

[462] The Necessarily Existent One possesses infinite beauty and perfection, for all the varieties of them dispersed through the universe are the signs and indications of His beauty and perfection. Those who possess beauty and perfection clearly love them. Similarly, the All-Glorious One greatly loves His beauty, and He loves it in a way that befits Himself. Furthermore, He loves His Names, which are the rays of His beauty, and since He loves them, He surely loves His art, which displays their beauty. In which case, He also loves His creatures, which are mirrors reflecting His beauty and perfection. Since He loves the creatures that display them, He certainly loves the creatures' fine qualities, which point to the beauty and perfection of His Names... And since He loves His art, He certainly loves Muhammad the Arabian (Upon whom be blessings and peace), who proclaimed His art to the universe in reverberating voice, making it ring in the ears of the heavens, and who with a tumult of glorification and recitation of the Divine praises, brought to ecstasy the land and the sea; and He loves too those who follow him. (Nursi, *The Letters*, 353-54.)

[463] M. Fethullah Gülen, *Gurbet Ufukları* (Istanbul: Nil Yayınları, 2010), 27.

that God will love you and forgive you your sins," the Qur'an explicitly points to this notion.[464] Implied in such a statement is that God loves the Prophet and loves the other believers to the extent that they emulate him.

The last issue that will be looked at with respect to acquiring God's love is enabling His servants to love Him. The *hadith*, "Make the servants love God so that God will love you"[465] is an articulation of this notion. To acquaint the people with God, making use of all the opportunities at hand to teach them about Him will bring with it God's love.

Servants' Love of God

Another aspect of love for God, which is of greater interest and relevance due to its pertaining to the human being directly, is the servants' love of God. While Sufi authors in general do not elaborate in depth on the nature of God's love for humanity due to the sensitivities associated with the concept of God's perfection and His having no equal, they provide a more detailed elucidation in relation to human beings' love for God.[466] One of the central threads woven through the literature about the heart is that it—from the perspective of its being the center of a person's feeling and perception—has been created with an innate capacity to love. In other words, the heart functions as the source and center of love, as is the case in virtually every other matter. Although the meaning people construct when love is mentioned is in general a shared one, it is also generally accepted that love can be of varying degrees and have diverse manifestations in differing conditions. This notion can be summarized briefly with

---

[464] (3:31)

[465] at-Tabarani, ed. *al-Mu'jam al-Awsat*, 10 vols. (Riyadh: Maktaba al-Ma'arif,1985), IV:32.

[466] In his work on love in Sufism, Süleyman Derin argues that the Qur'an's describes God in two different ways of *tanzih* and *tashbih*—His being incomparable to any other creature or concept and His being described in ways with which the human mind is already familiar, allowing God to be more accessible to the human mind, respectively. Derin discusses the caution that is required when handling topics of God's Attributes, in order to avoid placing God on par with human beings with respect to a particular attribute or quality. He states that while classical Sufi authors have understood the concept of love in different ways, the notion that God has no equal is common to them all and is an "idea [which] pervades all the Sufi interpretations of love extant in the classical literature." Süleyman Derin, *Love in Sufism: From Rabia to Ibn al-Farid* (Istanbul: Insan Publications, 2008), 30.

the statement that love is relative. The situation and direction of love in the heart can change according to the disposition, taste, advantage and aesthetic appreciation of a human being. In the Islamic understanding, the most encompassing and perfected manifestation of the ability to love given to the human heart and its most perfect reflection is that which is directed to the Creator, that is, the love of God. The definitions of love to be presented henceforth have been made in the context of Sufism from this specific standpoint.

In describing the first Sufis of Baghdad, Ahmet Karamustafa lends space to the views of Abu Sa'id al-Kharraz (d. 277/890), author of one of the earliest extant Sufi texts, and one of the famous Sufi renunciants Abu al-Husayn al-Nuri among others. According to Abu Sa'id al-Kharraz, there are veils between God and the human beings. Preventing people from reaching God, these veils can only be removed with *shawq* (joyful zeal) and *mahabba*.

Abu al-Husayn al-Nuri's approach can be summed up as follows: The believer, while endeavoring to reach God, turns their face away from everything other than God, turns to God with their entire being and begins their period of 'active waiting.' This connotes waiting, with worship and devotion, for the spiritual blessing that is to come from Him, which continues until they find the way to reach God in their heart. And such a moment comes that God creates a light in that servant's heart. This light dulls and discolors the attraction of the world and everything in it. The heart becomes estranged towards the world. As the Divine light in the heart increases, the expectations with respect to the Hereafter also disappear. The heart then eschews both the world and the Hereafter and becomes completely annihilated in God. In this way, the body, heart, speech and every state of this believer becomes light. After expressing thus, Nuri cites the Qur'anic verse "...Light upon light! God guides to His Light whom He wills."[467] He concludes with the words: "When the light of God completely covers the heart of His servant, the spiritual stage of 'unification' of (*jam'*) becomes dominant and, completing the path they found in their heart, the Sufi reaches their Lord."[468]

---

[467] (24:35)

[468] Karamustafa, *Sufism: The Formative Period*, 15.

According to Shibli (d. 334/945), one of the leading figures of Islamic spirituality, love is the natural indication and result of *ma'rifa*, experiential knowledge of God. This is because the way leading to love of God passes through knowledge of Him.[469] Discussing love in his famous work, Abu Nasr Sarraj draws a close connection between awe[470], experiential knowledge and love, expressing this by means of the rhetorical question: "How can you know God intimately when awe of Him does not rule your heart? And how can you be mindful of God and love Him without experiencing His graciousness in your heart, heedless of what He had in mind for you before He created you?"[471]

This approach is significant in terms of stating that the experiential knowledge required for love needs to be felt in the heart as awe. For Sarraj, in the heart that knows God should also be fear and reverence for Him. With this interpretation, Sarraj gives precedence to fear of God over love of Him and posits that these are formed not simultaneously, in the heart, but sequentially.

Qushayri quotes Shibli's statement that, "Love is named *mahabba* because it erases (*tamhu*) everything from the [lover's] heart except the beloved," demonstrating the scope of his viewpoint.[472] Shibli asserts thus because of the connection between the root of the Arabic word *mahabba* and the word *maha*, which means to 'eradicate and destroy.' Due to this meaning, *mahabba* functions to eradicate all interest and attachment towards anything other than the beloved and reserve the heart solely for them.

Abu Talib al-Makki views love as one of the highest states of believers who know God.[473] He cites Sahl at-Tustari's following expression to describe distinction of those favored with love of God:

---

[469] Sarraj, *Kitab al-luma,'* 67.

[470] While awe (*khashya*), which assumes an important place in the Sufi lexicon, is taken to be synonymous with the word denoting fear, *khawf*, *khawf* is used rather to describe a fear that is material and based on observable reasons, while *khashya* has been used to refer to a fear born of reverence, directed towards hope and expressing the situation of feeling a fear that accompanies exaltation. Thus *khawf* has come to bear the meaning of a worldly fear and *khashya*, a spiritual and Divine one.

[471] Sarraj, *Kitab al-luma,'* 89.

[472] Al Qushayri, *al-Risalah*, 298.

[473] Makki, ed. *Qut al-qulub*, I:243.

All people other than the learned are dead; and the learned are asleep, except for those who fear God; and those who fear God are cut off, except for the lovers; and the lovers are living witnesses who give God precedence over every spiritual state.[474]

These statements describe love of God and the condition of those who possess that love. Believers who love God prefer their Beloved to everything else; the love of God in their hearts places utmost priority to their Lord and His will and they are thus able to realize this elevated level of spiritual life.

Known for his views and interpretations in this field, Qushayri sees that the precondition of love as complying with the beloved's wishes "openly and secretly" and "to agree with the beloved in his presence and his absence." Likening love to "a flame in the heart that burns down everything except what the beloved wishes," he understands love to be "the substitution of the attributes of the lover for those of the beloved."[475] As in evident, Qushayri constructs his description of *mahabba* based on its manifestations.

In weaving the fabric of his views on *mahabba* in his work *Manazil al-Sa'irin* (The Hundred Fields), 'Abd Allah al-Ansari (d. 481/1089) first underlines experiential knowledge of God, and the proceeds to discuss the three doors opening onto it. The first of the doors is knowledge of the Divine existence and unity. The second is knowledge of the Divine omnipotence, omniscience, and generosity. And the third one is knowledge of good deeds, friendship and intimacy. The first one of these doors opens to Islam itself, the second one to faith, and the third to sincerity (*ikhlas*). Ansari describes the path leading to the third door as being for those who have attained experiential knowledge of God—those who love God. "It is the path of the elect, the path by which the heart is adorned, by which joy is enhanced and affection expanded."[476]

Through these evaluations, Ansari creates an important link between sincerity and love of God. A person who loves God will reach the point where they will perform their worship solely to earn His approval and

---

[474] Ibid.

[475] Ibid., 300-04.

[476] 'Abd Allah Ansari, ed. *Manazil al-Sa'irin (Resting Places of the Wayfarers)*, Knowledge of God in Classical Sufism: Foundations of Islamic Mystical Theology (Tunis: Dar al-Turki lil-Nashr,1989), 100.

pleasure, and attain tranquility as a result. Inversely, it is possible to say that a person who both claims to love God and at the same time taints their good deeds by paying regard to the approval of others does not feel the love of God in real terms.

Ansari's description indicates that these doors of knowledge are not located side by side but nested within each other. The first door opens to the edifice of Islam and takes one to knowledge of Divine existence and unity, while the second door opens to the those who have already entered through the first, taking them to deeper knowledge of God. At this point is a more profound awareness and comprehension of God vis-à-vis His Names and Attributes. For those using these two doors and heading towards the inner door, is one opening to intimate knowledge and friendship, sincerity and righteous action. From this point on, there is present that which enables them to attain all of these—the love of God. A believer who has passed through this door has attained Divine love and, as a manifestation of this love, they are sincere in their every act of worship and righteous in their every deed and feel their closeness to their Lord in their conscience and, so as to speak, see nothing but Him.

In his discussion of Divine love, Ghazali lists the necessary conditions that need to be present for a person to love something. For Ghazali, one who has the attributes of benevolence, beauty and perfection is loved and deserves to be loved. It is applicable in both human relations and in the relationship between human beings and God. For instance, just as a person feels indebtedness, gratitude and love towards one who does good to them, they thank their Creator for the innumerable bounties that He has bestowed upon them and love Him. Human beings have a tendency towards beauty, without any expectation. That is to say, human beings love beauty in and of itself. In the Islamic understanding, God is the source of all beauty. One of his ninety-nine Names is *Jamil* (The Beautiful); for this reason, He deserves to be most loved. Perfection and goodness constitute another reason for love. There is in the human heart an innate inclination towards perfection, just as there is towards beauty. The precondition for perfection is not becoming tainted, deficient or being annihilated. Because everything other than God is mortal, the perfection perceived with regard to everything other than Him is a perfection doomed to deficiency. Worldly life and everything pertaining to it are a case in point. Hence, God is most deserving of love on the basis of perfection.[477] Ghazali, in this way, discusses the reasons for love and explains just how and why the tendency to love, inherent in the human heart, should be directed to God.

Abu Hafs 'Umar as-Suhrawardi (d. 632/1234), the author of what is often acknowledged as the last of the classical Sufi compendia, is another author who affords an important place to the love of God. In his view, just as *tawba* (repentance) is the head of all spiritual stations, love is the head of all spiritual states. The terms 'station' (*maqam*) and 'state' (*hal*) employed here belong to the Sufi lexicon. Accordingly, *hal* denotes a temporary stopping place for the traveler to the truth in raising their spiritual standing, wherein they wait until progressing to the next spiritual stop. *Maqam*, on the other hand, is the name given to the station where the believer advancing from state to state is able to reach and where they stay for a relatively longer time. The latter, in other words, is the stable continuation of the former. As can be gleaned from these descriptions, inherent in 'state' is change, while 'station' implies stability. It can be said that the possessor of a particular spiritual station acquires a 'second nature,' so to speak.

Closer examination of Suhrawardi's work reveals his reduction of love to a single unit. He underlines the need for a believer who loves God to realize every inclination and desire in their life in orientation to this love. According to him, every kind of opposition to the Beloved, experiencing weariness from His remembrance, abandoning His will and command to pursue other objectives is impossible for a believer who possesses love of God. On the contrary, one who loves devotes their life to the Beloved. Even the smallest means and opportunity for togetherness with Him constitutes great privilege and bliss. The regard of the Beloved is everything for them and remembering the Beloved is the greatest happiness.

Following his evaluations Suhrawardi, with reference to God's being infinite, expresses that love for Him must also be infinite. In his view, the signs of love are innumerable. Love of God is so expansive and so grand as not to fit into a single book.[478] With his perspective, Suhrawardi associates love within the Sufi understanding with the boundless Names and

---

[477] al-Ghazali, *Ihya,'* IV:393.
[478] al-Suhrawardi, *'Awarif al-Ma'arif,* 18.

Attributes of God, and thus brings a theological dimension and depth to the topic. The notion that when the one who is loved is Eternal, the love for Him must also be eternal is unique to him.

Ibn Qayyim al-Jawziyya, author of *Madarij al-Salikin*, also offers a broad, detailed discussion on *mahabba*. With a clear command of the topic, Ibn Qayyim describes love by means of about thirty definitions, and provides a list of the conditions necessary for its emergence in the heart. He emphasizes that in order for love to emerge in the heart the believer should, first and foremost, turn to the Beloved with their entire being. In other words, if they love, they should make it known and demonstrate this in every possible way, both materially and spiritually. They should be in harmony with Him in public and in private, but should also feel themselves as wanting and lacking in their love for Him. As can be seen, Ibn Qayyim, like his predecessors, is rather exuberant in relation to the love of God, even to the point of jealousy. His expression, "Devoting everything that it is yours to the Beloved is leaving nothing in you of you,"[479] supports this argument.

After concluding his definitions of love, Ibn Qayyim relates an event narrated by Abu Bakr al-Kattani (d. 322/933). According to his account, a group of people gathered in Mecca during the time of pilgrimage, and began to discuss the topic of love of God. The youngest among them was Junayd Baghdadi. While others expressed their views, Junayd remained silent, until he was pressed to say something. With his head bowed down and tears swelling in his eyes, he said:

> The lover of God is he who forgets his own self, remains engaged in God's remembrance with due regard to all its requirements; sees God with the eyes of his heart, which is burnt by the heat of God's fear; Allah's remembrance affects him like a cup of wine, he speaks the word of God as if All-Mighty God speaks through his mouth; if he moves, he does so under the command of God; he finds rest only through the obedience of God; and when such a stage is reached, his eating, drinking, sleeping, awakening and, in short, all his actions are for the pleasure of God; he neither pays heed to the worldly customs, nor does he attach any importance to unfriendly criticism by people.

---

[479] al-Jawziyya, *Madarij al-Salikin*, III:656,58.

His response brings those present in the gathering to tears, prompting them to remark: "What more can be said after this? O master of the Gnostics! May God reward you with goodness."[480]

Among scholars most stressing the theme, Ibn Qayyim also elaborates on the reasons for love of God. If, as mentioned earlier, a believer needs to turn to the Beloved with their entire being in order for love to materialize in the heart, then there is much that that believer needs to do. For Ibn Qayyim, some of those things that are means for God's love to emerge in the heart are reading the Qur'an by considering its meaning, pursuing nearness to God through supererogatory worship in addition to the obligatory, not neglecting remembrance of God in any circumstance, preferring God's love even in situations where the carnal self holds sway, preoccupying the heart with the Names and Attributes of God, becoming one who possesses spiritual discernment and *ma'rifa*, reflecting on His goodness and His every bounty—hidden or manifest—being in seclusion with God, being in gatherings of the lovers of God and staying away from everything coming between the heart and God.[481] It can be said that a believer undertaking these and similar forms of worship and exhibiting such behavior makes an active prayer to God for Him to create love in their heart. In other words, in order to attract God's regard, they turn to Him first, as though inviting it.

From another perspective, Ibn Qayyim sees the love of God as the most important matter in the spiritual journey. For him, love of God is just like the sincerity contained within worship. Just as deeds without sincerity are not acceptable in God's eyes, a spiritual journey without love of God is also not acceptable or admissible. If there is no love, then all the spiritual stations relating to belief and Islam also become null and void. Love is the soul of every station, stage and deed. It is sincerity and Islam itself. This is because Islam is obedience and submission to the Creator, through love and worship. It is not possible to speak of true submission and surrender for one without love.

Consistent with the views of other scholars, Ibn Qayyim argues that love of God comes just before *fana*, or annihilation in God. The proponents of this view claim that those favored with love of God have no imagina-

---

[480] Ibid., 659.
[481] Ibid., 660.

tion other than that pertaining to God. In other words, the first thing to be annihilated in the *muhib*[482] is their memory pertaining to anything other than God.[483]

Renowned for his grasp of the Islamic tradition, contemporary religious scholar Said Nursi places significant emphasis on love like his predecessors, at times presenting differing interpretations and evaluations while at others accepting their views. His relaying the approaches of his antecedents is important in terms of demonstrating his embracing those ideas. Nursi, like Ghazali before him, makes categorizations and, like him, mentions the 'bestowal, beauty, and perfection' triad. In his view, there is in the nature of human beings a love of beauty, a regard for perfection and again a love for munificence. That love and regard increases in accordance with the degrees of beauty, perfection and munificence, and can even reach the highest point of love. God possesses an endless beauty, an infinite perfection, and boundless benevolence. That is precisely why He deserves to be loved by humankind.[484]

At another instance, Nursi refers to the causes of love as "either pleasure, benefit, resemblance (that is, inclination towards creatures of same kind), or perfection."[485] Stating that the human being has an innate love for God's perfection in and of itself and without cause, Nursi asserts that God has planted love of eternity in the nature of human beings as a shadow of one of His Names. In his view, God is worthy of being loved without any necessity, reason or cause other than Himself.[486] Nursi posits

---

[482] Literally meaning 'lover'; a traveler on the path.

[483] al-Jawziyya, *Madarij al-Salikin*, III:670.

[484] Said Nursi, *The Flashes*, trans. Şükran Vahide (Istanbul: Sözler Neşriyat, 2009), 90-91.

[485] Nursi, *The Words*, 647. The relevant section reads: "Sayyid Sharif al-Jurjani wrote in *Sharh al-Mawaqif*: "The cause of love is either pleasure, benefit, resemblance (that is, inclination towards creatures of same kind), or perfection. For perfection is loved for itself." That is to say, if you love something, you love it either because of the pleasure it affords, or the benefits it brings, or because it is similar in kind, like the inclination towards children, or because it possesses some perfection. If it is for perfection, no other cause or purpose is necessary; it is loved purely for itself. For example, in the olden days everybody loved people who possessed perfection; even if they had no connection with them they would still love them admiringly. Thus, since all God Almighty's perfections and qualities and all the degrees in His Beautiful Names are true perfections, they are loved for themselves."

[486] Nursi, *The Rays*, 71.

that the desire for eternity innate to human beings was given to them by God. One of the Divine Names, *Baqi* expresses God's being Eternal. This Name is manifested in the human being in the form of a yearning for eternal life and desire for immortality. It is God, the Eternal, who will fulfil this desire and it is for this reason that He most deserves to be loved. According to Nursi, another perfection that is particular to Him is his existence out of Himself, or that His existence is not contingent upon anything or anyone else. Possessing greatness and power beyond human comprehension in terms of His Essence, in addition to His Names and Attributes, God, the Lord of all the Worlds is most worthy of being loved.

In the his introduction to the Twentieth Letter, Nursi states:

> Be certain of this, that the highest aim of creation and its most important result is belief in God. The most exalted rank in humanity and its highest degree is the knowledge of God contained within belief in God. The most radiant happiness and sweetest bounty for jinn and human beings is the love of God contained within the knowledge of God. And the purest joy for the human spirit and the sheerest delight for man's heart is the rapture of the spirit contained within the love of God.

> Yes, all true happiness, pure joy, sweet bounties, and untroubled pleasure lie in knowledge of God and love of God; they cannot exist without them. The person who knows and loves God may receive endless bounties, happiness, lights, and mysteries. While the one who does not truly know and love him is afflicted spiritually and materially by endless misery, pain, and fears."[487]

Nursi refers to a succession of four elements: belief, experiential knowledge, love and rapture of the spirit. What draws immediate attention in this sequence is that the first two are voluntary and the other two develop virtually automatically in connection with the former ones. In a believer who knows the Creator in Whom they believe and who as a result widens their horizon of experiential knowledge, love of God and its associated pleasure of the spirit emerge. So as to express precisely this notion, one of the prominent figures of the *Tabi'un*[488] period, Hasan al-Basri, says "One

---

[487] Nursi, *The Words*, 262.
[488] The term used to refer to the immediate successors of the Companions of Muhammad.

who knows God, loves Him." A believer, who aspires to advance in their knowledge of the God in Whom they believe, begins to experience indescribable pleasure of the spirit in their worship and endeavor in their travels to Truth. In the language of Sufism, diverse perceptions, feelings and emotions referred to as Divine gifts start to flow into that believer's heart. A rapture of the spirit, encompassing everything from shedding tears during worship to the inspiration that comes to the heart when discussing spiritual matters, envelops the individual. This is the purest happiness and bliss for the human heart.

As can be understood from the abovementioned definitions, experiential knowledge is indispensable for reaching God's love and worship is the absolute reflection of this love. In order for a person to love someone, it is necessary that they know them first. One cannot love someone they do not know. A person's loving God is contingent upon their knowledge of Him. Just as one who loves Him fears His wrath, they at the same time love Him. Their love for Him is proportionate to their knowledge of Him.

With regards to the articulation of love of God in daily life, it is unconditional obedience, surrender and acquiescence to the True Beloved. Love is realized with a person's turning to God with their entire being, their being with Him, their perceiving Him and their eschewing completely all other desires and wishes. Love of God has two important elements. The outward of these is to perpetually pursue the approval of the Beloved, while the inward element is to close oneself off completely to everything estranged from God.[489]

The following words of famous Sufi saint Rabia al-Adawiya (d. 135/752) are important in terms of illustrating that the indication of love is submission:

> You talk about loving God while you disobey Him; I swear by my life that this is a great surprise, If you were truthful in your love, you would obey Him, For a lover obeys the one he loves. [490]

Muhammad's supplication bears special significance also and serves as a summation of the arguments presented thus far:

---

[489] Gülen, *Key Concepts in the Practice of Sufism 1*, 149.
[490] al-Bayhaqi, *Shu'ab al-Iman*, 7 vols. (Beirut: Dar al-Kutub al-'Ilmiyya, 1990), I:386.

O God! O God! I ask You for Your love and the love for him who loves You, and for the deeds which will cause me to get near to You; make Your love dearer to me than myself, my household and cold water. [491]

Fear of God

As mentioned earlier, fear of God, like love of God, is directly related to and is viewed as a natural result of knowledge of God. This approach can be formularized as "One who knows God fears Him just as they love Him." The Qur'an describes this relationship between knowledge and fear with the verse, "Of all His servants, only those possessed of true knowledge stand in awe of God."[492] While Ibn 'Abbas interprets this verse as "Everyone that stands in awe of God possesses true knowledge"[493], he emphasizes that fear of God cannot be without knowledge. With his statement, "I am the one among you who fears God most and who avoids His prohibitions most"[494], Muhammad draws attention to the close connection between knowledge and fear.

The center of the fear of God—an important dimension of the attitude the believer needs to adopt in relation to God and what is presented in *hadith* as "the beginning of wisdom"[495]—in the human being is the heart. In associating the concept to the heart, the Qur'an uses the term *wajal*, meaning "to be afraid, to shudder and to feel fear":

> The true believers are only those who, when God is mentioned, their hearts tremble with awe.[496]
> ...Who do whatever they do, and give whatever they give, in charity and for God's cause, with their hearts trembling at the thought that they are bound to turn to their Lord (remaining anxious, for they are unsure whether God will accept their deeds from them and be pleased with them) It is those (illustrious ones) who hasten to do all kinds of virtuous deeds, and they are in a virtuous competition with one another in doing them.[497]

---

[491] Tirmidhi, Dawa'at 73, Tafsir al-Qur'an, 39.
[492] (35:28)
[493] Darimi, Muqaddima, 30.
[494] Bukhari, Adab, 72; I'tisam, 5; Muslim, Fada'il, 127, 128.
[495] 'Abd al-Ra'uf al-Munawi, *Fayd al-Qadir*, 6 vols. (Beirut1682), III:57.
[496] (8:2)
[497] (23:60-61)

According to these verses, one of the most marked qualifications of believers who have perfected their belief is their possession of hearts which tremble when God is mentioned. The verse, "And God warns you that you beware of Himself"[498] is important with respect to its emphasizing the necessity of such. Perhaps for this reason, believers are asked not to be lax in elevating their hearts to this level, but far from it, are warned to hasten in this regard: "Has not the time yet come for those who believe that their hearts should soften with humility and submit (to God to strive in His cause) in the face of God's Remembrance (the Qur'an) and what has come down of the truth (the Divine teachings)?"[499]

Alongside those who interpret the word *wajal* as being afraid of punishment,[500] there have also been those interpreting it as "quivering with fear before God's majesty as a result of knowing Him."[501] Contemporary Qur'anic exegete Yazir describes the word as "God's greatness and majesty pervading the heart with the hope of mercy and the joyful zeal of love, and the heart's resultant movement."[502] One of Muhammad's Companions, Umm al-Darda' (d. 30/650) explains fear of the heart as "something like the burning of the dry leaves of a date palm."[503]

From such a vantage point, it is clear that trembling is a characteristic belonging to a living, sensitive and tender heart. Not experiencing difficulty with regards to compliance to the Divine commands can be seen as an example of the manifestation of such trembling. The Qur'anic verse, "Who do whatever they do, and give whatever they give, in charity and for God's cause, with their hearts trembling at the thought that they are bound to turn to their Lord,"[504] is also significant in this discussion. When this verse was revealed, Muhammad's wife, 'A'isha (d. 50/670) is said to have asked him whether the people mentioned in this verse were those who thought that their worship would not be accepted because of the sins they had committed in the past, to which Muhammad answered: "No,

---

[498] (3:28)

[499] (57:16)

[500] Qurtubi, *al-Jami,'* VII:232.

[501] Rashid Rida, *Tafsir al-Manar*, 12 vols. (Beirut: Dar al-Kutub al-'Ilmiyya, 1999), IX:589.

[502] Yazır, *Hak Dini Kur'an Dili*, IV:2367.

[503] Ibn Kathir, *Tafsir*, III:552.

[504] (23:60)

O 'A'isha! The believers mentioned in the verse are those who, although they perform the Daily Prayers, fast and give in charity, tremble with trepidation that their worship might not be accepted."[505]

There are also terms other than the word *wajal*—such as *khawf*, *khashya* and *rahba*—which are employed in the Arabic language and which are also appropriated by the Qur'an to discuss this same theme. In defining these terms, Ibn Qayyim considers the nuances between them. In his view, *wajal* is the shaking or the shuddering of the heart upon remembrance or sight of someone whose might, punishment and wrath is feared, while *khawf* is the fear of punishment in return for something committed, the heart's quivering at the remembrance of that which is feared and its trembling with the dread that its fears will come true. *Khashya*, moreover, is a fear grounded in knowledge, weighted in calm and tranquility. As for *rahba*, it is to dread the realization of one's fears, escaping with all one's strength.[506]

Many verses in Qur'an are related, either directly or indirectly, with fear of God. Some of the verses dealing directly with fear of God are as follows:

So do not fear them, but fear Me, if you are (true) believers.[507]

...and of Me alone be in awe and fear.[508]

They (the angels) fear their Lord high above them (i.e., Who has absolute power over them), and they do what they are commanded.[509]

...calling out to their Lord in fear (of His punishment) and hope (for His forgiveness, grace, and good pleasure).[510]

Verses dealing with fear of God in an indirect manner, however, mention the possibility of certain unexpected and unforeseen things befall-

---

[505] Tirmidhi, Tafsir al-Qur'an, 23; Ibn Maja, Zuhd, 20.

[506] al-Jawziyya, *Madarij al-Salikin*, I:549-50.

[507] (3:175)

[508] (2:40); (16:51)

[509] (16:50)

[510] (32:16)

ing human beings in the Hereafter, and direct them to take precautions with an admonitory tone.[511]

Fear of God, found more or less in every believer, has been seen as a phenomenon that increases and gains strength as the believer knows God and grows close to him. The main elements serving as a basis for fear of God have been categorized differently, including such issues as facing punishment, experiencing concern for one's lot or reverence felt towards the essence of God Himself. All of these have been deemed to be acceptable and even encouraged from the Islamic perspective. Alongside this, acceptance and encouragement remaining in the believer as just a feeling or an attribute has not been viewed as satisfactory, and their natural benefits have been emphasized. The degree of fear of God in believers has been endeavored to be understood by means of the manifestations of such fear in the day-to-day lives of believers. That is to say, believers' saying that they possessed fear of God was not relied upon; on the contrary, the extent to which this was translated into action through their behavior was the basis on which their possessing this quality was expressed. For, it is fair to assume that one who fears, will endeavor to the utmost to be safe from that which they fear. It is precisely in this context that Muhammad states, "Whosoever fears, undertakes the night journey. One who makes headway at night reaches their goal."[512] The night journey mentioned here is interpreted by *hadith* scholars as the supererogatory prayer vigils in the middle of the night.

Islamic scholars, and especially Sufis, discussing fear of God, have offered different definitions, approaching the topic from diverse perspectives and various identifications from different perspectives. For instance, one of the great early masters of the spiritual path Hatim al-Asamm (d. 240/852) says "Everything has its ornament and the ornament of worship is *khawf*; the sign of *khawf* is to cut short worldly aspirations,"[513] drawing attention to the natural consequence of fear of God. Dhu al-Nun

---

[511] Examples of such verses are: "Something will confront them from God, which they never reckoned." (39:47); "Say: "Shall We inform you who are the greatest losers in respect of their deeds? Those whose endeavor has been wasted in this world (because it is directed only to this-worldly ends, and so it is bound to be wasted hereafter also) but who themselves reckon that they are doing good." (18:103).

[512] Tirmidhi, Qiyama, 19.

[513] Ibid.

connects people's being on the path of Truth to fear of God and describes the lack thereof as deviation.[514] This interpretation is important in terms of placing emphasis on fear of God for the protection of the religious vein. Here, a believer's or religious devotee's loyalty to their religion is tied first and foremost to reverence to and fear of Him Who reveals this religion to them.

Making mention of the various degrees of fear of God, great Sufi shaykh Abu Ali ad-Daqqaq lists them as *khawf*, *khashya*, and *hayba*. His sequence reveals a progressively increasing trajectory. Constituting the first step, *khawf* is a must for believers, on the basis of the verse, "Fear Me, if you are (true) believers."[515] *Khashya*, the second step, is a prerequisite of knowledge and is particular to those possessed of true knowledge. As for the last and highest step, *hayba* is the necessary condition of experiential knowledge such that only those who know God can possess this kind of fear. Ad-Daqqaq grounds this last step in the verse[516], "And God warns you that you beware of Himself."[517]

Abu Hafs 'Umar as-Suhrawardi lends a different perspective to the topic. Of special significance is the question of 'who' represents this viewpoint, rather than what this viewpoint actually is. With his approach, Suhrawardi draws attention to the fact that fear of God is a quality that needs to be more pronounced in those who are in a position to guide others. Their success in this duty of leadership, as guides of the community, and their being freed from being called to account in the Hereafter is tied to this. For they are "the pillars of the religion, lanterns dispelling the darkness of natural ignorance, the chief leaders of Islam's council, mines of the wisdom of the Book and the Sunna (Prophetic tradition), God's trusted ones in the midst of His creation... the bearers of the Divine trust."[518] It is possible to conclude from Suhrawardi's statement that fear of God assumes extraordinary importance for possessors of knowledge and is pivotal for their maintaining their privileged position.

---

[514] Al Qushayri, *al-Risalah*, 130.

[515] (3:175)

[516] (3:28)

[517] Al Qushayri, *al-Risalah*, 128.

[518] al-Suhrawardi, *'Awarif al-Ma'arif*, 344.

Also focusing on *khawf*, Nursi describes it as a 'whip' driving believers "into the embrace of His mercy."[519] A Muslim, who fears God and worries about their end, should take action and this action should lead them to the ways leading to God's mercy and compassion. Accordingly, fear of God should direct the person to good works and deeds leading them to Divine mercy. In this way, *khawf* would have fulfilled its function. In the reverse, it can be said that fear of God gives rise to hope and salvation, rather than hopelessness and eternal loss.

Another unique standpoint that Nursi offers in relation to fear of God is his correlating it to a Sufi term, *firar*.[520] Literally meaning to escape, *firar* is the natural consequence of fear. In the Sufi context, *firar* is interpreted as a flight to God's mercy. It is the effort of a Muslim who fears God's punishment and strives to attract His compassion and forgiveness so as not to incur His wrath, like the child who fears the admonition of its mother throwing itself in its mother's embrace. With his supplication, "O God, I seek refuge with You from You,"[521] and "O God, I seek refuge in Your pleasure from Your wrath, I seek refuge in Your forgiveness from Your punishment,"[522] Prophet Muhammad indicates the nature of *firar* and what form it should take.

When examined from yet another perspective, it becomes clear that fear of God is connected to not being secure from and assured of God's wrath. In relation to this point, Nursi underlines the necessity of continuously maintaining the balance between hope and fear.[523] This is because

---

[519] Nursi, *The Words*, 368.

[520] Nursi, in his work *Isharat al-I'jaz*, says, "For what occurs first to the heart of one who sees something terrifying is a sense of bewilderment, then he wants to flee..." (Nursi, *Signs of Miraculousness*, 32.) Denoting fleeing and getting away, *firar* in the Sufi context refers to the flight from the people to God, leaving the drop to turn oneself to the ocean, as illustrated in the Qur'anic verse: "So, flee to (refuge in) God" (51:50).

[521] Muslim, Salat 222; Abu Dawud, Salat 148; Nasa'i, Tatbiq, 71, Istia'dha, 62.

[522] Ibid. The entire supplication is: "O God, I seek refuge in Your pleasure from Your wrath, I seek refuge in Your forgiveness from Your punishment. O God, I seek refuge with You from You, I seek refuge in Your grace from Your torment, in Your mercy from Your majesty, and in Your Compassion from Your irresistible power. I am not able to praise You as You praise Yourself."

[523] Nursi says: "It is the mark of guidance to preserve the balance between hope and fear, in order that hope may induce striving and work, and fear may restrain from transgression, and a person will not despair of Divine mercy and opt out in

when this balance is not preserved, ideas completely at odds with the Islamic understanding, such as despairing God's infinite mercy or instead, being completely confident that they will not face His eternal punishment, can be entertained. From the Islamic perspective, however much it is deemed to be appropriate that one does not see themselves as secure from Divine punishment however pious and religious a person may be, it is as appropriate that they do not abandon hope completely, no matter how evil and sinful they are.

Nursi posits that the possessors of experiential knowledge derive great pleasure from the fear of God. By way of elucidating his argument, he provides the example of the relationship between a mother and her child. Referring to a child's throwing itself into its mother's tender embrace when it feels a fear of her and the resultant pleasure that the child experiences, Nursi argues that the same is true of the relationship between a person and God. In his view, for a believer who feels fear due to their wrongdoing and shortcomings and who feels anxiety about their end, turning to God with feelings of fear and hope and taking refuge in His mercy, engenders supreme pleasure and contentment.[524]

A final point to be related here with respect to Nursi's view on *khawf* is its turning the direction of the love in one's heart from the world to the Hereafter. He draws attention to another function of fear by describing the need to direct fear and love from the world and people.[525] Here, is the implication that a believing person who fears God as He should be feared and experiences concern about their end, can distance themselves in their hearts from the aspect of the world looking to vain pleasures and desires. For Nursi, the feeling of love in the heart can be directed to God by means of fear of God. He seems to be saying that fear of God potentially encompasses love for God. In other words, the fear of God is a person's capacity to turn the face of love and attachment for *masiwa*[526] in their heart towards God. Implied in such a notion is that the tendencies and inclinations of the heart do not happen by themselves. There is a

---

blameworthy fashion, or feel sure he will not be punished so unconcernedly go astray." (Nursi, *Signs of Miraculousness*, 71.)

[524] Nursi, *The Words*, 368.

[525] Nursi, *Mathnawi al-Nuriya*, 301.

[526] *Masiwa* literally means 'besides.' In the Sufi context it is used to refer to everything other than God.

need for certain premises in order to orient these towards the right direction. *Khawf* constitutes an important tool for directing the feeling of love in the heart, towards God.

Taqwa is another theme that needs to be examined alongside the fear of God. Literally meaning "to avoid," *taqwa* has been defined as the effort to avoid God's punishment by obeying the Divine commands and staying away from the prohibitions.[527] When the definitions are considered, *taqwa* can be seen as the natural result and consequence of fear of God. In consideration of the fact that a believer who fears God exerts an endeavor so as not to be subjected to Divine punishment, the similarity between *khawf* and *taqwa* becomes even more pronounced. Introduced to believers with the verse, "Surely the noblest, most honorable of you in God's sight is the one best in piety, righteousness, and reverence for God"[528], *taqwa*, or piety, has been pursued for centuries by Muslims as a goal which needs to be reached. In this verse, acquiring great value and esteem in the eyes of God has been associated with living a life in line with His will. Put differently, a person's putting the will of God in place of their own whims and fancies and living their life with this consideration and prudence will allow them to attain an elevated and esteemed level in the eyes of God. It is rather meaningful that the verse associates reaching an eminent status in the eyes of God, but with piety, which is characterized by fear of God.

Stating, "Keep from disobedience to God in reverent piety," the Qur'an again draws attention to *taqwa*. Alongside elucidating the value of piety in the eyes of God in yet another way, this verse also focuses on its aspect that looks to the human being. It suggests that the believer should not suffice with the degree of piety level they possess. Thus, it can be said that persisting and exerting effort to the utmost in this regard assumes an important position in religious terms.

On the basis of the Qur'anic verses, Nursi states that piety consists of three stages: abandonment of associating partners with God, abandoning wrongdoing and abandoning *masiwa*.[529] Through this interpretation it is possible to say that he narrows considerably the sphere of piety. Completely avoiding *shirk* (associating partners with God) is obligatory

---

[527] Ibn Manzur, *Lisan al-'arab*, 'q-w-y.'

[528] (49:13)

[529] Nursi, *Signs of Miraculousness*, 48.

upon every Muslim. A Muslim who commits *shirk* cannot be said to remain within the sphere of Islam. Piety in this regard, then, is mandatory and indispensable. The second degree of piety, refraining from sin and wrong-doing, in addition to changing according to the willpower of every person, is a feature that keeps the believing person within the boundaries of Islam. Although committing sin is not something that is acceptable, it does not take the Muslim outside the sphere of Islam. If the three degrees of *taqwa* are to be considered as three concentric circles, then the inner-most circle represents the third degree of piety. Accordingly, if this inmost degree is abandonment of *masiwa*, it is a matter pertaining to Muslims pursuing an elevated level of religious devotion. The Prophets and those ardent, strong-willed individuals closely following them, are those who succeed in keeping away from everything other than God, though they may be licit and permissible, and are those who are able to realize the deepest and most comprehensive level of piety in their lives.

Furthermore, Nursi also assesses *taqwa* within the scope of cleanli-ness of the heart. Stating, "As soon as the heart is purified of evils with *taqwa* it is immediately thereafter adorned with belief," Nursi sees *taqwa* as a medium of purification on the one hand and a means to orient the heart to God on the other.[530] For him, the heart is forced to embrace *taqwa* in order to be purged of every kind of *shirk*, sin and everything other than God, and at the same time be adorned with experiential knowledge of God and overflow with perfected belief.

In sum, fear of God and a concern of one's end—expressed in Arabic and within the Sufi context with the terms *khawf* and *makhafat Allah*—emerges as a feeling of fear present more or less in the heart of every Muslim. In the Islamic/Sufi thought, fear has been considered an argu-ment driving the individual to entertaining an anxiety of their end on the one hand, and as an instrument leading one to attain mercy on the other. As such, the possessor of fear takes action in order to lessen their fear and anxiety and this shows itself as an inclination towards God. This is because there is no feeling other than this hope of attaining Divine mercy that can suppress this feeling. In the life of the believer who strives to keep this feeling alive using their willpower, the notion of *istiqama* (straightforwardness)—which also holds an important position in Sufi ter-

---

[530] Ibid.

minology—emerges. Their way of life takes on a form attracting Divine approval and acquires continuity. It is precisely this situation that is aimed at with *khawf* and constitutes its chief gain.

Remembrance of God

Dhikr literally means remembrance, protecting the knowledge one has acquired and mentioning with the tongue or heart. It has also meanings like distinction, honor, prayer, supplication and Divine scripture.[531] The concept of *dhikr* is one of the central themes of Islam. Just as it is afforded significant space in Qur'anic verses and *hadith*, it also constitutes one of the basic elements of the Sufi discipline. As a result, in lieu of examining every aspect of *dhikr* that has thus far been presented, a brief summary of the concept will be offered, followed by an examination of the heart's inclination towards God by means of it.

Further to the definitions cited above, *dhikr* also denotes overcoming forgetfulness and heedlessness.[532] The reason for stating this definition separately concerns the direct association that it has to the topic at hand. Even though human beings seem to possess a nature prone to forgetfulness and heedlessness, Islamic teaching envisages that they must not forget or remain heedless of certain things. First and foremost is God Himself and responsibilities towards Him, because any forgetfulness or distraction with regard to these can give rise to negligence and result in sin. Going further, the approach that forgetfulness of God is the base of all sins is one that has been readily accepted in religious understanding. With the statement, "And do not be like those who are oblivious of God and so God has made them oblivious of their own selves. Those, they are the transgressors,"[533] the Qur'an asserts that such forgetfulness of God will come back to the person in the form of their forgetting their own self. One who forgets their Creator, or acts as though they have and abandons Him, actually becomes estranged to their own self, for the real identity of the person is in their attachment and devotion to their Creator and in their reflecting their belief in Him and the essentials of this belief, in their everyday lives. The similitude Muhammad offers in the statement, "The example of the one who celebrates the Praises of his Lord (Allah) in

---

[531] al-Isfahani, *Al-Mufradat*, 179-80. Al-Ghazali, *Ihya,'* I:390.
[532] al-Qashani, *Istilahat*, 277.
[533] (59:19)

comparison to the one who does not celebrate the Praises of his Lord, is that of a living creature compared to a dead one"[534] is meaningful in the sense that it indicates the spiritual state of a person who forgets God by failure to invoke Him. Expressed differently, this *hadith* points out that remembrance of God is an indispensable element in preserving the vitality of human emotions. In the Islamic understanding fundamentally, everything from the Prophets to Divine scripture, solar and lunar eclipses to natural disasters, and worship to illnesses are accepted as a means to remembrance of God and invoking His Names.

In this respect, believers are warned in the Qur'an against any activity and enterprise that will distract them from God, and preoccupation with such things as wealth, children and trade—which are in essence permissible—to the degree of heedlessness of God and thus destruction of a religious way of life are reproached.[535]

Moreover, Islam desires that believers mention God as much as possible[536] and praises those who constantly mention Him.[537] Persistence in this matter has even inspired the term *dhikr al-daimi* (continuous remembrance) in Sufi thought.[538] The verse, "So always remember and make mention of Me that I may remember and make mention of you"[539] plays a pivotal role in encouraging Muslims to remember God and invoke His Names. According to this verse, believers who mention God are favored with the honor of themselves being mentioned by God.

Prophet Muhammad draws attention to the importance of *dhikr* in many of his sayings. In one of these, he states that God mentions the servant that makes mention of Him, thus constituting a parallel with the verse just cited.[540] In another tradition he states: "Do not busy yourself with

---

[534] Bukhari, Dawa'at, 66.

[535] The related verses are: "Those guided are) men (of great distinction) whom neither commerce nor exchange (nor any other worldly preoccupations) can divert from the remembrance of God, and establishing the Prayer in conformity with all its conditions, and paying the Prescribed Purifying Alms; they are in fear of a Day on which all hearts and eyes will be overturned" (24:37); "O you who believe! Let not your wealth nor your children (distract and) divert you from the remembrance of God. Those who do so, they are the losers" (63:9).

[536] (33:41,42)

[537] (3:191)

[538] Necmeddin-i Kübra, *Tasavvufi Hayat*, trans. Mustafa Kara (Istanbul1980), 58.

[539] (2:152)

[540] Bukhari, Tawhid, 15; Tirmidhi, Dawa'at, 131; Ibn Maja, Adab, 58.

unnecessary talk by forgetting God, because unnecessary and long speeches without the remembrance of God harden the heart. The furthest from God is the possessor of a hardened heart."[541] This Prophetic Tradition is important in terms of prescribing incessant remembrance of God. It explicitly states that long periods of time in which God is not remembered and invoked cause the heart to harden and that this is turn gives rise to estrangement from God. In the Islamic understanding, becoming distant and estranged from God has been considered the greatest loss.

Although *dhikr* is considered in three ways—namely that done with the tongue, the body and with the heart—it quickly becomes apparent that it is the heart which actually performs *dhikr* and constitutes a foundation for all of these. To mention God with His 'beautiful Names,' to thank and praise Him, to read the Qur'an and make supplication are examples of remembrance with the tongue. The body's *dhikr* is using every bodily limb and organ in accordance with its *raison d'être*, performing worship and staying clear of the religiously prohibited. The heart's *dhikr*, however, is to contemplate the proofs of God's existence and unity, His Names and Attributes, His commands and prohibitions, and His glad tidings and warnings for His servants and by means of reading line by line and letter by letter the Book of Universe, observing the close relationship between the Great Artisan and His masterpiece. Ghazali's comparing transformative, purifying love to the good tree with its branches in the sky and whose root is firm, as emphasized by Schimmel, also points to this trifold remembrance and illustrates the interplay between these three elements: "...the fruits show themselves in the heart, on the tongue, and on the limbs. These fruits are obedience to the orders of God and constant recollection of the beloved, which fills the heart and runs on the tongue."[542]

In an active position in all of these is the heart. The Qur'an places intense and frequent emphasis on the relationship between the heart and remembrance. Sometimes this relationship is positive because the heart is said to find rest with remembrance of God,[543] and sometimes negative because of the heart's heedlessness and resultant hardening.[544]

---

[541] Tirmidhi, Zuhd, 62.
[542] Schimmel, *Mystical Dimensions of Islam*, 134.
[543] (13:28)
[544] (18:28); (39:22)

Because the opposite of remembrance is heedlessness, remembrance that cannot dispel heedlessness cannot be considered true remembrance. The Qur'an criticizes the heedless performance of prayer, one of the types of remembrance,[545] and praises those who perform it perfectly.[546] In the same way, the verse, "The true believers are only those who, when God is mentioned, their hearts tremble with awe"[547] indicates the necessary shudder that the heart needs to experience during remembrance and draws attention to sensitivity and delicacy of the heart.

As a final point in relation to *dhikr*, while the Qur'an at times states, "And keep in remembrance the Name of your Lord,"[548] it sometimes also directly commands, "remember and mention your Lord."[549] Remembrance and invocation of the 'Name' of God is clearly differentiated from remembrance and mention of Him, Himself. Fakhru'd-Din ar-Razi explains this nuance by saying, "The individual, at first, continues their *dhikr* for some time with their tongue and later leaves the Name and moves on to the Essence."[550] It is possible to conclude that the nuances of meaning in these verses are due to the different types of remembrance. That is, while the Qur'an wants God to be mentioned with His Names and Attributes when it states, "Keep in remembrance the Name of your Lord," it is possible to say that "Remember and mention your Lord" suggests a person's using all their bodily limbs and organs in line with their purpose of creation and seeing God's majesty through examining His creation. Furthermore, with reference to *dhikr*'s being defined as remembrance of God, we can even say that realizing and bearing in mind that He encompasses everything with His knowledge and that He sees everything can be included within the meaning spectrum of this kind of remembrance.[551]

---

[545] "And woe to those worshippers (denying the Judgment), Those who are unmindful in their Prayers." (107:4, 5)

[546] "Prosperous indeed are the believers. They are in their Prayer humble and fully submissive (being overwhelmed by the awe and majesty of God)" (23:1, 2).

[547] (8:2)

[548] (73:8)

[549] (3:41)

[550] al-Razi, *Mafatih al-Ghayb*, XXX:156.

[551] Some of the verses that mention God's existence in every place and every moment are: "And He is with you, wherever you may be." (57:4); "We are nearer to him than his jugular vein" (50:16); "God sees well all that you do" (2:10); (8:72).

In short, the heart emerges as a *jawhar*, or jewel with a very functional and highly complex structure. Alongside this, it fulfils perhaps its most important function, to turn towards God. This inclination of the heart manifests itself in such ways as belief in God, knowledge of Him, love and fear of Him. It is in a position to utilize such capacities mentioned earlier as knowledge, comprehension, reason, intellect, feeling, perception, turning and discovery, first and in the most comprehensive way for God. The Islamic understanding anticipates that the heart is created for this. However, it is also the case that the heart may not realize this potential function. In such cases, it is indicated that the heart loses its neutrality and tends towards the negative. Hence, the heart functions in exact opposition to what is expected of it and is oriented towards evil and Satan. As such negative functioning will be elaborated later under the "Negative qualities of the heart" heading, we will suffice with only brief mention here.

Conclusion

This fourth chapter constitutes the main chapter of this study. After having considered the heart's nature, functions and positive and negative qualities, this chapter demarcates the most important reason for the creation of the heart as according to the Islamic understanding, that is, its connection with its Creator. Here, the heart's reciprocal relationship with God is examined. The first aspect of this is God's disposal over the heart. The second aspect is the heart's turning to God. The central thread weaving the fabric of this chapter is that the sole, unique vehicle through which the human being can establish a connection with God, or the Divine Reality, is the heart. Notwithstanding the paramount significance of this relationship within the Islamic understanding, the heart's turning to God is elemental, as this is the human being's active pursuit of knowledge of the Divine and their achieving subsequent intimacy with and Love of Him. All of these exist as potentialities within the human heart. However, what is most crucial at this juncture is that the task here falls upon the human being to mobilize these qualities of the heart and attain resultant knowledge, fear and love of Him.

Part II

Ghazali, Said Nursi and
Fethullah Gülen's Approaches
to the Heart

I n the first part, I explored the Islamic approach to the heart. This entailed an examination of the evaluations and approaches of the Qur'an, Prophet Muhammad, and succeeding scholars taking these two sources as their primary references. Narrowing the viewpoint further in this part, I will analyze the views and interpretations of prominent Turkish scholar Fethullah Gülen in relation to the heart. However, before so doing, and in order to better appreciate his views on the subject, I will consider two key scholars influential in Gülen's thought, famous Muslim thinker Abu Hamid Ghazali and twentieth century Muslim scholar Said Nursi, who authored several volumes of Qur'anic exegesis known as the *Risale-i Nur* (Epistles of Light). The reason behind such a choice is, as mentioned, the great impact that these individuals have had on Gülen's thought and works. Another factor behind the importance of these two personalities is the former's being the most renowned scholar of the classical period and the latter's being among the most influential Muslim thinkers in the modern era. With their works being translated into innumerable languages, first and foremost English, they continue to affect and mold the thoughts and views of millions of people around the world. Moreover, an exposition of the viewpoints of these two scholars constitutes a very important means of drawing a connection between the classical and modern periods. Hence, a discussion of Ghazali's view of *qalb* will be followed by an overview at Nursi's approach and, thereafter, an analysis of Gülen's observations and evaluations on the topic. Furthermore, as the technical terms to be employed in the second Part were elaborated in some detail in the first part, they will not be expounded again in this Part.

Ghazali and the Heart

T his chapter deals with Ghazali's approach to the heart concept. This topic will be expounded under two subheadings, namely "The Heart's Functions" and "The Characteristics of the Heart." The fact that the very title of this thesis is a term coined by Ghazali himself, as one of the leading scholars of the Classical period, is demonstration of the pivotal position that he occupies in Islamic literature in relation to the concept of the heart.

The Heart's Functions

The era in which Ghazali, known as *Hujjat al-Islam* (Proof of Islam) because of his impact and influence, lived was an era in which there was great interest in *tasawwuf* and an increase in Sufi activities. The author of one of the classics of Sufism *Kitab al-Luma' fi'l-Tasawwuf*, Abu Nasr al-Sarraj, is one of Ghazali's fellow townsmen. The influence of one of the seminal Sufi texts, *al-Risala al-Qushayri* on Ghazali can also be seen. Ghazali travelled through the lands where leading Sufis resided, such as Iraq and Syria, met with them and benefited from them. Despite being well known in his youth, his inclination towards *tasawwuf* took place while in his fifties. Ghazali spent his remaining years as a Sufi, and wrote his famous *Ihya' 'Ulum ad-Din* which contains his evaluations of the heart, in his place of seclusion. In this work, Ghazali presents the character, essence and functions of the heart, while dealing with its actions, such as sincerity, patience and reflection in another book entitled *Kashf al-Qulub*. To the volume wherein he describes the heart, Ghazali gives the title, "Marvels of the Heart." Such a heading choice is noteworthy in terms of indicating just how intricate, convoluted and enigmatic the structure and composition of the heart is. Going into quite some detail regarding the heart, Ghazali discusses both 'what it is,' as well as 'what it does.' Before proceeding to a discussion of these views and the 'insights that will be delineated in subsequent subheadings, it is possible to make the following general observation. An examination of Ghazali's observations and interpretations pertaining to the heart reveal that he holds the heart in a neutral position. Despite the fact that in *tasawwuf* the heart is generally afforded a positive place, Ghazali has not understood it to be thus, but at the same time, he has not considered it to be negative either. Instead, he sees the heart to be equally distant from the two extremities and expresses, in his own way, that it is open to both good and evil. For instance, alongside seeing the heart as "the site of knowing God and getting close to Him," Ghazali also characterizes it as that which disobeys and rebels against God. Just as it is the heart which strives and exerts effort for God and endeavors to meet with Him, all the wickedness spreading to the bodily limbs and organs is its doing. The organ which attains salvation and happiness when it is purified, and which is deprived of mercy on account of its debasement and deviation is, again, always the heart. Just as all goodness seen in human beings stems from the heart, the source of all wickedness issuing from them is also the heart. A person's being in light or darkness is related directly to the state of their heart.[552]

Ghazali also considers knowledge of the heart's realities and qualities as equal to knowledge of the essence of religion. Leading him to such a notion is the equation he formulates between knowing the heart, knowing the carnal self, and in this way knowing God. In the exact opposite case, however, he states that the human being will consequently forget God and, therefore, remain estranged from the essence of religion.[553]

In Islamic tradition, direct proportion has been established between a person's realizing their true human potential and the strength of the connection between them and their Creator, known as *iman* (belief or faith). Belief is the name given to a person's connection with God. Serving as the center and source of such attributes as perception, feeling, inclination and learning, the most important duty of the heart is to believe in God, and perceive and know Him.

In addition, Ghazali employs categorization in order to illustrate the functions of the very multi-functional heart, referring to the three classes of "the armies of the heart." Inciters and instigators make up the first group, with these being separated into two: those which incite or insti-

---

552 al-Ghazali, *Ihya,'* III:3.
553 Ibid.

gate to the acquisition of that which is "profitable and suitable," such as *shahwa* (appetence), and those which ward off that which is "harmful and destructive," such as *ghadab* (anger). The total sum of these two components is the impulse known as *irada*. The second class is the power that acts to mobilize the organs in order to fulfil these desired ends, which Ghazali calls *qudrah* (power). These armies are "diffused throughout the rest of the members, especially the muscles and sinews." The third class is the power that understands and perceives creation, perceiving and gathering information "as spies." These are the power of the five sensory organs of taste, sight, touch, hearing and speech. These are known as *'ilm* (knowledge) and *idrak* (perception).[554]

Ghazali understands the actions of the five sensory organs in the last category, such as sight and hearing, to be the hidden powers of the heart and posits that in order for these *batini* (esoteric) characteristics to fulfil their functions, there is a need for certain *zahir* (outward) things or instruments. For example, touch requires the hands; sight the eyes, and hearing, the ears. However, visible organs such as the hands, eyes, ears and tongue are not Ghazali's concern. The matter that interests him and that he emphasizes is the knowledge acquired through these organs and its use by the heart.

The last part, expressed as the heart's knowledge and perception has also been categorized separately within itself. These can be listed as follows:

Quwwa al-hafiza: The recollection of something seen in the *hayal* (retentive imagination).

Quwwa al-mufakkira: The mind's preoccupation with that kept therein and holding these to analysis and scrutiny.

Quwwa al-mudhakkira: The feature of the heart allowing it to remember what it has forgotten.

Hiss al-mushtarak: common sense; the heart's gathering together all that it feels and knows.[555]

In this categorization, it is possible to see the broad-sweeping nature of the heart and its functions. Due to his being propounding such taxon-

---

[554] Abu Hamid Muhammad ibn Muhammad al-Ghazali, *The Marvels of the Heart: Book 21 of the Ihya' 'Ulum al-Din*, ed. Walter James Skellie (Louisville: Fons Vitae, 2010), 13-17.
[555] al-Ghazali, *Ihya,'* III:10-11.

omy, his expertise and command of the concept of the heart as well as his capacity for analysis and synthesis becomes evident.

Latifa al-Rabbaniya

In describing the heart, Ghazali first makes brief mention of the material heart and then proceeds to discuss the spiritual heart, which he defines as *Latifa al-Rabbaniya al-Ruhaniya*, or the spiritual Divine intellect. Despite stating the close connection between the material heart and the spiritual heart, he adds that there has not been anyone who could say anything definitive regarding this and, in addition, does not neglect providing examples to illustrate the relationship between these two hearts. Ghazali likens this relationship to the relationship between colors and forms, qualities with the objects they qualify, one who uses a tool with the tool itself, or the relationship between a person who resides in a particular place with that place.

The similitudes that Ghazali employs when describing the connection between these two hearts are noteworthy. One of these similitudes, as mentioned, is the relationship between the characteristics of a particular thing and that thing being characterized. This can also be referred to as the connection between the description and the described. For example, a pencil that has a red lead must write in red. It is futile to expect it to write in a different color. In a similar fashion, the association between the spiritual heart and the material heart is thus. With reference to Ghazali's association, it is possible to say that the physical heart covers the spiritual heart like a sheath, houses it like a home or encases and protects it like a suit of armor. However, all these approaches do not rescue the heart, both Divine and spiritual, entirely from abstractness and mystery.

Furthermore, Ghazali describes a person's bosom, on the basis of the heart's being located therein, as the locus, realm and vehicle of the spiritual heart. In making this characterization, he relates the saying of Sufi Sahl al-Tustari, "the heart is the *arsh* and the chest is the *kursi*," when he likens the heart to the Supreme Throne (*arsh*) and the chest to the Divine Seat (of dominion), or the *kursi*. And in order to prevent misconception, he explains the heart as the site of God's disposal over human beings.[556]

---

[556] Ibid., III:7.

Ghazali later discusses the terms which can be considered in the same category as the heart: *ruh*, *nafs* and *aql*, denoting the spirit, carnal self and intellect respectively, and focuses on their association with the heart. Alongside stating that each of these has more than just a single meaning in consecutively defining them, Ghazali asserts that all these terms can be considered within the broader meaning of the word *qalb*. For instance, he states that the meaning of the word *ruh* is twofold; on the basis of its second meaning that is, "an unseen, conscious and knowing part of the human being," Ghazali says that it corresponds to the heart. By means of reference to the carnal self as "the reality and self of a human being" and to the intellect as "the qualification which enables the qualified [person] to perceive knowledge and to think about the cognizable," he regards them as part and parcel of the meaning framework of *qalb*. From this perspective, it can be argued that the terms Ghazali employs to express the knowledge of *tasawwuf* are intimately related and even synonymous with the heart.

It is possible to say that the statement Ghazali makes regarding the heart as a "Divine subtle faculty" is the most striking of all definitions encountered during my research. Referring to it as 'Divine,' Ghazali relates the heart with is mystifying essence to God. This characterization succinctly expresses the notion that the heart belongs to God, rather than human beings. As such, it is possible to say that when God created the human being and willed for them to believe in Him, know Him and worship Him as He deserves, He gave them a subtle faculty known as the heart, belonging to and revealing Him, in order for them to realize all of these.

The Locus of Knowledge of and Nearness to God

As defined in the first part, *ma'rifa* denotes spiritual knowledge of God, while *qurbiyya* refers to nearness to God. By way of an introduction to his discussion, Ghazali has articulated the general Islamic approach, connecting the honor granted to human beings and their superiority to other creatures with their knowing God. A believer who knows God is the most esteemed and virtuous of creation. Humanity cannot know God with any organ other than the heart and again can draw near to Him only by means of it. As they know and become nearer to God, they are able to become aware of particular secrets in relation to Him. For this reason, the heart simultaneously assumes the position of discoverer of the Divine mysteries.[557]

Experiential knowledge of God and nearness to Him has a spiritual delight particular to it. Many a work and scholar has referred to this aspect of such knowledge of God. By way of example, the words of Malik b. Dinar (d. 131/748) are relevant: Once having stated, "The people of the world departed from it without ever tasting the sweetest thing," those around him asked what this was, to which he replied, "Knowledge of God."[558]

Ghazali associates two very important matters, namely knowledge of God and nearness to Him, with the heart and describes the heart as the locus of belief. In other words, he passes over the issue of the heart's believing in God, thereafter immediately mentioning knowing Him and being near to Him. In contrast, Nursi—as will be examined later—mentions belief in God as the single most important mission of the heart. It can be argued that Ghazali's omitting reference to belief is not a shortcoming, but related to his not feeling the need for such emphasis in his day. While, from the Islamic perspective, belief constitutes the most important issue for every age, disbelief was not viewed as a problem in the Islamic world in Ghazali's era. Nursi, however, considers the overarching problem of his day to be disbelief and, as such, directs his entire effort to this.

God's Addressee

While expounding the heart, Ghazali weaves his discussion around two central issues that he ascribes to it. These are the heart's being an addressee of God and its position as the master over all the other limbs and organs. Ghazali emphasizes that so long as it is able to fulfil its *raison d'être*, the heart will remain the most honored organ in God's eyes; otherwise, it will remain distant from God to the extent of its failure to do so. It is for this reason that the heart has been accepted by God to be His addressee and is thus held accountable. When it is normally the human being that is assumed to be held as an addressee of God, Ghazali's mentioning the heart instead of the human being as the direct addressee of God is significant with respect to his highlighting its nature and worth in

---

[557] Ibid., III:3.
[558] Murtada al-Zabidi, *Ithaf al-Sada al-Muttaqin Sharh Ihya' 'Ulum al-Din*, 10 vols. (Beirut: Dar al-Kutub al-'Ilmiyya, 1989), 365.

human beings. Here the heart is, as it were, the human being itself. Put differently, it is as though the human being is composed entirely of their heart. Another issue worthy of note in such an approach is the notion that being an addressee of God brings with it associated obligation. It is possible to infer from this that alongside the potential for every heart to listen to God, some hearts respond to this call with belief while others respond contrarily. From the inverse perspective, every heart that is an addressee of God is not necessarily going to be molded according to His will. Perhaps for this reason, just as it is the heart that is rewarded according to Ghazali, it is again the heart that is deserving of and subjected to Divine punishment. Ghazali, at this juncture, interprets God's intervening between a person and their heart and expresses this as His preventing their heart from *mushahada* (observation), *muraqaba* (self-supervision), and knowing His Attributes. In Ghazali's view, by means of coming in between that person and their heart, God refuses to allow them to know Him and become one of those possessing *ma'rifa*.[559] As can be understood from these explanations, the heart plays a key role in the God-servant relationship. However, a positive outcome is not always expected from this role that the heart plays. The human being who is to open the door eternity with the key of the heart can sometimes close the door to their eternal life with this same key. It is not possible to overlook the projections of the Qur'anic verses in Ghazali's emphasis. For this reason, the role that he cuts out for the heart should not be considered an exaggeration.

The Heart's Soldiers

Another important point that Ghazali develops is the comparison he makes between the heart and the other organs. Salient in this comparison is the heart's always being in a position of dominance and power over the other organs. According to Ghazali, the relationship between the heart and the other organs is akin to that between a ruler and his subjects, a commander and his men, and a master and his slaves and servants. Just as servants carry out every command of their master without hesitation, a human being's other organs and limbs carry out the orders and commands of the heart with the same submissiveness and obedience. The heart puts all the organs to work, while the organs execute its commands immedi-

---

[559] al-Ghazali, *Ihya,'* III:5.

ately and without delay. Such is Ghazali's belief and conviction in this approach that he sees no harm in comparing this relationship to the relationship between God and the angels. In his view, the obedience and compliance of the heart's soldiers to the heart resembles the obedience and compliance of the angels to God, with one notable difference being angels fulfilling these tasks consciously and the bodily organs fulfilling them unconsciously.

Ghazali focuses on the 'why' of this chain of command between the heart and the organs and, using the word 'journey,' states that "the heart undertakes a journey to God," and that it is "created to reach God." Hence, the true duty of the heart is to take its owner to their Creator. The vehicle that the heart uses on this journey is the human body with its provisions being knowledge. A person is required to set these provisions of knowledge and their body in motion, that is to perform good deeds, and only in this way continue on their journey towards God.[560] In light of this information that Ghazali provides, it is of course necessary that the leadership of the heart be understood as a spiritual one. However, one point that should not be forgotten here is that the ability of the other organs to be in harmony and effectual on a person's journey towards God is contingent upon the leadership of the heart. Otherwise, like the scattering of soldiers in an army that has lost its commander, without the leadership of the heart, all the other organs will lose their connection with each other as well as their purpose.

The Characteristics of the Heart

Furthermore, referring to the characteristics of the heart, Ghazali mentions *'ilm* and *irada* and states that by utilizing these, the human being increases in esteem and becomes worthy of attaining close proximity to God. He then goes on to reiterate that the site of knowledge is the heart and emphasizes the relationship between knowledge and the heart. In so doing, he elucidates the word *ma'lum* referring to 'the intelligible' or what is known. According to him, *ma'lum* is an expression for "the specific natures of things," while *'ilm* is "an expression for the representation of the image, or the *ma'lum*, in a mirror."[561]

---

[560] Ibid., III:23.
[561] Ibid., III:13.

At every opportunity mentioning the heart's difference and superiority to all the other human organs and faculties, Ghazali states that the responsibility of the concept of *amana* (Divine Trust) referred to in the Qur'an[562] is shouldered by the human heart. He says the following:

> To [the heart] is the reference in the statement of Him who is Mighty and Majestic, "Verily we offered the trust to the heavens and the earth and the mountains, but they refused to bear it, but man bore it" (Ahzab, 33/71). This refers to his possession of a special characteristic which distinguishes him from the heavens, the earth, and the mountains, by which he is enabled to bear the trust of Allah. This trust is experiential knowledge and the Divine unity (*tawhid*). The heart of every human being is, in its original constitution, fitted for and capable of bearing this trust...[563]

However, the heart is prevented from discerning these realities in certain situations. If the heart has been sullied with the impurity of sin and wrongdoing and has deviated from the straight way, or become veiled due to fulfilling its whims and desires, the real nature of things is unable to shine therein. For this reason, with the heart's being cleansed of the stains of sin and attaining a dutiful and righteous state, it is able to become a shining mirror of the lights of truth.[564]

Relating one of Ibn Ma'ja (d. 273/886)'s narrations, Ghazali draws attention to the importance of purity of heart, explaining this in the con-

---

[562] Suat Yıldırım says the following when clarifying the concept of 'Divine Trust': "*Amana* has been interpreted as religious obligations, responsibilities, obedience to God, intellect and the ability to think. There are also those who describe it as contentment with the secret of Divine Destiny (Qadar), or the will of God. The ego given to human beings also constitutes an element of the Divine Trust. Ego has been given to only human beings out of all creatures. If the ego given to human beings fails to understand its true essence and turn to its Lord, its nature changes into one that fills the world with oppression, disbelief and the horror of associating partners with God. And God knows best," Suat Yıldırım, *Kur'an-ı Hakim ve Açıklamalı Meali (The Holy Qur'an and its Translation with Commentary)* (Istanbul: Define Yayınları, 2006), 426. Explaining the trust here as *aql*/intellect, some Muslim thinkers raise Ghazali's relationship between the heart and *ma'rifa* to a more rational plane. See for example, Muhammad 'Abduh, *Tafsir al-Manar*, 12 vols. (Cairo: Matba'at al-manar, 1931); Ismail Albayrak, *Klasik Modernizmde Kur'an'a Yaklaşımlar* (Istanbul: Ensar Neşriyat, 2004).

[563] al-Ghazali, *Ihya,'* III:14.

[564] Ibid., III:13.

text of the knowledge-heart relationship. According to a narration by 'Abd Allah b. 'Umar (d. 72/692), Prophet Muhammad was asked about the best of people, wherein he answered: "Every believer whose hearts are *mahmum* (cleansed)." When he was asked, in turn, the meaning of a cleansed heart, he responded saying that "It is the God-fearing, pure heart in which there is no fraud, nor iniquity, nor treachery, nor rancor, nor envy."[565] Implied in purity of the heart is the establishment of the light of belief in the heart and the luminance of *ma'rifa* (gnosis) therein.[566]

Knowledge Being Associated with the Heart

In reference to knowledge being associated to the heart, Ghazali makes mention of three degrees of belief. These are the belief of the common people (*al-awam*), that of the theologians and the Gnostics respectively. Comprised of *taqlid*, purely blind imitation, the belief of the masses constitutes the lowest degree. The belief of the theologians,[567] alongside being intermingled with a sort of logical reasoning, is slightly better than that of common people, while the belief of the *'arifun* (Gnostics) is the perfected belief which is seeing clearly by means of the light of *yaqin* (certainty). The similitude given to describe the belief of these three types of people is that of a person believing that there is someone in a particular room after being told as such, or hearing the voice of that person in the room, or seeing that person themselves.[568]

---

[565] Ibn Maja, Zuhd, 22.

[566] Ghazali substantiates his approach with the Qur'anic verses, "Thus, whomever God wills to guide, He expands his breast to Islam," (6:125) and "Is he (who derives lessons from God's acts in the universe, and so) whose breast God has expanded to Islam, so that he follows a light from his Lord (is such a one to be likened to one whose heart is closed up to any remembrance of God and, therefore, to Islam)?" (39:22).

[567] Ghazali's putting theologians in the second category is arguably due to the fact of their placing excessive importance on rational proofs. The second group within this categorization is generally comprised of the *hawas*, scholars or elites, as representatives of a exalted Islamic understanding and way of life.

[568] Ghazali's categorization, as such, corresponds precisely to the degrees of certainty. Certainty has been categorized in accordance with the strength of belief and has generally been expressed by means of the example of fire. Accordingly, giving information regarding fire exemplifies *'ilm al-yaqin*, or certainty coming from knowledge, seeing fire is an example of *'ayn al-yaqin* or certainty that comes from direct

Another point worthy of note here is Ghazali's understanding the word *'ilm* to mean belief and *ma'rifa*, and expressing it as thus when stressing the knowledge-heart relationship. In actual fact, in his discussion of the heart concept the emphasis he constantly makes, sometimes overtly and at other times implicitly, is on belief. If implied in knowledge is the heart's accepting the existence and unity of God and acquiring experiential knowledge about Him, then the heart, at the same time, must be the locus of belief, a concept which completely coincides with Said Nursi's discourse, as will be discussed later.

The importance that Ghazali places on experiential knowledge of God was touched upon earlier. In the verse, "...their light shining forth before them and on their right hands,"[569] qualifying the word *nur* (light) with the concept of *ma'rifa*, he understands it to mean "the lights of *ma'rifa*." Again in his view, a person cannot remain indifferent to the knowledge that they acquired and their efforts to polish their heart and prepare it for the acquisition of this knowledge. That is to say, they will most certainly reap the rewards of such endeavors. For a believer, therefore, the means for true happiness is directly proportionate to their knowledge and experiential knowledge of God.[570] For, as far as they are concerned, there is no greater means for happiness than belief in and knowledge of God.[571]

---

observation, and burning in fire itself represents *haqq al-yaqin*, or certainty that comes from direct experience.

[569] (57:12)

[570] al-Ghazali, *Ihya,'* III:22.

[571] Said Nursi says the following in stressing this same notion: "Be certain of this, that the highest aim of creation and its most important result is belief in God. The most exalted rank in humanity and its highest degree is the knowledge of God contained within belief in God. The most radiant happiness and sweetest bounty for jinn and human beings is the love of God contained within the knowledge of God. Yes, all true happiness, pure joy, sweet bounties, and untroubled pleasure lie in knowledge of God and love of God; they cannot exist without them. The person who knows and loves God Almighty may receive endless bounties, happiness, lights, and mysteries. While the one who does not truly know and love him is afflicted spiritually and materially by endless misery, pain, and fears. Even if such an impotent, miserable person owned the whole world, it would be worth nothing for him, for it would seem to him that he was living a fruitless life among the vagrant human race in a wretched world without owner or protector. Everyone may understand just how forlorn and baffled is man among the human race in this bewildering fleeting world if he does not know his Owner, if he does not discover his Master. But if he does discover and know Him, he will seek refuge in His mercy and will

It is worthy of note that Ghazali ties worldly happiness to one of the most important functions of the heart, which is intimate knowledge of God. Hence, the greater one's experiential knowledge of God, the greater one's happiness.

Satan's Attack on the Heart

Ghazali examines Satan's entering the hearts of human beings under different headings. Leading in to this discussion, he defines the heart by means of various symbols. The heart, for instance, is like a pitched pavilion around which are doors through which external and internal states and circumstances pour into it, a target at which arrows from all directions are shot, a mirror reflecting assorted forms and images and a pool into which water from different channels opening onto it flow. As such, just as things that are good, becoming and beneficial can enter it, those that are harmful, repugnant and evil can also find room therein. The ways in which these things entering the heart, both positive and negative, come forth are either through the five senses or through intangible means such as anger, lust and imagination. The positive thoughts or suggestions entering the heart are referred to as *ilham* (inspiration), while the negative suggestions are called *waswasa*, or prompting and urgings to evil. The secondary cause for the inspiration is the angel, while the cause that prompts to evil is *Satan*.[572]

By virtue of its disposition, the heart is equally open to angelic inspiration and satanic whispering. Subjected to attack from two fronts, the heart is forced to choose one of these influences. When the assault is Satanic, the best defense is *dhikr Allah*, or remembrance of God. In order for the heart not to be defeated in the face of satanic prompting and suggestion, Ghazali presents remembrance of God as an alternative or means to prevailing over Satan. In his view, for a heart that remembers God and is occupied with invoking Him, the opportunity for Satan to intervene decreases or even totally vanishes. In such a situation, Satan's position is replaced by an angel who, in opposition to his whispering, provides inspiration. This approach, at the same time, serves as an elucidation of the Prophetic statement, "I too have a devil, but God helped me to overcome him and

---

rely on His power. The desolate world will turn into a place of recreation and pleasure, it will become a place of trade for the hereafter." (Nursi, *The Letters*, 262).

[572] al-Ghazali, *Ihya,'* III:36.

he has submitted to me, so he does not order anything except good."[573]
Its expression, in Ghazalian terms is thus:

> Purging the heart of Satan's promptings can only be possible through
> placing in the heart that other than that which is the source of these
> promptings. Whatever one places in the heart other than remem-
> brance of God and invocation of His Names can help Satan in his
> urgings. The only thing that protects the heart from Satan's urgings
> is *dhikr Allah*, or remembrance of God. Satan does not have a share
> of such remembrance. A thing is only treated with its opposite. The
> opposite of all the evil promptings of Satan is the remembrance of
> God by taking refuge in Him and disclaiming one's own strength
> and power.[574]

According to Ghazali, something else which needs to be done in order
to rescue the heart from the assaults of Satan is to cleanse it of *hawa*
(vain desires) and carnal desire. Those who follow their impulsive and
perverse human soul, as opposed to God's will, are slaves of their vain
desires. Stating, "Do you ever consider him who has taken his lusts and
fancies for his deity," the Qur'an[575] draws attention to this point.

The heart is a fortress and Satan, an enemy wanting to enter that
fortress, take possession of it and dominate it. Protecting the fortress from
the enemy can only be possible through securing its doors and covering
its gaps. The doors that Satan uses are such doors as lust, anger, greed,
envy, impetuousness, gluttony, love of adornment, ambition, appetence,
wealth and worldly possessions, stinginess, fear of poverty, enmity, arrogance, doubt in matters of faith and suspicion. It is imperative that these
doors be closed in order to avert Satan's intervention and assault.[576]

Maintaining that these doors can only be tightly shut through remembrance of God and through ridding oneself of idle passions, Ghazali moreover refers to *taqwa* (piety) and presents it in terms of the impact of such
remembrance. In his view, the heart's benefitting from the remembrance
of God is directly related to the heart's piety and purity. The remem-

---

[573] Tirmidhi, Rada, 17; Ibn Hanbal, *al-Musnad*, III:309.
[574] al-Ghazali, *Ihya,'* III:28.
[575] (45:23)
[576] al-Ghazali, *Ihya,'* III:34-36. Ghazali examines at length and in depth each of the
topics and themes briefly touched upon above.

brance of a heart that cannot remain pious and cleanse itself of its blame-worthy characteristics can only express carnality and cannot have any kind of positive effect on the heart. In such a case, Satan's assault becomes inescapable.[577]

Ghazali also refers to remembrance being realized with not only the tongue, but with the heart also; this is especially significant. Remembrance of God should not be carried out with the tongue only; on the contrary, the heart should also say what the tongue is saying. Only in such a way can Satan's urgings and evil promptings be prevented. In other words, while the tongue invokes God, the heart's preoccupation with other things and its disarray cannot provide the necessary protection and Satan's finding ways to enter the heart cannot be forestalled. According to Ghazali, the heart referred to in the verse, "Those who keep from disobedience to God in reverence for Him and piety: when a suggestion from Satan touches them—they are alert and remember God, and then they have clear discernment"[578] is such a heart.

Hence, the heart is shaped in accordance with the attributes that are dominant therein. When satanic attributes prevail, the heart becomes estranged from God and reaches the point of being a helper to Satan and the enemies of God. In so far as angels are dominant, however, it does not pay heed to the enticements and deceptions of Satan and, despite its ceaseless persistence, inclines towards worship and devotion.

On the basis of each organ of the human body having a *raison d'être* like the human being themselves, Ghazali makes mention of the duties of the heart and describes a heart which cannot realize these as diseased. For instance, the hand has been created to hold, the eye to see. The heart, too, has such duties in line with the purpose of its creation, such as knowledge, wisdom, gnosis, love of God, remembrance of God, spiritual pleasure, preferring God to all else and asking for God's help in the face of all the desires and pursuits of the carnal soul. A heart that cannot fulfil these is, therefore, diseased.[579]

---

[577] Ibid., III:42. In the same section, Ghazali defines the pious heart as the heart that is cleansed and purged of *shahwah* (appetence) or lust. The word *shahwah* is a concept comprehensive enough as to encompass every kind of desire and expectation outside of God in its scope of meaning.

[578] (7:201).

[579] al-Ghazali, *Ihya,'* III:62.

Putting forth such a rule, Ghazali then goes on to providing examples of his observation. For example, the manifestation of a heart's knowing God is love of Him. For one who does not possess knowledge of God does not have a share in love of Him. In the same way, if hoarding wealth and not giving it to the needy make a person happy, this means that they have become affected by the disease of miserliness. In order for that person to be freed from this illness, it is necessary that they donate their wealth in the path of God, for it is inconceivable for a heart that is miserly or stingy to be healthy and sound. It is virtually impossible for a heart wherein is held evil habits to safeguard itself from Satan's urgings and evil promptings. While finding the middle way of every task is important, it is at the same time very difficult. *Istiqama* (straightforwardness) caused even the Prophet to remark, "Sura Hud and others similar to it have made me old."[580] If even the Prophet of Islam expressed such difficulty in attaining the middle way, the path of straightforwardness, then the difficulty for average believers is axiomatic. Achieving this seems to be directly connected with the heart's soundness.

The Heart and Lust

Ghazali interprets the source of diseases of the heart to be the inclinations and desires felt for everything other than God. He uses the term *shahwa* to refer to this issue. The heart's death is realized in the event that it succumbs to its passions and becomes completely worldly. A heart that loses itself in the midst of worldly bounties and is contented with these and, in contrast, fails to ponder fear, sorrow, death and the afterlife is a lifeless heart. The verse, "Those who have no expectations to meet Us and are well-pleased with the present, worldly life, and (neither looking nor seeing beyond it) are content with it,"[581] explains the condition of those possessing such a heart. The only way to protect the heart from such a condition is again remembrance of God, obedience to Him, and keeping the heart away from all appetencies and passions, those within both the licit and the illicit sphere.[582]

---

580 Al-Tirmidhi, Tafsir al-Qur'an, 57.
581 (10:7)
582 al-Ghazali, *Ihya,'* III:68.

As can be seen, Ghazali, attributes meaning to the word *shahwa* as though he were interpreting the Qur'anic verse, "Made innately appealing to men are passionate love for women, children, (hoarded) treasures of gold and silver, branded horses, cattle, and plantations. Such are enjoyments of the present, worldly life; yet with God is the best of the goals to pursue," [583] considers it within a rather broad framework of meaning, and accepts it as the exclusive cause of the heart's disease and death. Moreover, he sees the soundness and health of the heart to be contingent upon its steering clear from these passions and weaves the pattern of his thought around this notion.

Alongside being the wellspring of goodness and prosperity, the heart can also serve as an accessory to evil and maliciousness. As conducive as it is to goodness, it is also open to wickedness. Just as it is the locus of belief and sincerity, the site of disbelief and dissension is also the heart. As figuratively expressed by Ghazali, just as it is "like a basin into which different streams of water empty from channels opening into it," it is also a pool into which murky and dirty waters are emptied. In addition to being like a target into which Satan shoots his poisonous arrows, it is also the mark for angels. Together with possessing such an impressionable and exceptionally changeable constitution, it has generally been viewed in the religious literature as always positive. For instance, virtually no one has understood from the expression "level of the life of the heart" the baseness of a wicked heart but far from it, has not entertained any doubt of it referring to an elevated level of spirituality. The heart, for Muslims, is always a precious faculty, the center of the human being and the place at which true humanity is revealed. It is the matchless, invaluable dimension that is the focus of God's constant sight, wherein a human being earns eternal happiness and Divine approval and pleasure.

Within this context, Ghazali has divided hearts into three from the perspective of those showing constancy in goodness and evil and/or those that oscillate between these two. This being so, hearts built up by piety, purified of wicked character and those fixed on good and which as a result find rest constitute the first type. Such hearts indicated in the verses, "Then, as for him who gives (out of his wealth for God's good pleasure), and keeps from disobedience to Him in reverence for Him and piety, And

---

[583] (3:14)

affirms the best (in creed, action, and the reward to be given), We will make easy for him the path to the state of ease (salvation after an easy reckoning),"[584] are receptive to and as a result are led to every kind of goodness. With goodness opening other doors of goodness for these hearts, they become with God's permission, closed to all evil and Satan.

The second type of hearts, in complete contrast to the first, are fastened shut to angels while at the same time giving right of way to Satan, sullied by evil characteristics and corrupted by the vain desires of the carnal soul. The Qur'an points to these hearts through such verses as: "Do you ever consider him who has taken his lusts and fancies for his deity? Would you then be a guardian over him (and, thereby, assume responsibility for guiding him)? Or do you think that most of them (really) hear or reason and understand? They are but like cattle, (following only their instincts). No, they are more heedless of the right way (and, therefore, in greater need of being led than cattle)."[585]

The third type of hearts, distinct from the first two and that of most people, are those which swing back and forth between the suggestion of the angel and that of Satan. While these incline to goodness on the one hand, they are subjected to the influence of evil on the other. While passion directs them toward evildoing, intellect invites them to goodness and while Satan assails them on the one hand, the angels strive to protect them against his promptings and whisperings. Hearts wavering between goodness and evil are these; they continue to do so until eventually their state becomes determined by the characteristics which reign dominant in them. Verses such as, "Thus, whomever God wills to guide, He expands his breast to Islam, and whomever He wills to lead astray, He causes his breast to become tight and constricted, as if he were climbing towards the heaven. Thus, God lays ignominy upon those who do not believe" [586] and "If God helps you, there will be none who can overcome you; if He forsakes you, who is there that can help you thereafter? In God, then, let the believers put all their trust," [587] describe the possessors of these hearts. Ghazali ascribes the condition of these hearts to God

---

[584] (92:5-7)
[585] (25:43-44)
[586] (6:125)
[587] (3:160)

and elucidates their condition by means of the terms Divine decree and destiny (*qadar*).[588]

Conclusion

While he does not explicitly express it as such, it is possible to say that Ghazali sees the heart to be the center of spiritual life or spiritual life itself. The matters that he attributes to the heart reflect his clear stance on this issue. In his view, a human being has both a physical heart and a spiritual heart and the second always holds a position of dominance over the first. In explaining this, Ghazali likens the heart to a sovereign over the other organs. In this way, human beings are always being directed by their heart, whether they are aware of it or not. This direction can be either good or bad, depending on the condition of the heart. If the heart is healthy, this reflects on the other organs in a positive manner and the human being continues their life as a good person. The opposite also being true, in cases where the heart is sick, sealed and rusted, the human being pursues an unhealthy life, materially as well as spiritually. And because it is either a means to goodness or transgression, it is again the heart which is deemed to be deserving of reward or damnation, which experiences happiness or is condemned to punishment. The heart, in Ghazali's belief, is the great reality making man into man or depriving him of his humanity. The extent to which the heart, which Ghazali situates at the center of a person's spiritual faculties also, holds command over a person's material being can in this way be seen. A person is thus 'as human as their heart.'

---

[588] al-Ghazali, *Ihya,'* III:63-66.

Nursi and the Heart

S aid Nursi also explores the heart concept and deals with it at length in his works. Like his predecessors, Nursi—one of the most prominent scholars of the contemporary period—prioritizes the functions of the heart as opposed to its essence and provides simple examples by way of explaining his purpose. In this section, an overview of Nursi's thought on the essence of the heart will be presented, followed by his understanding of the heart's functions and purpose.

The Essence of the Heart

While Nursi examines the descriptions of preceding scholars in focusing on 'what' the heart is, his own personal interpretations and readings also attract attention. One of the famous statements he makes about the heart's essence is as follows:

> What is meant by the heart is the Divine subtle faculty—not the piece of flesh shaped like a pine-cone—the emotions of which are manifested in the conscience and the thoughts of which are reflected in the mind. [589]

In introducing the heart, Nursi mentions the physical heart first and then asserts that it is not the physical, material heart to which he would devote his attention. The heart in question is the spiritual one, which is the "Divine subtle faculty." Ghazali before Nursi employed this expression, as mentioned in the relevant section.[590] The heart, in addition to pertaining to the human being, is attributed to God through reference to it as 'Divine.' This attribution holds within it very important clues in terms of revealing the ultimate mission of the heart. Accordingly, despite the

---

[589] Nursi, *Signs of Miraculousness*, 86. For Nursi's definition of the heart as a Divine subtle faculty (*latifa al-Rabbaniya*) see: Said Nursi, *The Reasonings*, trans. Hüseyin Akarsu, The Risale-i Nur Collection (New Jersey: Tughra Books, 2008), 121.

[590] This was the first theme explored in the section entitled 'Ghazali and the Heart.'

heart being intrinsic to the human being, it is more a part belonging to God. As such, it is as though the heart, as well as belonging to God, is a mechanism given to the human being in trust. As we have seen, for Ghazali, a person knows their Lord, believes in Him and acts with their heart. This is can be expressed in the following way also: The Creator, Who created humanity and then asked them to believe in Him, gave them a faculty called the heart with which they could realize this. Humanity is in a position of using this *batini* (esoteric) heart in order to actualize their purpose of creation, know their Lord and believe in Him.

In Nursi's view, this "Divine subtle faculty" has two very important dimensions: *wijdan* (conscience) and *dimagh* (mind). Of these, *wijdan* is the heart's wellspring of emotion, while the *dimagh* (which can be referred to with the terms intellect (*aql*) or consciousness (*shu'ur*) constitutes the place where thoughts and imaginations pertaining to the heart are reflected.

From this vantage point, Nursi approaches the heart as a roof or an umbrella and presents the conscience and intellect as its two complementary elements. As such, the heart arises from *wijdan*, which is the source of spiritual perception, discernment and emotion, and *dimagh*, which projects ideas, thought and knowledge. Put differently, the heart's representative with respect to perception and feeling is the conscience, and its representative in terms of knowledge and thought is the mind. This being so, these are not completely disconnected and separate entities, but on the contrary, are the elements that make up the heart.

This approach also bears importance in the sense that it enables certain Qur'anic verses to be better understood. For instance, in its chapter entitled Hajj, the Qur'an describes reason as a function pertaining to the heart.[591] A verse in the chapter called Tawba (Repentance) explains how certain people are deprived of their ability to reason due to their hearts being sealed.[592] Through such verses, mental capacities such at

---

[591] The particular verse reads: "Do they never travel about the earth (and view all these scenes with an eye to learn lessons), so that they may have hearts with which to reason (and arrive at truth), or ears with which to hear (God's call)? For indeed, it is not the eyes that have become blind; it is rather the hearts in the breasts that are blind" (22:46).

[592] The verse states: "They are well-pleased to be with those (women and children) bound to stay behind, and a seal has been set upon their hearts, so they cannot ponder and penetrate the essence of matters to grasp the truth" (9:87). The

understanding, perception and thought are ascribed to the heart. In the event of the intellect being considered as a faculty entirely separate to the heart, these verses become rather difficult to comprehend. When *aql* is accepted as a dimension of the heart, however, this difficulty is immediately lifted and a more plausible understanding gains ascendance. Asserting that, "The light of reason comes from the heart" and that "There can be no reason without the heart,"[593] Nursi expresses the heart-mind connection in yet another way. The mind cannot be present where the heart is not.

Assessing the servanthood of a believer, Nursi says they are charged in three respects: "In respect of their hearts, with submission and obedience; in respect of their intellects, with belief and affirming Divine unity; and physically, through action and worship."[594] As such, he assigns reason the responsibility of belief in the unity of God. Serving as a mirror for the thoughts occurring to the heart, *aql* also fulfils such a function in relation to knowing God.

In addition to this categorization, Nursi presents another where he takes the conscience and the soul to be a roof with four elements constituting its foundations:

> Will, mind, emotion, and the subtle inner faculties, which constitute the four elements of the conscience and four faculties of the spirit, each have an ultimate aim. The ultimate aim of the will is worship of God; that of the mind is knowledge of God; that of the emotions is love of God; and that of the inner faculties is the vision of God. [595]

---

verse rebukes those who seek permission to stay behind due to their fear when the situation of fighting in God's way arises. They are unable to grasp the wisdom behind such struggle and the delicacy in obeying the Messenger's commands and experience serenity and happiness. Their failure to fulfil the command has resulted in their hearts becoming sealed. For information about the heart's being sealed, refer to the relevant section of the thesis.

A directly related verse reads: "Surely, among the jinn and humankind are many that we have created (and destined for) Hell (knowing that they would deserve it). They have hearts with which they do not seek the essence of matters to grasp the truth, and they have eyes with which they do not see, and they have ears with which they do not hear" (7:179).

593 Nursi, *The Words*, 739.

594 Nursi, *Signs of Miraculousness*, 173.

595 Said Nursi, *The Damascus Sermon*, trans. Şükran Vahide (Istanbul: Sözler Publications, 1996), 117.

With this approach, Nursi refers to four elements that make up the conscience or spirit, which he uses synonymously. These are willpower, intellect, feeling and the subtle faculty that can be referred to as the spiritual intellect. It can be argued that in place of the word *dhihn*—the second of these four elements—the words *dimagh*, *aql* and *shu'ur* (consciousness) can also be employed. That Nursi understands the Divine subtle faculty to be the heart was previously mentioned.

In this category *wijdan* or *ruh* (the spirit) are the essence, while the four elements referred to constitute this essence. In addition to their having other functions, these four elements have uses which serve their *raison d'être*. In accordance with these, *irada* has been given to worship God and to realize a perfected level of servanthood, *dhihn* has been given to know God and deepen in experiential knowledge, *hiss* (feeling) to overflow with love of God and *qalb* to ascend to a level of closeness to God as though seeing Him.

As can be seen, Nursi, like Ghazali, uses certain terms like spirit, conscience and heart synonymously, and sees no harm in doing so. Distinct separations between these complementary concepts—as terms which are used to express aspects of spiritual life—are virtually impossible to encounter in literature.

Although he appropriates the term 'Divine subtle faculty' when describing the heart, Nursi's reference to, "the fair gifts of the Compassionate One such as the intelligence, the heart, the eye and the tongue, given to you to make preparation for the foundations of everlasting life and eternal happiness in the hereafter,"[596] reveals an additional nuance of meaning, with the heart being described as a Divine gift.

Also clear in this statement is the notion that all the limbs, organs and faculties—material and spiritual—are not given for this world, but in order to earn eternal happiness. In line with this, the heart has the capacity to allow human beings to attain eternal bliss in the Hereafter. As such, the heart becomes a Divine gift and bestowal, which allows the person to feel eternity, satisfies this need and enables them to reach their ultimate objective. In this respect, the heart is a *buraq*[597] taking the human

---

[596] Nursi, *The Words*, 40.

[597] Buraq is the name of the horse-like creature that is said to have carried Prophet Muhammad during his Ascension to Heaven.

being to eternity, a pointer to God and a means to know Him, and a great bounty bestowed upon humanity by God Himself.

An analogy that Nursi uses with respect to the relationship between a person and the heart is relevant here. Stating, "The inner dimension of creation is called the *malakut* and the outer dimension is called the *mulk*. In this respect, a human being and the heart are both the envelope and the contents for one another. This is because with respect to the latter, corporeal dimension, a human being is an envelope and the heart is its contents. With respect to the former, incorporeal dimension, the heart is an envelope while the human being is the contents," [598] Nursi draws attention to the close relationship between a human being and their heart. Accordingly, because the heart is physically, outwardly located in the human body, it becomes the contents. Conversely, as the heart spiritually is in a position of rule and dominance over the person and all their faculties and organs, the human being is, so to speak, like the letter within their heart, or in other words its contents. Nursi's description of the essence of the human heart is constructed around this likeness.

The Heart's Functions

According to Nursi, the heart's most important function and mission is its being the locus of belief and experiential knowledge of God. His general emphasis and focus in relation to the heart can be situated within the framework of these two key understandings. As can be understood from Nursi's expression and style—in all the similitudes and symbols he employs when describing the heart—he sees the heart, much like Ghazali, as the site of belief in God and the place wherein and source wherefrom God is recognized and known experientially. An attempt will be made to classify these approaches under separate headings.

The Locus of Belief

For Nursi, the first of the two vital duties of the heart is its being the site of belief in God. It is always the heart which has faith in God and the other essentials of belief—such as belief in God's oneness, the Prophets, the Hereafter, angels and Divine decree and destiny—and which accepts

---

[598] Nursi, *Mathnawi al-Nuriya*, 91.

the existence of the realities of the unseen and incorporeal. In this respect, it is the place and wellspring where belief is born and nurtured.

In interpreting the verse, "God has set a seal on their hearts and on their hearing," he focuses on the heart and explains important issues in relation to it in the following manner:

> The word "their hearts (qulûbihim)" precedes hearing and sight because it is the seat of belief; and because the first evidences of the Maker are manifested from the heart's consultation with itself, and from the conscience referring to the innate disposition. For when a person consults himself, he feels an acute sense of power-lessness that drives him to seek out a point of support, and he per-ceives his clamoring need to fulfil his hopes and is compelled to find a source of assistance. But there is no support to be found and no help except in belief. [599]

In these statements, another function of the heart is stressed, in addition to its housing belief. This is its seeking God and its showing His existence through its signs and proofs. According to Nursi, the heart has two deeper dimensions, which he calls the "point of reliance and point of seeking help." Using these two factors, it seeks and wants God and points to Him. It is possible to express Nursi's view in this way:

Whenever the heart, in continuing its worldly life, experiences a sense of powerlessness, it looks for someone who will rescue it from this pre-dicament, make it forget its deficiency and offer it true consolation. This is the natural state of the heart. It is precisely in such a situation that the authority on which the heart will depend and thus be free of its distress is God. Again in the same way, when the heart experiences inclination, desire and expectation in relation to the world or to the Hereafter, its seek-ing someone who possesses the power to fulfil its needs and wants also comes naturally to the heart. It is again God, the Owner of Infinite Power, Who can meet the needs that the heart so strongly feels. It is at these two points, therefore, where the heart indicates God and attests to His existence.

Asserting, "There is no support to be found and no help except in belief," Nursi adds that those who do not have belief are deprived of these points of reliance and seeking help. Frequently using these two concepts

---

[599] Nursi, *Signs of Miraculousness*, 85.

in favor of finding God and knowing Him, Nursi uses the word *wijdan* in place of heart and draws attention to the same issue:

> Like the darkness of the night shows up light, so through his weakness and impotence, his poverty and need, his defects and faults, man makes known the power, strength, riches, and mercy of an All-Powerful One of Glory, and so on... he acts as a mirror to numerous Divine Attributes in this way. Even, through searching for a point of support in his infinite impotence and boundless weakness in the face of his innumerable enemies, his conscience perpetually looks to the Necessarily Existent One. And since he is compelled in his utter poverty and endless need to seek for a point of assistance in the face of his innumerable aims, his conscience in that respect all the time leans on the Court of an All-Compassionate One of Riches and opens its hands in supplication to Him. That is to say, in regard to this point of support and point of assistance in the conscience, two small windows are opened onto the Court of Mercy of the All-Powerful and All-Compassionate One, which may all the time be looked through. [600]

Through this statement, he initially uses the interplay of day and night as a metaphor for his particular purpose. The existence of night is proof of the existence of day and as a result of light also. Similarly, a person's being, by virtue of their nature, weak, powerless, poor, deficient and imperfect makes known One Who is absolutely free of any of these qualities particular to the created, and points to His strength, power, wealth and mercy; human beings in this sense reflect Divine Attributes. Beyond this, the endless impotence of the human being and their countless weaknesses cause them to seek someone who can rescue them from this helplessness and weakness. Again, in the same way, their possession of innumerable desires and ambitions directs them to one who is capable of fulfilling these wants and desires. And so, the One on Whom human beings can rely and in Whom they can seek refuge in the face of worldly trials and tribulations, and turn to so as to fulfil their worldly expectations and goals, is God Himself.

It becomes clear at this point that Nursi's point of departure is the precept, "things are known through their opposites," which he cites at every

---

[600] Nursi, *The Words*, 719.

opportunity throughout his works. As is well known, this approach is used in various disciplines. One of the methods human beings have used in order to give meaning to creation is their attempting to interpret things by means of finding their opposites. Nursi first determines the weaknesses and flaws of human beings and then, on the basis of God's being free from all these, goes on to express their need for Him. These needs being addressed appears in the form of the heart's turning to God with such feeling. People utilize their point of reliance when they turn to God wholeheartedly with the purpose of having their needs met and use their heart's point of seeking help when they turn to Him to have their wants fulfilled. Finally, Nursi's assertion that the heart has the function of seeking as much as that of knowledge, brings into question one of the mysteries of the creation of the human being, that is examination. The heart's knowing its Creator is connected with the effort it exerts in seeking Him. Consequently, Nursi's view of the heart should not be seen as one that is static. On the contrary, his approach to the heart is considerably dynamic.

Windows Opening onto Reality

One of Nursi's interpretations in relation to the heart's functions is its serving as a window opening to the sun of truth. Not all hearts, however, are like this. "All those luminous hearts, turned and joined to the truth and manifesting it, each a small throne of Divine knowledge, a comprehensive mirror of God's Eternal Besoughtedness, were like so many windows opened onto the Sun of the Truth."[601]

Nursi, in this text, lists the characteristics of hearts that he terms windows opening to the truth. The most salient characteristic of such a heart is its being "turned and joined to the truth and manifesting it." An understanding of the word Nursi uses, *haqiqa*, will be useful in understanding this statement. The words *haqq* and *haqiqa*, which are more often than not mentioned and considered in juxtaposition, come to mean such things as truth, being constant, right, as well as knowing something decisively and something whose existence is certain. As God exists and His existence is accepted as absolute truth, He has been referred to as 'al-Haqq.' In expressing the meaning of *haqq* as something whose existence is real and certain from the perspective of creation, in the legal sense it

---

[601] Nursi, *The Rays*, 166.

implies the "remuneration for labor or services" and something belonging to someone. In the religious context, however, it is a term which signifies "everything belonging to God." In the Islamic discourse, everything pertaining to God's Essence, Names, Attributes and actions expresses the truth, or *'Haqq* and *Haqiqa.'*[602]

Raghib takes these words to mean "truth and something fit for truth." In his view, everything bearing on each of God's Names and Attributes is truth and reality. As everything in the created realm reflects one of His Names, everything that rests on this Name is also truth and reality. He says that all created things were created in accordance with a particular benefit or within a certain order and that created things are truth and reality to the extent that they realize the benefit or service for which they were created.[603] Sharif al-Jurjani defines *haqq* as "a thing whose existence is so certain that it cannot be denied," while Taftazani (d. 792/1390) describes it as "a judgment which concurs with the truth." It is for this reason that the mainstream Muslims (Ahl al-Sunna wa'l-Jama'a) has also been referred to as *Ahl al-Haqq*, or the People of Truth.[604]

Mentioned in hundreds of verses in the Qur'an, the word *haqq* has generally been used as the opposite of *batil* (falsehood).[605] It has also been used to mean, "a report truthful to an event," [606] "accurate news"[607] "the true way"[608] "knowledge and belief based on fact"[609], "evidence"[610] and "the inner reality of an event."[611] Prophet Muhammad's use of the word also corresponds with its Qur'anic meanings. For instance, in the *hadith*, "O Allah! You are the Truth and Your Promise is truth, And to meet You is true, Your Word is the truth And Paradise is true And Hell is true And all the Prophets (Peace be upon them) are true; And Muhammad is true, And the Day of Resurrection is true,"[612]it is clear that the term is used to

---

[602] Ibn Manzur, *Lisan al-'arab*, 'h-q-q.'

[603] al-Isfahani, *Al-Mufradat*, 156.

[604] al-Jurjani, *al-Ta'rifat*, 'haqq.'

[605] (2:42); (4:105); (5:57)

[606] (7:169); (38:84)

[607] (23:62)

[608] (10:35)

[609] (53:28)

[610] (10:76, 77)

[611] (12:51)

[612] Bukhari, Tahajjud, 1.

mean "things whose existence is certain." Ibn Hajar, in his interpretation of this Prophetic tradition, characterizes the truth and reality as "the entirety of things belonging to God."[613]

Just as it is possible to understand from Nursi's "windows opening onto the truth" expression that hearts have been illumined with their own light of belief, that they have completely grasped the truth, have attained it and have become a source of truth, it can also be sensed that these hearts have the added duty of carrying other hearts to the truth. His making reference to such hearts as 'windows' evokes this meaning. They are representatives of the truth and the luminous sites which serve as the means to reaching it. The truth does not endure any change, become tarnished or soiled in them but remains as it is, and their light is reflected, with all its brightness, to other hearts.

In this paragraph are included two other definitions of the heart that Nursi offers, namely "Throne of Divine Knowledge" and "Mirror of God's Eternal Besoughtedness." However, these will be elaborated under separate subheadings below.

Throne of Divine Knowledge

The second expression in Nursi's aforementioned statement is the heart's being the Throne of Divine Knowledge. The word *arsh* (throne) literally means ceiling. It is used to refer to the higher section of a building or place. A house's ceiling, the ceiling's roof or dome are also included in the scope of the word's meaning. In addition, anything which towers and provides shade like a tent or gazebo can also be called *arsh*. As can be understood from these meanings, the term connotes loftiness and superiority. The thrones of rulers have also been called *arsh*, with allusions also being made to their associated requirements—namely dominion, greatness and sovereignty. Apart from these, the term has also been used to refer to something supporting a thing, a thing's essence and the leaders managing a society's affairs.[614]

It can be argued that the correlation between the heart and the word *arsh* stems from its being considered—from the perspective of its mean-

---

[613] Ibn Hajar, *Fath al-bari*, VI:4.
[614] Ibn Manzur, *Lisan al-'arab*, 'a-r-sh.' Yazır, *Hak Dini Kur'an Dili*, III:2176-77.

ing and functions—within a very broad spectrum.[615] In this context, it is possible to say that the expression which is quite problematic in view of the criteria determined in *hadith* studies, "Neither the heavens nor the earth can contain Me, save the heart of My believing servant,"[616] has encouraged Sufis to assert the heart's greatness over the *arsh*. For instance, on the basis of this statement Ibn 'Arabi claims that the heart is wider than even God's all-encompassing mercy.[617] Mawlana Jalal al-Din Rumi says that the seven heavens would disappear within the heart and become invisible as "the mirror of the heart hath no bound."[618] His explicit reference to the heart as God's throne and the implications of such is as follows:

---

[615] As a natural extension of this perspective, there have also been views along the lines of the Ka'ba also being the heart. Ibn 'Arabi connects the heart's being the Ka'ba to its being the wellspring of experiential knowledge of God. (Ibn al-'Arabi, *al-Futuhat*, IV:7.) On the basis of its being the site where God directs His gaze, Hujwiri states that it is even more valuable than the Ka'ba. (al-Hujwiri, *Kashf al-Mahjub*, 204.) Mawlana Jalal al-Din Rumi describes the heart's superiority over the Ka'ba in the following manner: "The Ka'ba is a structure built by Azar's son Ibrahim. The heart however is where God, the All-Majestic the All-Great, directs His gaze." (Tahir al-Mawlawi, ed. *Sharh al-Mathnawi* (Istanbul: Dehliz Books,2008), couplet 6196.) The second couplet reads: "Never since God made the Ka'ba hath He gone into it, and none but the Living (God) hath ever gone into this House (of mine)." (Rumi, *The Mathnawi of Jalalu'ddin Rumi*, 337, couplet 2246.) In reference to the early Sufis, Schimmel states that many of them frequently performed the pilgrimage to Mecca and "knew that the true seat of the Divine spirit was not the Kaaba made of stone but the Kaaba of the faithful worshiper's (*sic*) heart in which God might reveal Himself." (Schimmel, *Mystical Dimensions of Islam*, 106.) All these approaches need to be evaluated not in terms of the heart's being superior to the Ka'ba in reality, but in terms of its importance and value for the human being and God. It is also important to state that the heart which Sufis see as greater and more valuable than the Ka'ba is not the heart of every human being, but the heart of the perfected believer. *Hearts that have not been purged of masiwa*, or everything other than God, bear no relation to the topic at hand. Also see: Titus Burckhardt, *An Introduction to Sufi Doctrine*, trans. D. M. Matheson (Bloomington (IN): World Wisdom, 2008), 134.

[616] al-Ghazali, *Ihya,'* III:127; Ibn al-'Arabi, *al-Futuhat*, I:216. Ahmad Faruq (Imam Rabbani) Sirhindi, *al-Maktubat*, 3 vols. (Cairo: Matba'a al-Miriyya, 1899), II:30. Iraqi, who undertakes the *takhrij al-hadith*, or the process of *hadith* extraction and authentication—in Ghazali's Ihya' 'Ulum ad-Din says that he is unable to find the source of this Tradition. Ajluni recounts Ibn Taymiyya's statement that "This expression is aforementioned in the Isra'iliyyat (stories of the Children of Israel). There is no such *isnad* (chain of narrators) communicated from the Prophet. (*al-Hujwiri, Kashf al-Mahjub, II:255.*)

[617] Ibn al-'Arabi, *al-Futuhat*, IV:6.

[618] Rumi, *The Mathnawi of Jalalu'ddin Rumi*, 190, couplet 3488.

(If) the throne of the heart has become restored to soundness and purged of sensuality, thereon *the Merciful God is seated on His Throne* (emphasis in original). After this, God controls the heart without intermediary, since the heart has attained to this relation (with Him).[619]

Furthermore, some Sufis have articulated the heart's expansiveness with the following likeness. "If the *arsh* and everything it encompasses were to be placed in the heart of the *'Arif* (gnostic), they would not even feel it. For the heart is as expansive enough as to embrace the *Arsh*, the Divine Seat (of dominion), the carnal self, and everything within or outside space."[620]

Imam Rabbani (Shaykh Ahmad Sirhindi, d. 1033/1624) does not concur with the Sufis on this question. In his view, these kinds of expressions are the product of confusion. The truth is that the heart is a *jawhar* (literally meaning jewel, but also used to mean substance) which expresses the *'alam-i amr*, or the 'world of command,' and the encompassing reality of the human being.[621] Such statements pertaining to the heart's broadness should be assessed not in the sense of their being expressions of a truth, but within the framework of the Sufis' own understanding. This is because the manifestation in the heart, when compared with that of the Supreme Throne constitutes but a glimmer. From this standpoint, real superiority with respect to Divine manifestations belongs to the Supreme Throne. For Imam Rabbani, the views of Junayd (297/910) and others who see and present the heart as bigger than the Supreme Throne is the result of confusing the essence of a thing with its representation. That is, when they saw the exemplification of the Supreme Throne and its contents in their hearts, they ruled what they saw to be the truth and fell into error.[622]

Coming through these statements, Imam Rabbani's definition of the heart is noteworthy. He describes the heart in a way analogous to the descriptions mentioned earlier and states that in addition to the belong-

---

[619] Ibid., 199.

[620] For detailed information see: Sirhindi, *al-Maktubat*, I:100. Ismail Haqqi Bursawi, *Kitab al-Natija*, ed. Ali Namlı and İmdat Yavaş, 2 vols. (Istanbul: İnsan Yayınları, 1997), I:417.

[621] The term Jawhar "refers to the idea that the substance is the most valuable thing" for consideration. See, Alam, *Faith Practice Piety: An Excerpt from the Maktubat-i Imam-i Rabbani*, 66.

[622] Sirhindi, *al-Maktubat*, II:30-31.

ing to the realm of the unseen, the heart is a reality and *jawhar* which combines many qualities of the human being within it. The 'world of command' that he refers to is synonymous with the world of the unseen and that which is the opposite of the 'world of creation' or 'world of witnessing' which is known as the corporeal, visible world. The world of command is the otherworldly, invisible realm which is not contingent upon space or time. One of the most famous examples provided by way of explaining this difference is the human body being of the world of witnessing and the spirit being of the world of command.

For Imam Rabbani, alongside the heart being a *jawhar* from the world of command, it constitutes the most important facet of the human being because of its bringing together many of the qualities that make a person human. However closed the world of the unseen is for human beings, irrespective of this, they carry within them something of that world, called the heart. When considered in this light, it is possible to say that the human being is not just an entity of the world of witnessing that we can perceive, but is at the same time a part of the world of command. However connected the human being is to this world, visible and material, that is how connected and related they are to the world of the unseen.

Not only seeing the human being as essence of all creation and likening the human heart to the Supreme Throne, Sufi thought has in addition characterized the heart of the perfected believer as *arsh al-akbar*, or the Greatest and Supreme Throne.[623] Imam Rabbani approaches the matter just touched upon from yet another perspective:

> The human being is a miniaturized summary of this realm. In this regard, an example of everything in this world is present in the human being. For instance, the counterpart in the human being of the Supreme Throne is the heart. Just as there is an intermediate realm between this world and the world of command, the heart in the same way is an intermediate realm between this world and the world of command.[624] The heart and the Supreme Throne therefore, despite

---

[623] Muhammad 'Ali al-Tahanawi, *Kashshaf istilahat al-funun* (Beirut: Dar al-Sadir, 1745), III:981.

[624] "The heart is the focal point of all forces and is situated right at the center of all these powers. That is, it is a vehicle between spiritual forces and bodily organs. In this respect, it is in a position of both receiving and giving spiritual blessings." (Bursawi, *Kitab al-Natija*, I:341.))

being considered part of the world of creation with respect to their corporeality, are accepted to be from the world of command in terms of their other aspects. However, coming to a realization of the essence of these kinds of jewels, according to the Sufis, is a situation unique to saints (*awliya*) who have rightfully completed their *suluk*, or spiritual initiation.[625]

The word *barzakh* comes to mean "a thing that intervenes between any two things: or a bar, an obstruction, or a thing that makes a separation between two things."[626] It is an intermediate realm. Previously ascribing the heart and the Supreme Throne to the world of command, Imam Rabbani here likens them to an intermediate realm sandwiched between the world of witnessing and the world of command. *Qalb* and *Arsh* in his view are each like a veil located between these two realms and looking unto them. They are akin to veils that are in close connection to these two worlds, have a face looking towards them but which simultaneously separate and even conceal them from one another.

As highlighted, Nursi does not term every heart the Throne of Divine Knowledge, as his predecessor Imam Rabbani[627], but makes such a comparison in relation to those hearts illumined with the light of belief.[628] Hearts can be called the Throne of Divine Knowledge so long as/to the extent to which they remain celestial. As far as we can understand, Nursi, with this expression, puts forth the notion that the faculty which can know God and do this in the best possible way is the heart.

He has approached commentaries on the heart and *arsh* from the perspective of comparison and contrast, making the following observations:

> The sun has manifestations from a fragment of glass and a droplet of water to a pool, the ocean, the moon, and the planets. Each contains the sun's reflection and image in accordance with its capacity, and knows its limits. In accordance with its capacity, a drop of water says: "There is a reflection of the sun on me." But it cannot say: "I am a mirror like the ocean." In just the same way, the ranks of the

---

[625] Sirhindi, *al-Maktubat*, II:18.

[626] Lane, *An Arabic-English Lexicon*, I:187.

[627] Imam Rabbani's clear influence over Nursi's thought is the chief reason why myriad references are made to the former's works and ideas in this section.

[628] Nursi, *The Rays*, 111.

saints have degrees, in accordance with the variety of the Divine Names' manifestations. Each of the Divine Names has manifestations like a sun, from the heart to the Divine throne. The heart too is a throne, but it cannot say: "I am like the Divine throne."

Thus, those who proceed reluctantly and with pride instead of knowing their impotence, poverty, faults, and defects, and prostrating entreatingly before the Divine court, which form the basis of worship, hold their miniscule hearts equal to the Divine throne. They confuse their droplet-like stations with the ocean-like stations of the saints. They stoop to artificiality, false display, and meaningless self-advertisement in order to make themselves fitting for those high ranks, and cause themselves many difficulties.[629]

Nursi makes these observations with a view to human beings knowing their limits and refraining from erroneous expression or belief. He draws attention to the need for human beings to experience a constant consciousness of servanthood. So long as feelings at the core of servanthood such as deficiency, shortcoming and diffidence before God actively continue, there would be no change in the servant's humble standing before their Creator. The reverse, however, causes a person's believing they have a series of virtues, which in turn can mislead them to such incorrect thought and belief as to see their heart as equal to the Divine throne or even greater. Nursi's aim seems to be to curb such mistaken belief, reminding human beings of their vulnerability to such feelings of arrogance and presumption. Moreover in Islamic tradition, a person's perpetually viewing himself or herself as imperfect and flawed before their Lord has been considered the befitting attitude to adopt as His servant.

Another instance of Nursi's mentioning the terms heart and supreme throne in juxtaposition is in the context of a person's being able to make direct contact with God.[630] Every believer who possesses experiential knowledge of God can establish a relationship with their Lord in accordance with their capacity. Every believing heart knows God to the extent of their belief in Him. Their God, so to speak, is a God Who they can know and recognize. God, who manifests Himself in their heart, is not the God

---

[629] Nursi, *The Flashes*, 136. Nursi, *Mathnawi al-Nuriya, 145.*
[630] Nursi, *The Words*, 125.

Who is the Lord of the Worlds but the God in respect to the degree of their belief. That is why a *wali* (friend of God), for instance, when communicating with God through supplication can say, "My heart is a mirror of my Lord," but cannot say, should not say, "My heart is the Supreme Throne of the Lord of the Worlds." For when they pray, they are favored with an address according to their own degree and capacity.

Nursi's words, "The heart too is a throne"[631] should be evaluated along the same lines. In other words the heart, like the supreme throne, belongs to the world of command and is a mechanism that presides over the human being. As mentioned earlier with reference to Ghazali, all the feelings, limbs and organs belonging to a human being are like slaves and servants while the heart is like their sultan. The sultan commands anything he wishes to his slaves and servants, and they in turn fulfil his commands without hesitation.[632] Nursi does not see the human heart as the supreme throne of God. On the contrary, just as the supreme throne symbolizes God's administering the universe, the heart also administers the human being, and reigns over all their faculties and organs, physical and immaterial. In his view, the relationship between the supreme throne and the heart is explored in this way.

---

[631] Nursi, *The Flashes*, 180-81. Nursi, *Mathnawi al-Nuriya*, 145.

[632] The commentary of the Qur'anic verse, "He established Himself on the supreme Throne" allows one to draw this conclusion. Suat Yıldırım says the following in relation to the meaning of these verses: *Is'tawa*, literally means stability, resolving on something, establishing oneself and ascending. *Arsh* refers to the throne on which sovereigns are seated. The Salaf-i Salihin (prominent guides among the Companions and their followers) accept such *mutashabih* or allegorical, multifaceted verses of the Qur'an as they are, without commentary, only holding God above any similarity to His creation and above the imperfections that these words express in relation to human beings. As for the late scholars, so as not to fall into the danger of the common people, they interpret these in the light of *muhkam* verses and take them to mean dominance, invasion, ownership and dominion. While this verse explains God's limitless actions in the universe, His creating the heavens and earth in six days and His commanding the sun, moon and stars, it asserts His Lordship in directing all affairs in the universe, and presents a sovereign's establishing themselves on the throne and decreeing one thing after another and controlling all things in this way. Becoming established on the throne and reigning over is mostly used in this sense. While the expositions of the late scholars are acceptable, the manner and approach of the *salaf* is considered more secure. (Yıldırım, *Kur'an-ı Hakim ve Açıklamalı Meali*, 156.)

Mirror of God's Eternal Besoughtedness

One of the original characterizations that Nursi makes of the heart is its being the mirror of God's Eternal Besoughtedness. His statement, "the inner heart is the mirror of the Eternally Besought One,"[633] also depicts this same notion. At another point at which he explains that the heart has been created for an eternal love, he again describes it as "the mirror of the Eternally Besought One."[634]

It is noteworthy that in these statements there is a special insistence on the Name *Samad* (Self -Sufficient). In order to understand this, it is necessary to examine Nursi's views on the Names of God. When categorizing *Asma al-Husna* (The Most Beautiful Names), used to refer to the ninety-nine Names of God, he states:

> Know that a portion of the Names of the Necessarily Existent One are those pertaining to His Essence, which point to the Most Sacred Essence from every aspect. It is His Name and His title. There are many Names such as "Allah, the One, the Self-Sufficient, the Necessarily Existent." Another portion of these Names pertain to various sorts of action. For instance, "Forgiving, Provider, Giver of Life, and Dealer of Death."[635]

As can be seen, Nursi has categorized Divine Names into those of His Essence and those of His action. He provides the Names *Allah, the Unique One, Self-Sufficient* and *Necessarily Existent One* as examples of the former and *Forgiving, Providing* for the latter. Accordingly, the first Names are the Names of the Creator Himself and His titles and, in his words, show God from every aspect. On this basis, as far as we can understand, Nursi's choice of the Name *Samad* is due to this Name showing God from every facet. He could, for instance, have used the Names *Allah* and *the Unique One*, which also express God in every way. But because such Names

---

[633] Nursi, *The Words*, 670.

[634] He states: "A beloved who is hidden through setting is not beautiful, for those doomed to decline cannot be truly beautiful. They may not be loved with the heart, which is created for eternal love and is the mirror of the Eternally Besought One, and should not be loved with it." (Ibid., 228.) "Do not give any opportunity to other loves to enter into your inner heart because the inner heart is the mirror of the Eternally Besought One and pertains only to Him." (Nursi, *The Words*, 670.)

[635] Said Nursi, *Emirdağ Lahikası (Emirdağ Letters)* (Istanbul: Şahdamar Yayınları, 2010), 322.

such as *Providing*, *Giver of Life* which express God's actions as distinct from to His Essence, as they do not encompass all of God's Names and show God's Essence directly, Nursi has not chosen them within this context.

Nursi not only uses the Name *samad* here, but in most places where he feels the need to mention a Name unique to God. When explaining the universe, for instance, he describes it as a letter belonging to God, seeing all creation as "a missive of the Eternally Besought One."[636] And when describing all the beauty, splendor and perfection in the world of creation, he uses the expression "transcendent Attributes."[637] Nursi also uses the expressions "power of the Eternally Besought One,"[638] "brilliant miracle of the Eternally Besought One's art,"[639] "manifestation of the Eternally Besought One,"[640] "imprint of eternal besoughtedness,"[641] "stamp of 'eternal besoughtedness,'"[642] "utterly perfect beauty of that Eternally Besought One,"[643] in addition to those formerly expressed.

Seat of Love and Hate

Also part of Nursi's discourse on the functions of the heart is the idea of the heart as the seat of love and hate. It becomes apparent that he uses such wording when interpreting particular Qur'anic verses. For instance, when examining the verse about backbiting in the chapter entitled Hujuraat which reads "...do not backbite (against one another). Would any of you love to eat the flesh of his dead brother?"[644] Nursi interprets the word love, stating "Is your heart, the seat of love and hate, so corrupted that it loves the most despicable thing?"[645] Two aspects will be elaborated here. The first is that even though only the words love and hate have been mentioned here, other words related to these two concepts are also included within their meanings. For instance, taking an interest in or giving impor-

---

[636] Nursi, *The Words*, 65, 229, 553, 653. *Nursi, The Flashes, 19.*
[637] Said Nursi, *Tarihçe-i Hayat* (Istanbul: Şahdamar Yayınları, 2010), 327.
[638] Nursi, *The Words*, 52.
[639] Ibid., 35.
[640] Ibid., 141.
[641] Ibid., 226.
[642] Ibid., 620.
[643] Nursi, *The Rays*, 13.
[644] (49:12)
[645] Nursi, *The Words*, 392.

tance to, having respect for, being excited about, having an attachment towards can be evaluated within the concept of love, while having an aversion to, being repelled by, holding in detestation can be considered within the concept of hate. All of these thus emerge as functions of the heart.

The second point warranting attention here is Nursi's placing emphasis on a corrupted heart's being able to love even the most detestable thing. It becomes apparent that when the heart is sound and healthy it realizes its own functions in the best possible way, but when it becomes corrupted, for various reasons, it faces the exact opposite situation. When, under normal conditions, something that is loved is not repugnant, a corrupted heart reaches such a point that it experiences just this. Nursi's approach reveals that because the heart has its own particular equilibrium, when this balance is destroyed the heart can take on a completely conflicting character.

Stating, "...he was given a heart with an infinite capacity to love in order to direct it toward One possessing infinite undying beauty,"[646] Nursi draws attention to the heart's capacity to love, one of its most important functions, and where this love needs to be spent. Here, on the basis of God's being Eternal, he underscores the need for the love which is directed toward Him to also be eternal. This notion can be expressed thus: The heart's capacity to love is boundless, because it has been given to love God Who is Eternal. When the fact that there is no limit to loving Him is taken into consideration, a progressively increasing love for His sake is one which is desirable.

In his examination of the characteristics of the heart, Nursi refers to its two facets, the inner heart and outer heart, and their particular purposes. In his view, God created the inner heart for belief, knowledge and love of Him, while the outer heart is aimed at all other things.[647] It is normal for the heart to love certain things other than God. That is, there is room in the heart for love of other things also. For example, there is no harm, in religious terms, in a person's loving their mother and father, their spouse and children. However, the entirety of the heart's potential to love being directed to the *masiwa* has been viewed as wrong and mistaken. The outer heart might be preoccupied with this, but as for its

---

[646] Nursi, *The Flashes*, 14.
[647] Nursi, *The Damascus Sermon*, 124.

essence and profundity—known as the inner heart—it belongs/must belong only to and be reserved solely for belief in God, experiential knowledge and love of Him.

In his work, *Sincerity and Brotherhood*, Nursi focuses on the animosity and enmity that emerges between believers and discusses the great damage that such things which cause this hostility—including taking sides, obstinacy and jealousy—pave the way for. In expressing this issue he states, "If you wish to nourish enmity, then direct it against the enmity in your heart, and attempt to rid yourself of it."[648] Denoting enmity or hostility, the word *'adawah* in this sentence has been ascribed to the heart. Just as the heart serves as the wellspring of many positive emotions, it is also the dwelling place of such negative feelings as obstinacy, jealousy and enmity.

The last matter that will be touched upon under this heading is the heart's becoming wounded. When the heart fails to use the feeling of love for its True Owner but spends it elsewhere, because it is either not reciprocated or because it loses it with time, the heart becomes wounded, is left in agony or falls into heedlessness. The safest way to be followed in order not to be afflicted thus, is allocating the love in one's heart to its True Owner.[649]

Map of Thousands of Worlds

In his examination of such broader topics as Sufism and *tariqa* and their technical aspects like *walaya* (sainthood) and *sayr u suluk* (spiritual journeying and initiation) and where he needs to make mention of the heart, Nursi describes the heart as the "map of thousands of worlds." He views the human heart as the "place of manifestation of innumerable cosmic

---

[648] Nursi, *The Letters*, 309. That is to say, if a person insists on harboring feelings of hatred and enmity, they should hate the feeling of hatred that they hold in their heart and try their utmost to annihilate it.

[649] Nursi, *The Words*, 368. As such, Nursi states: "Indeed, man loves firstly himself, then his relations, then his nation, then living creatures, then the universe, and the world. He is connected with all these spheres. He may receive pleasure at their pleasure and pain at their pain. However, since nothing is stable in this world of upheavals and revolutions swift as the wind, man's wretched heart is constantly wounded. The things his hands cling onto tear at them as they depart, even severing them. He remains in perpetual distress, or else plunges into heedless drunkenness."

truths" and their pivot and seed. The works of many saints demonstrate this to be the case.[650] This is precisely the reason behind God's willing that human beings use their heart, bring it out from the potential to the actual, develop it and put into action. In order for this to be enabled, according to Nursi, the heart must engage in recitation of His Names and turn itself towards the truths of belief.[651]

It is possible to argue from the context that the "innumerable cosmic truths" that Nursi refers to are the truths of belief. The heart, then, is the place wherefrom these truths are manifested and revealed. The heart assumes, at the same time, the position of being both the cause and the ocean of these. These truths have each been placed, or planted in the heart as seeds, so to speak. God, the "Heart's Creator" who sprinkles these seeds in the heart—in Nursi's words—wills that it should be worked. When it is worked, the truths of belief that have been planted in the form of seeds will develop, the heart's faith in the truths of belief will increase and belief will advance to *tahqiq*, or realization. The heart must fulfil yet another task, namely to move from the potential to the real, which can be expressed as "righteous action." The heart's being worked and its transformation therein will be ensured by orienting itself to the truths of belief via recitation of God's Names, endeavoring to better understand these and deepening in its understanding.

As a final point, Nursi's reference to the "heart's Creator" also warrants closer attention. The word used in the original text, *fatir*—derived from the root f-t-r—comes to mean "to split." Raghib says that this is to split something vertically. In the Islamic context however, being one of God's ninety-nine Names *Fatir* refers to "creating out of nothing"[652] and has become famous with this meaning. In light of these details, it is possible to express the implication of Nursi's statement in the following manner: the heart is like a field into which all truths, God first and foremost, are sown like seeds. A person is in a position to cultivate these seeds in

---

[650] Nursi, *The Letters*, 428.

[651] He states: "...certainly the heart's Creator willed that it should be worked and brought out from the potential to the actual, and developed, and put into action, for that is what He did. Since He willed it, the heart will certainly work like the mind. And the most effective means of working it is to be turned towards the truths of faith on the Sufi path through the remembrance of God in the degrees of sainthood." (Ibid., 508.).

[652] Yazır, *Hak Dini Kur'an Dili*, VI:3972.

their heart. Like seeds sprouting through the field, these truths of faith would break through the soil surface, as it were, and show themselves, even sometimes becoming great trees according to the heart's capability. But of course the one doing all of this, placing these seeds in the heart is none other than *al-Fatir*. That is to say, both the Creator of Hearts and the one cultivating the seeds in hearts and transforming them into grand trees is again only God Himself.

As such, it is axiomatic that a heart which develops the faculties inherent within it is akin to a spiritual map encapsulating "the parts and components of an eternal, majestic machine pertaining to the hereafter."[653] It possesses the ability to show the roads leading to the thousands of celestial worlds, which can be defined as the purpose of creation and matters pertaining to belief, setting and charting out a course therein. It is arguably for these reasons that Nursi attributes the word map to the heart.

Mainspring of the Human Machine

Another unique definition of the heart that Said Nursi presents is its being the "mainspring of the human machine." He touches upon this issue in his discussion on the benefits and advantages of Sufism, stating:

> Since the Sufi path is a means of working the heart, the mainspring of the human machine, and of causing the heart to stir the other subtle faculties into motion, it drives them to fulfil the purposes of their creation, and thus makes a person into a true human being.[654]

As such, Nursi likens the human being to a machine, with its heart as its central unit and mainspring. What he terms the "mainspring" is the principal power spring driving the mechanism, being its chief driving force. On this basis, it would not be erroneous to suggest that he presents the heart as the most important part of the human being. That Nursi views the heart as the sole vehicle for human beings to reach the level of true humanity, is evident. For the machine known as the human being to be put into action, according to the example he provides, it is pivotal that the heart be worked first. When the central spring in the mechanical device is spurred into action, the other faculties of that device will

---

[653] Nursi, *The Letters*, 508.
[654] Ibid., 522.

also function and, in this way, the machine with all its components will operate at best performance. In this example, the first action is given to the mainspring of the machine. Like so, a person's using their other emotions also and attaining the level of "a true human being" is contingent upon a heart-centric motion.

The heart's being propelled into action is possible only through remembrance of God and recitation of His Names.[655] Nursi expresses this with the phrase "working the heart." In taking into consideration all the connotations of *dhikr*, Nursi deems such remembrance of God to engender stirrings in the heart and later spark action. His mentioning that working the heart can be achieved through the Sufi path is perhaps due to the importance placed upon recitation of God's Names in *tariqa*, with *dhikr* constituting its mainstay. Failure to take this argument into consideration would lead one to the conclusion that a believer who does not follow the Sufi path would never be able to develop their heart. Put differently, there is no attitude in the Islamic tradition as to spiritual development not being possible without entering a Sufi path. The benefits of *dhikr* were discussed in depth in the section regarding the heart's finding inner peace and reassurance.[656]

Nursi's use of the word mainspring, or *zemberek* in the original text is rather striking. *Zemberek* denotes "the principal spring in a watch or clock that drives the mechanism by uncoiling."[657] As evident in its definition, the mainspring is the most important component for the operation of a clock, or similar mechanism. This is because the functioning of the hour and minute hands and the clock's displaying the time depends on it. The connection between winding the timepiece and the clock's regular functioning—within Nursi's reasoning—is also present between a person's heart and themselves. A person's proper functioning—with all their dimensions such as the biological, psychological, emotional—has been directly associated with their heart's realizing its functions in the best possible way.

Becoming a perfected human being has been seen as possible only through putting the heart to work and keeping it perpetually dynamic.

---

[655] Ibid.

[656] Refer to Section I, "Heart in the God-Human Relationship."

[657] Turkish Language Association (TDK), *Great Turkish Dictionary*, ed. Mehmet Doğan (Ankara: Vadi Yayınları, 2001), 'Zemberek,' 2:2504.

The heart's dynamism will in turn motivate a person's other feelings and in this way human beings will be able to fully realize their reason for existence. In discussing this topic, Nursi employs a term assuming special importance in Sufi terminology—*al-insan al-kamil*, or the perfected human being. It is important, at this point, to consider Nursi's grasp of Sufism and the value that he places on it.

In the same section where he elucidates the benefits of the Sufi path, he again refers to the heart from diverse standpoints. He draws attention to the importance of the heart and its advantages for the human being by appropriating such terms as *intibah al-qalbi* (awakening of the heart), *dhikr al-qalbi* (recalling God with the heart) and *sayr u suluk al-qalbi* (journeying with the heart). The first of these expressions implies spiritual wakefulness of the heart and is used in the context of comprehending and appreciating the subtle truths contained in the religious obligations.[658] Accordingly, only a believer whose heart is spiritually awakened is able to perceive the realities at the essence of the religiously ordained. Remembrance of God is indispensable.

In the same section stating, "Through the regard, sense of the Divine presence, and powerful intentions of the Sufi path, gained by recalling God with the heart and reflecting on Him with the mind, this is to transform customary actions into worship,"[659] Nursi employs yet another approach of the Sufi path. Even though the topic at hand is his evaluation of the heart rather than *tariqa* itself, Nursi makes significant reference to it due to the central place that the heart and its functions holds in *tariqa*. In this statement, remembrance is ascribed to the heart and reflection to the mind. As such, when the heart remembers God and the mind ponders God's creation, a regard for the Creator develops in the human being as well as a consciousness of forever being in His presence. In addition, good will and intention also emerge in that person's heart. All of these signify the transformation of everyday actions into worship, and represent a position unique to Nursi.[660] When the heart operates with all

---

[658] Nursi, *The Letters*, 522.

[659] Ibid., 523.

[660] With his expression, turning "customary actions into worship," Nursi presents following the tradition of Prophet Muhammad as the way to attaining endless reward in the world and explains that so long as this is the case, even worldly actions can be transformed into worship and yield rewards. He illustrates this notion by

its capacities, a person's habitual, natural acts become acts of worship and earn them reward.[661]

The last point that will be referred to from Nursi's discussion on the benefits of *tariqa* is the value that he places on the heart in spiritual advancement. He mentions spiritual progress as one of the many benefits and fruits of *tariqa* and posits that this can be realized as a result of development of the heart and advancement of the spirit.[662] The connection Nursi draws between development of the heart and becoming *al-insan al-kamil* warrants attention. According to his discourse, the Sufi path is the means to such development and human beings in this way reach maturity and virtue. That is to say, the spiritual growth and development that a person displays plays a pivotal role in their reaching perfection. It is possible to extract the following equation from Nursi's views presented thus far: *dhikr* + *tafakkur* = development of the heart = *al-insan al-kamil*.

It is also useful to present Nursi's words articulated within the same context, which have become famous. He exemplifies the importance of the life of the heart thus:

> Since worldly life and the life of the flesh and animal life are thus, shake free of animality, leave behind corporeality, enter the level of life of the heart and spirit! You will find a sphere of life, a world of light, far broader than the world you imagined was broad. The key to that world is to make the heart utter the sacred words "There is no god but God," which express the mysteries of Divine unity and knowledge of God, and to make the spirit work them.[663]

---

way of the example of a transaction. In his view, if a person undertaking a mundane action such as shopping at that moment implements the relevant religious ruling, this situation reminds them of the Prophet and therefore constitutes worship. Recollection of the Prophet at that instant evokes being in God's presence and because this engenders turning to God, is considered a form of worship. For detailed information see: Nursi, *The Flashes*, 82.

[661] Due to Nursi's characterization of the mind as the heart's dimension of idea and thought, this was not mentioned separately. For a discussion on the mind's being a dimension of the heart, see: Nursi, *Signs of Miraculousness*, 86.

[662] He says: "The ninth [benefit] is to struggle to be a perfect human being through journeying with the heart and striving with the spirit and spiritual progress; that is to say, to be a true believer and total Muslim." (Nursi, *The Letters*, 523.)

[663] Nursi, *The Flashes*, 180-81. Nursi, *Mathnawi al-Nuriya, 215.*

Here, making work is attributed to the spirit, while making utter is attributed to the heart. That Nursi more often than not uses the words heart and spirit synonymously was touched on earlier. In this particular paragraph, a narrower boundary has been drawn for the heart and the spirit to be put to action, with remembrance of God not mentioned in general terms, but rather the declaration of faith—There is no god but God—brought to the fore. It would be erroneous to presume that other invocations would not be useful in working the heart and spirit, on the basis of this statement. It would prove to be more useful to focus on the importance of the Islamic declaration of faith with respect to reaching the objective.

Seed of the Human Being

According to Nursi, the human being is both the fruit and the seed of the tree of creation.[664] A seed of the human being is their heart. He thereafter discusses some of the characteristics of the heart. Accordingly, the heart has been created as needy and dependent. The heart is in need of all the lights of the Divine Names. This is because just as they have needs as much as the world, they have just as many adversities and enmities. The satisfaction and contentment of the heart that has such worldly desire and expectation as well as a world full of enemies, can only be possible with God. The heart, by virtue of its constitution and creation, cannot be content with anything other than the eternal and perpetual. Nursi, therefore, brings a very different perspective to the heart's finding peace and reassurance.

At this instance likening the heart to a seed, he consequently likens the human being to a tree. If the purpose of the seed that is planted in the earth is for it to become a tree, then the purpose of humanity is for them to attain the elevated rank of the perfected human being by means of developing their heart.

Said Nursi's Positive Allusions to the Heart

In his elaboration on the heart, Nursi makes reference to its certain positive characteristics, in view of facilitating understanding. These characteristics will be discussed under the sub-headings 'The Heart Telephone,' 'The Eye, Ear, Feet of the Heart' and 'The Sustenance of the Heart.'

---

[664] Nursi, *Mathnawi al-Nuriya*, 175.

The Heart Telephone

Nursi views the heart as a means enabling humanity to reach God directly and because he sees it thus, he employs the metaphor of the telephone. He argues that by using the telephone of the heart, the human being can call upon God and entreat Him without any intermediary.[665] In Islamic understanding, there is no intermediary between God and the human being, the Prophet included. Every individual can make contact with God directly, entreat Him and ask what they will from Him. A person can realize this by way of their heart. Nursi refers to this notion with the figurative "telephone of the heart" expression. By virtue of this quality, the heart can also be called the meeting point between a person and their Lord.

For Nursi, God makes known His presence and existence to His servants in two ways: in deed and by speech. The first of these is His God making His existence and presence perceptible in deed. This manifests itself in the form of meeting all the needs of and protecting the human being who is by nature weak and indigent. As for the second, it is His making His presence felt through the 'heart telephone' by means of veracious inspiration which is a kind of "Divine speech." All of these are requirements of God's mercy and compassion.[666]

Elsewhere, he mentions that the Prophets and saints conduct their communication with God via 'telephones' and clarifies in a footnote what is implied in the use of the word telephone as follows:

> As for the telephone, it is a link and relation with God that goes forth from the heart and is the mirror of revelation and the receptacle of inspiration. The heart is like the earpiece of that telephone.[667]

---

[665] Nursi, *The Words*, 148.

[666] Nursi, *The Rays*, 168, 70. Nursi states: "God makes His existence, presence and protection perceptible in deed to His most weak and indigent, His most poor and needy, conscious creatures, that stand in great need of finding their Master, Protector, Guardian, and Disposer. It is a necessary and essential consequence of His Divine solicitousness and His Divine compassion that He should also communicate His presence and existence by speech, from behind the veil of veracious inspiration —a mode of Divine discourse— to individuals, in a manner peculiar to them and their capacities, through the telephone of their hearts."

[667] Nursi, *The Words*, 65.

In this text, the heart resembles that telephone's earpiece, while the telephone itself is defined as a relation with God extended from the heart. Consequently, for the Prophets, the heart is the place where revelation is reflected, while for saints it is the place where inspiration appears; the telephone, then, is the channel for communication stretching from this site of revelation and inspiration to God Himself. The communication between Messengers and saints, and God is actualized via both this telephone and its earpiece, which is the heart. As communication is again by means of the heart, it is perhaps not incorrect to use the expression, the 'ear of the heart.' That is to say, it is fair to argue that there is no difference between the heart's being the earpiece and the telephone itself.

As stated by Nursi himself:

> In the same way, the Creator of the universe, the Monarch of Pre-Eternity and Post- Eternity, has made numerous causes and intermediaries a veil to His execution of affairs and has demonstrated the majesty of His divinity. But He left private telephones in His servants' hearts so that they might leave causes behind and turn directly to Him, and might say: You alone do we worship and You alone do we ask for help![668]

However much God has made means and causes as veils to His actions, He has nonetheless placed a special telephone, as it were, in the hearts of His servants so that they may put causes aside and make two-way contact with Him directly. Every human being possesses the opportunity to communicate with their Lord using this personal telephone. While Nursi does not use the term "telephone of the heart" here, he expresses this same meaning in a different way.

The Eye, Ear, Feet of the Heart

What can be gleaned from the analysis thus far is Nursi's frequent use of figurative language in his discourse on the heart. Under this heading, his reference to the eye, ear and feet of the heart will be examined. Nursi underscores the importance of looking at the Qur'an with the eye of the heart in order for it to be properly understood[669] and, in presenting to readers a tableau pertaining to the Hereafter, he states that the eye of

---

[668] Ibid., 646.
[669] Ibid., 316.

the heart will enable one to see that the past is not a vast grave but the place where groups of great spirits fly to elevated abodes.[670] In reference to the witnesses and proofs of experiential knowledge of God, he again asserts the need for looking at them with the "heart's eye and spirit's vision."[671] It is interesting to note that he uses the expression "light of insight" to elucidate the expression, "the heart's eye." In actual fact, in the Islamic religious terminology, the use of the word *basira*, translated as insight, to refer to the eye of the heart is quite widespread.[672]

In addition, Nursi also refers to 'looking at' God by means of the heart.[673] He uses such a manner in drawing attention to the role of knowing the Divine Names in attempting to understand Divine wisdom. If humanity dwells on these causes, they will be unable to see the Creator who gives them that impact. Under these circumstances, instead of attributing creation to God, they attribute it to other things and their deviation becomes inescapable. So as not to fall into such error and delusion, they need to bear in mind the Divine Names when looking at the universe. In order to see the Great Craftsman of creation and the hidden hand—so to speak—behind causes, it is necessary to observe the universe with the heart. In other words, the human eye is not sufficient to see that hidden hand. That is why the heart must look at God with the binoculars of the Divine Names.

Nursi puts forth the notion of listening with the 'ear of the heart' in order to hear the lessons in belief offered by the Qur'an.[674] He also posits that the testimony of the world of creation can be heard with the heart's ear,[675] and again uses the same expression when examining the wisdoms of illness. In his view, sicknesses whisper into the ear of the heart a person's helplessness, responsibility, the purpose for which they were sent to this world of their Creator.[676]

---

[670] Ibid., 322.

[671] Nursi, *The Flashes*, 176.

[672] According to Sayyid Sharif al-Jurjani, *basira* is "the strength of a heart illumined with sacred light, so much so that the heart with this strength sees the inner faces, meanings and realities of things." (al-Jurjani, *al-Ta'rifat*, 39.)

[673] Nursi, *The Rays*, 191.

[674] Nursi, *The Words*, 374. Said Nursi, *Münazarat*, ed. Abdullah Aymaz (Izmir: Şahdamar Yayınları, 2006), 46.

[675] Nursi, *The Words*, 714.

[676] Nursi, *The Flashes*, 269.

As for the metaphor of the "feet of the heart," Nursi employs this in his discussion on the spiritual journeying in Sufism referred to as *sayr u suluk*. On one such occasion he states:

> The aim and goal of the Sufi path is—knowledge of God and the unfolding of the truths of faith—through a spiritual journeying with the feet of the heart under the shadow of the Ascension of Muhammad (pbuh), to manifest the truths of faith and the Qur'an through tasting and certain enhanced states, and to an extent through direct vision; it is an elevated human mystery and perfection called the Sufi path or Sufism.[677]

The expression *sayr u suluk* is the name given to the immaterial journeying and initiation undertaken in conforming to particular criteria belonging to the discipline of Sufism.[678] This journey is to God, while the one to undertake it is the human heart. It can be argued that Nursi associates the word 'feet' to the heart on the basis of the connotations of the word *sayr*, which refers to going, walking, advancing and journeying.

That Nursi appropriates metaphor when describing the heart was mentioned earlier. As is evident, he ascribes such words as eye, ear, feet and even wing[679] to the heart and expresses himself in such a fashion.

The Sustenance of the Heart

Where Nursi refers to the 'sustenance of the heart' he says:

> O my stomach-worshipping soul! Every day you eat bread, drink water, and breathe air; do they cause you boredom?

> They do not, because since the need is repeated, it is not boredom that they cause, but pleasure. In which case, the five Daily Prayers should not cause you boredom, for they attract the needs of your companions in the house of my body, the sustenance of my heart, the water of life of my spirit, and the air of my subtle faculties.

---

[677] Nursi, *The Letters*, 507. In relation to the same topic, see: Nursi, *The Letters*, 39, 515. Nursi's use of the expression, "feet of love" is also interesting. In much the same way, one needs to turn towards experiential knowledge of God with such 'feet.'

[678] *Sayr u suluk* will be discussed in detail under the heading "Fethullah Gülen's Understanding of the Heart."

[679] Nursi, *The Flashes*, 91.

> Yes, it is by knocking through supplication on the door of One All-Compassionate and Munificent that sustenance and strength may be obtained for a heart afflicted with infinite griefs and sorrows and captivated by infinite pleasures and hopes.[680]

For Nursi, every effort to direct one's attention and regard to God can be referred to as the heart's sustenance. After all, it is again the heart itself that is to realize this orientation. Nursi characterizes the Daily Prescribed Prayers and recitation of the Qur'an[681] as the heart's sustenance. Accordingly, while at first glance it appears that it is the body which performs these forms of worship, which in actual fact worships God and turns to Him is always the heart. Of course there are aspects of worship that need to be performed with the body. However, the heart's accompanying the body therein bears importance both in terms of performing worship in the best possible sense and for the heart's receiving nourishment with that worship.

It will prove to be useful, at this point, to mention another one of Nursi's arguments which follows a similar trend. In reference to Prophet Job he again ascribes servanthood to the heart. When afflicted with various illnesses and wounds, Job entreated God; his supplication was thereafter accepted and he was cured of his ailments. Nursi expresses Job's appeal to God with the words, "O Lord! Harm has afflicted me; my remembrance of You with my tongue and my worship of You with my heart will suffer."[682] As is clear in this statement, servanthood, which encompasses every act and form of worship of God, is characterized as an action of the heart. As touched upon earlier, even though there are forms of worship that need to be carried out externally, what is essential in servanthood to God is the heart's actualizing that servanthood and worship; in other

---

[680] Nursi, *The Words*, 277.

[681] Nursi, *Mathnawi al-Nuriya*, 34. In analysing the use of repetition in the Qur'an, Nursi asserts that the Qur'an constitues sustenance and strength for hearts. For a discussion of this same point, see: Nursi, *Signs of Miraculousness*, 37.

[682] Nursi, *The Flashes*, 21. The Qur'an explains this situation as follows: "And (mention) Job (among those whom we made leaders): he called out to his Lord, saying: 'Truly, affliction has visited me (so that I can no longer worship You as I must); and You are the Most Merciful of the merciful.' We answered his prayer and removed all the afflictions from which he suffered; and restored to him his household and the like thereof along with them as a mercy from us and, as a reminder to those devoted to our worship." (21:83-84)

words, the essence of worship not being sacrificed to form has been given great importance in Islamic understanding. This issue, moreover, constitutes one of the central topics of Sufism.

Other than these, Nursi also refers to the heart's shuddering[683], tranquility[684], wakefulness[685] as well as its ambitions.[686]

Nursi's Negative Allusions to the Heart

Just as Nursi examines the positive aspects of the heart, he characterizes it using negative ones. This in fact stems from the heart's being just as susceptible to evil and vileness as it is to goodness and beauty. The Qur'an too characterizes the heart with certain negative characteristics such as its hardening, being sealed and corrupted as described in detail earlier. Here, Nursi's views within this context will be explored and examined.

Satanic Centre

The first negative characterization that Nursi makes of the human heart is its possessing an inner faculty which is the means of diabolical suggestions. He explains this notion thus:

> ...everyone has experienced in himself the inner faculty situated in a corner of the heart which is the means to diabolical suggestions and temptations and is a satanic tongue that speaks at the promptings of the surmising faculty and the corrupted power of imagination, which becomes like a small Satan and acts contrary to its owner's will and opposed to his desires—these are certain evidences of the existence of great satans in the world. And since the inner faculty which is the means of diabolical suggestions and the power of imagination are an ear and a tongue, they infer the existence of an external evil individual who blows on the one and makes the other speak.[687]

The word used for Satanic center in the original text, *lümme*, has such meanings as mark, insignia, stamp, point, evil suggestion and delu-

---

[683] Nursi, *The Words*, 661.
[684] Ibid., 49.
[685] Nursi, *The Rays*, 777.
[686] Nursi, *Mathnawi al-Nuriya*, 157.
[687] Nursi, *The Flashes*, 120.

sion.[688] When this term is considered as a characteristic pertaining to the Satan, such expressions as "the point at which Satan prompts to evil" and "Satan's mark and insignia" can also be developed. Nursi makes reference to this expression in his evaluations pertaining to Satan. He verbalizes this expression as "means to diabolical suggestions" and "power of imagination." Adopting Sufism's classical view, Nursi accepts the human being as a miniature universe. As such, the human is a micro-universe and the universe is a macro-human being. Just as there is a source of evil named Satan in the macrocosm, there is a point within the human being that directs them to evil, being the center which Satan uses as a means for diabolical suggestion and groundless fear and fancy. Fethullah Gülen too, in examining the matter of Satan and satanic whispering, touches upon this issue and asserts that this is a crucial point in the believer's heart center constituting a target for Satan. In his view, next to the place which receives angelic inspiration there is in the human heart a place where Satan aims his arrows of doubt, hesitation and prompting to evil. When explaining the angel and Satan's taking aim at these two points so close in proximity to each other, Gülen uses the example of a mirror. This situation is akin to a mirror's transparent and polished face being in juxtaposition to its black and matt one. Another such example is a believing person and non-believing person being in the same room. He also indicates that these two aspects or central points in the heart complete one another, as do the two poles on a battery.[689]

Satan's point is the center wherein he whispers every kind of thought, fancy, suggestion, intention, baseless fear and urging aimed at wickedness and wrongdoing. The part of the heart open to evil has been named as such by Nursi. In the same section, he indicates that angels represent and manage the laws in effect in good deeds and issues.

Blindness

Nursi defines a heart that is unperceiving and uncomprehending as "blind." Such blindness, in his view, stems from not being able to discern God's handiwork in the universe. The Creator does everything with perfect ease,

---

[688] Abdullah Yeğin et al., eds., *Ottoman Turkish - Turkish Encyclopaedic Great Dictionary*, 2 vols. (Istanbul: Türdav,1981), II:850.

[689] M. Fethullah Gülen, *The Essentials of the Islamic Faith* (New Jersey: The Light Publishing, 2006), 78.

balance and order. Within this ease and order He simultaneously creates His handiwork with complete and perfect measure and craftsmanship. It is God only who does a thing both with perfect ease and speed, and with highest artistry. A person's looking around them with even the slightest attention is enough for them to wake to this truth. It is precisely the hearts that cannot see this beauty, orderliness and beauty that are those that are blind.[690]

On the basis of Nursi's views, it is possible to infer the following: One who is able to see the beauty and perfection around them, read the seal and imprint belonging to their Creator upon them and see that everything actually serves their purpose of creation is delivered from such blindness. Nursi, moreover, makes mention of the Qur'an's assuring the ability to see truth and reality with the eyes of the mind and heart and stresses that God's Word is the light of these 'eyes.'[691]

The Heart's Being Pierced

In Nursi's view, certain emotions that cannot be directed towards goodness and virtue have a negative effect on the heart. As a case in point, the feeling of greed that is not used in accordance with its *raison d'être*, or in other words is misused, can pierce the heart and cause those things that are pursued with such greed and ambition to take the form of idols within it. He states:

> Criminal greed pierces the heart, and introduces idols into it. God is displeased and punishes the greedy person with the opposite of his purpose.[692]

He refers to a greed that can become fatal as a result of abuse. Generally having negative connotations and causing humanity's loss when directed towards wickedness and vice, greed punctures the heart and fills it with false deities. The implication here is that due to its becoming absorbed in worldly desire and expectation, the heart can fall into many an error and wrongdoing. It can therefore be said that a heart that ambitiously pursues worldly whim and fancy would fail to stop where required

---

[690] Nursi, *The Words*, 302.
[691] Said Nursi, *The Staff of Moses* (Istanbul: Sözler Publications, 2006), 243.
[692] Nursi, *The Damascus Sermon*, 120.

and put forth what was expected of it. For example, a person wanting to attain a certain rank or position with greed and ambition, idolizes that position, so to speak, and sees every means to this end as permissible. When it becomes thus, God does not grant the heart that which it wants, instead punishing it with the opposite of its objective. It is possible to say that with this view, Nursi directs the human being to watchfulness and advises them to exercise great caution so as not to allow their heart to be pierced by its weaknesses.

The Heart's Being Gnawed At

Nursi discusses the heart's being bitten within the context of its becoming blackened with sin. He states:

> Sin, penetrating to the heart, will blacken and darken it until it extinguishes the light of belief. Within each sin is a path leading to unbelief. Unless that sin is swiftly obliterated by seeking God's pardon, it will grow from a worm into a snake that gnaws on the heart.[693]

The heart becomes charred and hardened because of sin and wrongdoing. When, however, they are not immediately dispelled with repentance, the heart is as though being bitten by a snake. The heart's being bitten in this way can be understood to mean its facing much doubt and uncertainty in belief due to the influence of sin. Nursi's making mention of sins eliminating the light of belief in the same sentence and the potential that each sin possesses in the way of paving the way to disbelief makes such a reading possible. By way of illustration, he provides two examples. The first of these reads:

> Similarly, one who does not perform the obligatory prayer and fulfil his duty of worship will be affected by distress, just as he would be in case of the neglect of a minor duty toward some petty ruler. Thus, his laziness in fulfilling his obligation, despite the repeated commands of the Sovereign of Pre-Eternity, will distress him greatly, and on account of that distress he will desire and say to himself: "Would that there were no such duty of worship!" In turn, there will arise from this desire a desire to deny God, and bear enmity toward Him. If some doubt concerning the existence of the Divine Being

---

[693] Nursi, *The Flashes*, 22.

comes to his heart, he will be inclined to embrace it like a conclusive proof. A wide gate to destruction will be opened in front of him. The wretch does not know that although he is delivered by denial from the slight trouble of duty of worship, he has made himself, by that same denial, the target for millions of troubles that are far more awesome. Fleeing from the bite of a gnat, he welcomes the bite of the snake.[694]

In the same section, Nursi connects the heart's being bitten by sins with the statement, "Nay but their hearts are stained,"[695] from the Qur'an.

The Heart's Illness

The notion of the heart's becoming diseased was examined in light of verses from the Qur'an and Prophetic traditions. The reason for referring to this again is the different outlook that Nursi brings to the topic. He establishes his framework on the basis of the notion of the different degrees of the *nafs*, or the carnal self, which assumes quite a significant place in the Sufi tradition. As such, even if the carnal soul advances and becomes refined, it transfers its attack on the nerves. The resultant anger and irritation from the nerves fulfilling their function continues until death. That is to say, some saintly people who have been successful in training their carnal soul and who have reached elevated stages of the *nafs* in their journeying of the soul can sometimes display behavior that lends the impression that they still possess a *nafs al-ammara*, or the Carnal, Evil-Commanding Soul. For instance, they can display a strong reaction to a small incident and demonstrate an attitude not expected from them. Whereas, this is not expected of them due to their assuming a superior level of humanity. As for those saintly people with a deeper spiritual knowledge of God, exhibiting surprising deportment, they have complained of their carnal, evil-commanding soul and have bemoaned that their hearts were afflicted with spiritual ailments. Right at this very point, Nursi asserts that there is no reality to this view that saintly people have of themselves, that their situation arose from nerves, as already mentioned, and that that which they deemed sickness of the heart was in actual fact an imag-

---

[694] Ibid., 23.
[695] (83:14)

inary affliction. He connects, furthermore, the continuation of these states to the continuation of struggle in the path of spiritual progress.[696]

The Heart's Death

In Nursi's view, a heart without belief is a heart that is dead. As he frequently argues, the heart's greatest and most important function is belief in God, knowing and loving Him. This being the purpose of its creation, when the heart is deprived of the light of guidance, it is unable to reach its goal and there is virtually no difference between its existence and non-existence. And this constitutes its death. Saying, "Moribund hearts were raised to life through the light of guidance,"[697] he elucidates this point and emphasizes that even if it dies, it can be revived by means of the "light of guidance."

Conclusion

In his examination of the heart, Nursi on the one hand defines it, while on the other hand presenting its functions by means of his figurative method of expression. The heart, in his view, is a "Divine subtle faculty" and "Divine gift" and, as the locus of belief in and knowledge and love of God, it is assigned a fundamental mission. God, who creates humanity, wants of them to believe in Him, know Him and submit to Him in a complete consciousness of servanthood, and bestows them with a heart with which all these can be realized. God has thus made the heart of the human being the focus of His gaze and deals with them on the basis of their heart.

According to Nursi, qualities such as *wijdan* (conscience), *aql* (reason), *dimagh* (the mind), *shu'ur* (perception), *irada* and *hiss* (feeling) are the dimensions of the heart which fulfill its diverse functions. With all these features and profundities, the heart is, as it were, akin to a mirror reflecting God's manifestations of His Names.[698] Furthermore, his use of such words as throne, spiritual map, center, mainspring and seed when

---

[696] Nursi, *The Letters*, 380.

[697] Nursi, *The Words*, 263.

[698] Nursi articulates the heart's being such a mirror in the following way: "...man, who is the fruit of the tree of the universe, is the purpose of its creation and existence and the aim of the creation of beings. While his heart, which is the seed of the fruit, is a most brilliant and comprehensive mirror to the universe's Maker. (Ibid., 642.)

describing the heart is noteworthy. When focusing on the heart's functions, he ascribes such terms as telephone, eye, ear, feet, wing and sustenance to the heart. For Nursi, that which believes, denies, loves, hates, is sincere, deviates, allows entry to both satan and the angel, hopes, falls into despair, experiences wakefulness, falls prey to heedlessness, shudders, expands, contracts, suffers hunger, is sustained, speaks, develops, sees, becomes blind, hears, becomes deaf, receives pleasure, endures anguish, finds health, is afflicted, comes to life, dies, guides to God, mentions Him, turns to Him, walks and worships...is always the heart.

Apart from these, employing such expressions as "heart's blindness," "heart's sickness," which are part of Islamic religious discourse, Nursi also introduces novel expressions to the lexicon, such as the heart's being 'pieced' and 'bitten,' thus adding a richness to the terminology.

Nursi attaches great emphasis, beyond even that which is presumed, to the heart and a life of the heart and lends weight to its development. As he vividly and succinctly states:

> Since worldly life and the life of the flesh and animal life are thus, shake free of animality, leave behind corporeality, enter the level of life of the heart and spirit! You will find a sphere of life, a world of light, far broader than the world you imagined was broad. The key to that world is to make the heart utter the sacred words "There is no god but God," which express the mysteries of Divine unity and knowledge of God, and to make the spirit work them.[699]

It thus becomes clear that Nursi, like Ghazali before him, sees the life of the heart as a person's actual identity and selfhood and encourages the human being to advance in the way of spirituality for their attaining such a level of life.

---

[699] Nursi, *The Flashes*, 186. Nursi, *Mathnawi al-Nuriya*, 157.

Gülen and the Heart

ethullah Gülen's view on the concept of *qalb* and the factors determining and influencing his approach and his contributions to the concept will now be examined. Gülen focuses on the heart in many of his writings, taking the thoughts and works of certain scholars as his base, and elaborates its dimensions, depths and functions. The section will be structured according to his views in general, with each comprising a separate subheading. Before proceeding with these, however, it will prove useful to define his particular standpoint with respect to knowledge and tradition, as these have a direct bearing on his thoughts and works. Rooted in the tradition of classical Islam and reverent to the Salaf-i Salihin, the prominent guides among the Companions of Muhammad and their followers, Gülen is one of the contemporary representatives of the Sunni tradition. As such, his command of classical Islam's intellectual heritage, known as *turath*, becomes evident. He thus fulfils a very important mission with regard to the fourteen-century-old knowledge tradition and heritage being known in the present day. Quite naturally, he has benefited from texts belonging to virtually every discipline as well as from leading scholars. The same issue is applicable for Sufism in the broader sense and the concept of heart more specifically. An examination of his works in relation to these topics makes it possible to refer to a wide-reaching field of influence from Qushayri, Ghazali, Mawlana Jalal al-Din Rumi and Ibn Qayyim al-Jawziyya to Imam Rabbani and Said Nursi. That he has also benefited from Persian and Turkish literature in expressing his thoughts and views is also evident.

The Heart and Its Functions

In making an introduction to the heart, the spiritual aspect of which is the subject matter of Sufism, Gülen first focuses on the material heart. Accordingly, the heart, which predecessors liken to a pine cone, "With respect to its structure and tissue, the heart is different from all other bodily parts: it has two auricles and two ventricles, is the origin of all arteries and veins, moves by itself, works like a motor, and, like a suction pump, moves blood through the system."[700] In making such an introduction, Gülen follows Ghazali's method. Beginning his discussion on the heart, he too studies the physical heart, mentions that it is the cone-shaped organ of flesh and that by virtue of its composition it is of a different and particular make-up (lahmun makhsus). He states that this physical heart belongs to the visible material world and animals and that even the dead have this heart of flesh, and then proceeds to a discussion of the immaterial heart which he describes as latifa rabbaniya ruhaniya, or a 'subtle tenuous substance of an ethereal spiritual sort,' and focuses on it at length.[701]

After a look at the physical heart, scholars dealing with the issue of the spiritual heart have necessarily considered the relationship between these two hearts. Some have dwelt upon this issue at length, while others, due to its hidden nature, have only briefly indicated it and guarded against attempts to explain or disclose it. Ghazali for instance, alongside stating that the majority of people "have been mentally bewildered when they tried to perceive the nature of this connection," has attempted to make it somewhat more comprehensible by way of a few examples. In his view, the connection between these two hearts resembles the connection between qualities and the things they qualify, the user of a tool with the tool itself and that which occupies a place with the place itself.[702] Gülen too analyzes this connection and suffices with saying that nothing clear has been said on the nature of this connection which has been discussed by philosophers and Muslim sages for centuries. In his view, the intrinsic connection between the biological heart and its spiritual counterpart is just as vague and hazy as the relationship between the heart, spirit, mind and perception.[703]

---

[700] Gülen, Key Concepts in the Practice of Sufism 1, 22.

[701] Saying, "What is meant by the heart is the Divine subtle faculty—not the piece of flesh shaped like a pine-cone," Nursi also underscores this same issue. (Nursi, Signs of Miraculousness, 86.)

[702] Abu Hamid Muhammad ibn Muhammad al-Ghazali, Wonders of the Heart, trans. Walter James Skellie (Islamic Book Trust, 2007), 6.

[703] Gülen, Key Concepts in the Practice of Sufism 1, 25.

Evaluating the heart from a rather broad perspective, Gülen posits that it serves the function of a bridge enabling the transfer of all goodness and blessing to the human being, and that it is simultaneously susceptible to all kinds of satanic and carnal urging and imagination.

> When set on God and guided by Him, it resembles a projector that diffuses light even to the furthest, remotest, and darkest corners of the body. If it is commanded by the carnal (inherently evil) self, it can become a target for Satan's poisonous arrows. The heart is the native home of belief, worship, and perfect virtue; a river gushing with inspiration and radiation arising from the relationships among God, humanity, and the universe. Unfortunately, innumerable adversaries seek to destroy this home, to block this river or divert its course: hardness of heart (losing the ability to feel and believe), unbelief, conceit, arrogance, worldly ambition, greed, excessive lust, heedlessness, selfishness, and attachment to status.[704]

As is evident, the heart, within Gülen's approach is a subtle faculty that is open to beauty and virtue as well as vice and vileness. In this sense, Gülen holds the belief that the heart is in need of protection and 'quarantine' and supports his view with Qur'anic verses and *hadith*. In his view, with the verse, "Our Lord, do not let our hearts swerve after You have guided us," the Qur'an[705] and the Prophet's stating "O God, O Converter of hearts! Establish our hearts firmly on Your religion"[706] in his common supplication is reminiscent of this protection and quarantine.

This subtle faculty has been deemed by Muslim scholars as a Divine gift and blessing bestowed upon human beings in order for them to recognize God, know and love Him and to worship Him as He deserves to be worshipped. It is due to this belief that notwithstanding scholars' maintaining that the heart is inherently receptive to both good and evil, they have in general viewed it positively and have taken into account its aspect that is open to virtue in their evaluations. It is possible to see this approach in Gülen's works also. It would thus be more accurate to evaluate Gülen's interpretations from this standpoint.

---

[704] Ibid.

[705] (3:8)

[706] Tirmidhi, Qadar, 7; Ibn Hanbal, *al-Musnad*, VI:302.

The Biological Heart's Spiritual Aspect

For Gülen, "heart' signifies the biological heart's spiritual aspect."[707] The function that the biological heart serves in the human body, the spiritual heart fulfills in a person's spiritual life. It is in this sense the counterpart of the physical heart. Like the biological heart's pumping blood to the human body and giving it life, as it were, the spiritual heart serves the same function in a person's spiritual life, keeping them alive and animate. The word *malakut*, used in the original text, comes to mean "a thing's inner face, inner aspect or reality."[708] In this sense, it can be said that the spiritual heart is the invisible facet, the essence and reality of the physical one.

Gülen defines the heart as "the center of all emotions and (intellectual and spiritual) faculties, such as perception, consciousness, sensation, reasoning, and willpower," such that this is reminiscent of Nursi's categorization in relation to *wijdan*.[709] As such, Gülen buttresses Nursi's view and also sees willpower, intellect, the inner power of perceptiveness (sensation or feeling) and consciousness as each a separate function of the heart. Due to its capacity of intellect, perception and awareness, the heart is able to know, perceive, and understand. Because it possesses *irada* (willpower), it is addressed by God, undertakes responsibilities, suffers punishment or is rewarded, is elevated through true guidance or debased through deviation, and is honored or humiliated.[710] The concept of *irada* has been brought into question by scholars examined previously; however, Gülen's approach to the matter encompasses not only a mystical dimension but a theological dimension also. Theologically speaking, the heart is the name of the organ that makes a person religiously and morally accountable. In Gülen's approach, it is the organ that makes a person human, renders them addressees of Divine commands and, most importantly, is the key to eternal life.

In the same section, Gülen directs attention to what is considered the heart's most important quality, namely, "the 'polished mirror' in which Divine knowledge is reflected." With this outlook, he expresses his adop-

---

[707] Gülen, *Key Concepts in the Practice of Sufism 1*, 22.

[708] Yeğin et al., eds., *Ottoman Turkish - Turkish Encyclopaedic Great Dictionary*, II:925.

[709] In this categorization, Nursi refers to the four elements constituting the conscience, namely: "will, mind, emotion, and the subtle inner faculties." (Nursi, *The Damascus Sermon*, 121.).

[710] Gülen, *Key Concepts in the Practice of Sufism 1*, 22.

tion of the general view of the heart as the 'site of knowledge of God.' With such an approach, Gülen considers the heart within a rather broad framework. Accordingly, the heart is the center of *shu'ur* (perception), *idrak* (awareness), *aql* (reason) and *irada* (willpower), or these together make up the heart. When the heart uses these capacities in the proper way and sufficiently, it elevates a person to the level of true humanity. For it is always the heart that thinks, learns, knows, perceives, comprehends, understands, feels and discerns.

Being the headquarters of such abilities as understanding, perception, discernment and desire and inclination, the heart that utilizes these capabilities is able to comprehend and understand creation. In this sense being 'that which perceives,' the heart is at every moment the focus of God's gaze and is constantly held under His control. And in this sense it is also 'that which is perceived.' It is due to this characteristic that it has been called *nazargah-ı İlahî*, or the focus of God's sight.[711] Gülen derives this understanding from the Prophetic tradition which states, "God considers not your bodily statures, but your hearts."[712]

He posits that in order for the heart to put these capacities to work in the best possible way, it is necessary that it is healthy. In his words, if the heart is alive, all of these elements and faculties are alive; if the heart is diseased, it is difficult for it to realize its duties of "reason, knowledge, knowledge of God, intention, belief, wisdom, and nearness to God Almighty."[713] Here, Gülen indicates that the heart becomes diseased with sin and wrongdoing and that when it cannot function healthily it is unable to use the aforementioned faculties. It becomes clear that in addition to those capacities he mentions earlier, Gülen also adds such previously unmentioned elements as intention, wisdom and nearness to God. These, like the others are included among the duties of the heart. This being so, it is perpetually the heart which inclines to something and intends, procures benefit, knows God and at the same time draws near to Him.

According to Gülen, God addresses the human being in line with their spiritual development and level and treats them in keeping with this. Accordingly, for instance, His relationship with a heart that possesses an elevated level of experiential knowledge of God and knows Him very

---

[711] Ibid., 23.

[712] Muslim, Birr, 33.

[713] Gülen, *Key Concepts in the Practice of Sufism 1*, 23.

well is much deeper and more profound than that with a heart that is not of that level. If the heart, by committing major sins, has dulled and weakened its capabilities, the abovementioned faculties are negatively impacted and experience great difficulty in actualizing their mission. This difficulty, in turn, appears to drag the human-God relationship to undesirable levels.

Source of Feeling and Belief

The heart, for Gülen, is "humanity's most important, most vital aspect, the expression of their spiritual existence, the wellspring of their feelings and beliefs and is both the longest of the paths leading to human profundity as well as its first station."[714] In line with this notion, the heart constitutes the entirety of a person's spiritual existence. When 'heart' is mentioned—as touched upon earlier—all the faculties making up a human being's spiritual being such as intellect, feeling, perception and awareness are implied. It is clear, after all, that those who do not put such qualities to work are unable to represent humanity with only their material, corporeal beings. Hence it can be said that it is a human being's spiritual aspect that rules over their physical aspect and that a person's humanity actually stems from here. It for this reason that Gülen, like Ghazali and Nursi, sees the heart as commander with the inner and outer feelings and emotions as its soldiers. For Gülen, the heart is a resplendent lamp and the other organs, moths flying around it.[715] As is evident from the metaphors mentioned here, the heart does not merely direct the organs surrounding it but, on the contrary, constitutes their source of life and they will eventually unite with the heart and become one with it.

The Combination of Divine Favor and Essence of Human Existence

One of Gülen's characterizations of the heart is its having emerged from the combination of "Divine favor" and "the essence of human existence" and its bearing "the seal of the Creator." In this respect it is intimately connected with both the spiritual and material realms.[716] This view is impor-

---

[714] M. Fethullah Gülen, *Zamanın Altın Dilimi* (Izmir: Nil Yayınları, 2002), 133.
[715] Ibid., 136.
[716] Ibid., 135.

tant in terms of highlighting the significant role the heart plays between God and the human being and the value it holds as an indispensable faculty for the human being aspiring to know God. The word Gülen uses in the original text, *'inaya*, denotes goodness, perfect virtue and grace.[717] On the basis of Gülen's choice of words, it is possible to suggest that God has done humanity a great favor by bestowing them with the faculty known as the heart. This is such a kindness that human beings, who have been given such responsibilities as belief, worship and morality, have not been left to their own devices, but on the contrary, have been supported with a mechanism, known as the heart, with the capacity to fulfil all of these in a perfect way.

In the same text, Gülen also explains the heart's purpose as "forming a friendship with God." That is to say, in addition to such issues as the heart's believing in God and its knowing Him, it also possesses the ability of friendship with God and attaining closeness to Him. It can be argued that concepts that come to mean nearness in the Sufi lexicon, such as *qurbiya* (nearness) and *unsiya* (intimacy), give voice to this meaning.

Projection of the Realms Beyond in the Corporeal World

When defining the heart, like virtually all other scholars and thinkers, Gülen appropriates metaphor and similitude. In one particular sentence, he employs five metaphors simultaneously. He describes the heart, therein, as "a stairway leading to human perfection, a projection of the realms beyond in the corporeal world, the largest door within the human body open to spirituality, the sole laboratory where our selfhood is formed, and the most important criterion of telling right from wrong."[718]

The first metaphor used in this sentence is the heart's being a 'stairway' extending towards human perfection. This expression underscores the heart's capacity to take the human being to perfection. As discussed earlier, it is imperative that the heart be developed and worked in order to attain true humanity. It is useful at this point to recall earlier Muslim intellectual and philosopher Muhammad Iqbal's (d.1359/1938) identify-

---

[717] Ibn Manzur, *Lisan al-'arab*, 'a-n-y.'

[718] M. Fethullah Gülen, *Speech and Power of Expression: On Language, Esthetics, and Belief* (Istanbul: Tughra Books, 2010), 51.

ing the Daily Prescribed Prayers as an 'ascension' (*mi'raj*) that a person undertakes to their heart, five times a day. Denoting ladder or stairway, *mi'raj* in the Islamic tradition has more often than not been understood to mean ascension, at the individual level, to the heart or with the heart.

The heart is, at the same time, a projection of the realms beyond in the visible corporeal world. In the Sufi tradition, the corporeal realm which humanity perceives has been given such names as "material realm" or "witnessed realm" (*'alam shahada*), "realm of creation" (*'alam khalq*), "realm of physical reality" (*'alam nasut*), and "realm of dominion" (*'alam mulk*). The realm containing those things that are unseen but whose existence is believed in, on the other hand, has been called the "spiritual realm," "realm of the unseen" (*'alam ghayb*), "realm of command" (*'alam 'amr*), "realm of Divinity" (*'alam lahut*) and "angelic realm" (*'alam malakut*). It can therefore be argued that the meaning conveyed through Gülen's use of the expression "realms beyond" is the realm termed *ghayb*, *'amr*, *lahut* and *malakut*. Precisely at this juncture, the heart becomes a pivotal faculty given so as to allow the invisible realm to be understood, as well as the unique place wherein the realities pertaining to the realms beyond can be known in this world. Moreover, when touching upon this function of the heart, Gülen asserts that it is a *barzakh*, or intermediary realm between the realm of witnessing and realm of the unseen. As for the *barzakh* metaphor, it plays a very important role in determining the heart's position and standing as an isthmus between two worlds. The single, unique place of contact between the physical and metaphysical realms is the heart.[719] The word 'projection' has been described as 'forming an

---

[719] When describing the heart's being a *barzakh*, Gülen states: "With its intermediary existence between this world and the next, the inner and outer dimensions of existence, the physical and metaphysical worlds, the heart, which has been created at the intersection point of spiritual and material realms...has a very extensive area of contact. With such extensiveness, it is that which is enveloped at the same time as it is that which envelops, and something which encompasses while it is encompassed." While the literal meaning of the word *barzakh* is 'barrier' and 'veil,' it is also defined to mean the long, narrow stretch of land dividing two land masses and the barrier between two seas, or canal-passageway-strait. The barrier between two objects, the hiatus separating two objects or veil are also called *barzakh*. The heart's being a *barzakh* between the lived realm of matter and the world of the unseen leads to its possessing a very wide-reaching field of contact. In other words, the heart's being located at the point of intersection between

image onto a screen or other surface for viewing with the beams emitted from a light source.' Therefore, the heart is the place where the celestial spectra of light coming from the realms beyond descend. Given that there is no other projection of the metaphysical realm in the world than the heart, the realms beyond can only be perceived via the heart.

It is possible to evaluate the ensuing expression, "the largest door within the human body open to spirituality" in the same vein as the preceding one, with there being one notable difference: the heart's being referred to with the word 'door' is evocative of such qualities as its being opened, shut and being locked. Just as the door of the heart is amenable to opening and perceiving spiritual realms, there will also be human beings who will be unable to open it and what is more, who will never be able to enter that realm due to their having locked the door of their heart. The metaphor of the lock is a matter which has its foundation in the Qur'an directly. It can be argued that Gülen, with the metaphor in question, adds a different interpretation and dimension to Qur'anic verses.

In addition to all of these, the heart is at the same time "the sole laboratory where our selfhood is formed." To elaborate the 'laboratory' metaphor in Sufi understanding, a person is only a human being and reaches perfection only to the extent of their rehabilitating their spiritual life, or the life of their heart. However, its development is not at all easy. They must attend to their heart with the delicacy and precision employed within a laboratory and carry out its maintenance and protection faultlessly. Only in such a way can a person attain a level of the life of the heart. As already mentioned, Gülen sees the heart as commander over the other bodily limbs and organs. So long as the commander is fully trained, all their needs are satisfied and they are brought to perfection, all its instructions and commands to the other limbs and organs—each like soldiers at its command—will be of the same perfection and in this way the human being will likewise become perfected and attain strength of character.

The last expression is the heart's being "the most important criterion of telling right from wrong." The original Turkish text actually reads: "...the most important testing center of both good and evil." It can be said that this is a function of the heart's developed state. That is, a person

---

these two realms evokes the notion that it has a connection with both worlds, that it is like a window or eye opening up to each and, moreover, that it possesses or can possess knowledge about them.

who has made headway in terms of the life of the heart can differentiate between right and wrong, good and evil, the beneficial and the damaging. The other side of the coin is that a person who does not live a life at the level of the heart, even though they be Muslim, will not be able to distinguish between good and evil; moreover, they will not even attach importance to such a distinction or, even worse, will not even be able to perceive that there is in fact any difference between the two. That such a predicament would amount to great decline and deterioration for humanity is self-evident.

From another perspective, the "testing center" expression also suggests that the heart functions as a kind of indemnity, or protection against future loss. It can be said that as a person lives their life moment to moment, they are in actual fact spending their life either at odds with their heart or at peace with it. When they do those things that their heart affirms, they are reconciled with it and at ease; when they do that of which the heart disapproves, they clash with it and are agitated. It is, moreover, possible to substitute the word 'conscience' for 'heart' in this statement. As discussed earlier, being the heart's dimension of feeling and perception according to Nursi's taxonomy, *wijdan* (conscience) either leaves a person in peace or tortures them. It possesses the feature of giving a person comfort when they do what it approves of, and leaving a person in anguish and misery when they do the opposite. The heart, in this sense, serves as a person's insurance, so to speak, and perpetually tests life and all that is part of it. Gülen's interpretations are as though presented within the framework of Nursi's observations.

Another salient sentence in this article is the following: "So it is this heart which becomes over time the sight and hearing of our spirit; in accordance with the "point of reliance and point of seeking help" (*nokta-i istinat, nokta-i istimdat*), which are deeper dimensions of the heart, our sensations and perceptions become the heart's sight, our mind becomes its analyzer, and our willpower its director and administrator."[720]

Here, like Nursi, Gülen more often than not mentions the word heart in conjunction with the word spirit. While this joint reference brings to mind the synonymity of these terms, it also serves as an indication of the spirit's encompassing the heart and all its associated faculties, like an

---

[720] Gülen, *Speech*, 51.

umbrella. The expression, "an ascending development, or spiritual journeying in the form of spirit heart or heart spirit, heart *sirr, sirr khafi, khafi akhfa*,"[721] can be provided as a case in point. The synonymity of the two terms *qalb* and *ruh* is cleared indicated. And as can be gleaned from the statement, "...and the spirit embraces all these faculties like an atmosphere and connects them to the heart,"[722] the spirit encompasses all of the other feelings and faculties. For Gülen, the sight and hearing of the spirit is the heart which has attained spiritual growth and development. The phrase, "over time" stresses that every heart is not the 'eye' and 'ear' of the spirit; on the contrary, only a heart that is able to reach the point of actualizing its purpose of creation can realize this mission.

It is a heart at this level that can reach the point of using the "point of reliance" and the "point of seeking help" dimensions contained within it[723] to the highest possible degree. Gülen later presents the words perception, *aql* (reason) and *irada* (willpower) as deeper dimensions of the heart and states that perception determines outlook, the mind makes evaluations and that willpower, in the end, directs and manages. Reference to Nursi's definition of *wijdan* (conscience) will prove to be useful here. He makes mention of four components of conscience: willpower, the power of perceptiveness, the mind and *latifa al-Rabbaniya*. It is possible to refer to the last of these as *qalb*. Taking *irada* as it is, Gülen replaces *hiss* (sensation) with *sezgi* (perception) and *dhihn* (mind) with *aql* (intellect). The mechanism that Nursi calls *wijdan* and *ruh*, Gülen refers to as *qalb*.

One point in particular is worthy of note here. There is an important principle in Islamic jurisprudence referring to the notion that there is no conflict between the names used for a concept, so far as the concept is the same. That is, the terms themselves do not matter; it is the concepts themselves that matter.[724] Modern names can be adopted for ideas and concepts so long as their aims and objectives remain the same. In relation to the topic at hand, the synonymous use of the words *wijdan* and *qalb* can be provided as an example. There is therefore no contradiction or

---

[721] M. Fethullah Gülen, *Kalbin Zümrüt Tepeleri 4* (Istanbul: Nil Yayınları, 2009), 66.

[722] Gülen, *Key Concepts in the Practice of Sufism 2*.

[723] These concepts were elaborated in the previous section.

[724] This is expressed in Arabic as "La mushahhata fi l-istilah," literally meaning, "There is no harm in using particular terminology." Refer to Majma' al-Lughah al-'Arabiyyah, *Al-Mu'jam al-Wasit*, 2 vols. (Cairo: Arabic Language Academy, 1962), 474.

error in Gülen's saying *qalb* where Nursi refers to *wijdan*, or using other terms interchangeably, as the essential meaning remains one and the same. Moreover, it appears indispensable to accept such a principle given the vague and hazy nature of these issues for human beings. This difference in terminology appears not to stem from a confusion of concepts, but on the contrary, from these matters not being able to be comprehended in their entirety by the human mind and consciousness. Within this context, Gülen's frequent use of the words *ruh* and *qalb* interchangeably is evident. Defining *ruh* as "a gift from a realm having nothing to do with materiality to the corporeal realm," he sees it as a manifestation from both the Realms of Divine Existence and Knowledge because of its relation to the Divine Essence, and due to its perfect capacity to learn and know its Creator via its luminous and transparent nature.

Implied in this view, on the basis of the verse, "I breathed into him (Adam) out of My spirit," is that the spirit[725] is a part, so to speak, belonging to *Wajib al-Wujud*, The Necessarily Existent One,[726] and because it is thus, that it possesses a true existence. The spirit's connection with the Realm of Knowledge is its being open to advancement. That is to say, whoever wants to have a grasp of Divine mystery, they can again only do this with their spirit and heart.[727]

In this regard, Gülen sees the heart as both *mazruf* (contents of an envelop) and *zarf* (envelope), as well as *muhat* (that which is enveloped) and *muhit* (that which envelops). That Nursi also describes the heart as both the envelope and the contents of that envelope was mentioned in the previous section.[728] The heart's being *muhat* and *muhit* indicates that

---

[725] (15:29)

[726] Muslim thinkers have accepted the God's Essence is "Necessarily Existent." That is, God exists necessarily and by Himself. Even the very idea of His nonexistence is enough to make the entire universe meaningless. Scholars of theology are in agreement that all other things and/or beings are contingent in essence. Their existence is within the sphere of possibility, with there being no difference between their existence and non-existence. In other words, God's existence is essential. All other beings can be or not. Their existence or non-existence would have no impact on the order and functioning of the universe.

[727] In relation to this, Gülen states: "As the secrets related to the truth of Divinity can be viewed only from the horizon of the heart through the eye of the spirit, so nearness to God beyond intellect, logic, and reasoning, and beyond all causes can be realized only by means of the spirit and the rules of the heart." (Gülen, *Speech*, 54.)

[728] Under the heading "The Characteristics of the Heart."

it, by nature, can both be enveloped and also envelop. Its being *muhat* is presumably only possible from God. The One who completely envelops it, perceives and knows it is only God. The heart which is enveloped by God is also the human being's *muhit*. It is the heart which altogether envelops a person, directs them and governs all their physical and immaterial faculties. By way of summary, the heart, then, is God's *muhat* and the human being's *muhit*. This is important in terms of illustrating the value that the heart holds within the human being. God's treatment of human beings is thus viewed to be in relation to the state of their heart.

Point of Observation

The expression, 'Horizon of Observation' is one that Gülen frequently resorts to in his explanation of the heart. Denoting gaze, the word in the original text, *rasat*, has found a place with varying versions in his vocabulary. In his view, the heart is the site of manifestation of Divine Names and Attributes.[729] Such an approach entails a triadic classification, including God's Names, Attributes and Essence. According to this classification, alongside being able to know God with His Names and Attributes, the heart possesses certain feelings and perceptions pertaining to His Essence that is beyond comprehension.

Gülen's views are reminiscent of Nursi's argument that God is known through His Names, is encompassed with His Attributes and is existent but unknown with respect to His Essence. When explaining this point, Gülen states that all creation is in actual fact a result of the manifestations of God's Names, which is in line with Nursi's view. Giving the example of uninterrupted projection of images in the 'film' of things and events due to their swift projection, he explains the way in which God's Names give existence to creation. In his view, God's Attributes are the source of His Names. That is, God's Names emerge from His Attributes. Names such as *Muqaddir*, *Musawwir* come forth from the Divine commands pertaining to creation. When it comes to God's Essence, He is the Existent One whose existence all creation attests to, but there is no such thing as knowing Him completely. In this sense, He is Unknown.[730] However, as touched upon, Gülen posits that while God is existent but unknown in

---

[729] Gülen, *Prizma 6*, 80.
[730] M. Fethullah Gülen, *Prizma 3* (Izmir: Nil Yayınları, 1999), 196.

terms of His Essence, those who know Him through His Names and Attributes can again acquire certain feelings and perceptions with respect to His Essence with their hearts. His description of the heart as *rasat ufku*, or "point of observation" is identical in meaning to his characterization of it as a "special observer" (*müşahid-i has*).[731] Gülen's assertion is significant with respect to its implying that the heart can transcend Names and Attributes. Also relevant to this discussion is Nursi's reference to the concept of *mushadat Allah*, or 'vision of God,' which he describes as the ultimate aim of *Latifa al-Rabbaniya*, or the subtle inner faculties. Being the highest state of a developed heart in Nursi's view, *mushadat Allah* within Gülen's characterizations is reaching the level of seeing God by means of observing the manifestations of His Names with the eye of the spirit, and the condition of sensing, perceiving and experiencing the Divine Names and Attributes.[732] This being its greatest aim, the heart, which is at the same time the "eye of the spirit,"[733] is its "special observatory" and the secrets related to the truth of Divinity can be viewed only from the horizon of the heart through the eye of the spirit.[734] The heart thus appears to be the sole conduit through which God is known both with His Attributes and above and beyond these, with His Essence. The heart seems to possess such depths, as will be mentioned below, that God becomes known and even 'observed' when these are used properly by the human being.

Sirr, Khafi, Akhfa

The words *sirr* and *akhfa*, albeit being used frequently in the Sufi discourse, are terms belonging to the Qur'an. Consequently, before moving on to the evaluations of Gülen who makes frequent use of these key Sufi concepts, it will be useful to consider the evaluations of the primary sources of Islam and certain Sufis, chiefly Imam Rabbani, who assign great room to these concepts in their works. For instance, the Qur'an uses these terms, in the verse, "If you say something aloud (or keep it to yourself), He surely knows the secret as well as (whatever you may be keeping as) the more hidden. He surely knows the secret as well as (whatever you may

---

[731] M. Fethullah Gülen, *Key Concepts in the Practice of Sufism 3*, trans. Ali Unal (New Jersey: Tughra Books, 2009).

[732] Gülen, *Key Concepts in the Practice of Sufism 2*, 112.

[733] Gülen, *Key Concepts in the Practice of Sufism 1*, 22.

[734] Gülen, *Speech*, 54.

be keeping as) the more hidden."[735] In commenting on this verse virtually every Qur'anic exegete has avoided a Sufi interpretation and has interpreted it on the basis of the literal meanings of these terms.

According to Sufi understanding, the word *sirr* has been used in a number of ways. The special knowledge that is known only by God, or by a small number of people,[736] constitutes one of these. Scholars basing their assertions on this meaning take as their reference the Prophetic tradition which states, "If you knew what I know, you would laugh little but weep a lot."[737] As for the second meaning, to be stressed here, *sirr* is "a faculty which has been entrusted to the human mold." Placing such a meaning upon *sirr*, Qushayri proceeds with the expression, "seat of observation"[738], thus elucidating its purpose for creation. In his view, the seat of love is the spirit and that of experiential knowledge is the heart.

In such an understanding, *qalb*, *sirr* and *ruh* appear as separate elements making up human spirituality. Albeit seemingly such, it is not inaccurate to suggest that these are each different dimensions pertaining to human spirituality. For, as mentioned previously, the heart, for instance, is able to serve many diverse functions such as willpower, feeling, cognizance, perception and understanding. For this reason, rather than seeing these elements as distinct and separate to one another, it is more plausible to suggest that these need to be evaluated as different parts of a single whole. However much the words *sirr*, *qalb* and *ruh* play a part in Sufi texts of the classical period, it is Imam Rabbani who considers these as different dimensions and depths of human spirituality, ascribes them a particular mission and, in this way, has enabled them to be concepts specific to the discipline of Sufism.[739]

At the fore of all issues that Gülen emphasizes in relation to the heart are the concepts of secret, arcanum and super-arcanum. It is important to note from the outset that in his discussion of these concepts, Gülen frequently resorts to the views and interpretations of Imam Rabbani. For this reason, the views of the latter will first be examined briefly, followed by an analysis of Gülen's approach. This does not imply, however, Gülen's

---

[735] (20:7)

[736] Gülen, *Key Concepts in the Practice of Sufism 2*, 66.

[737] Bukhari, Manaqib al-Asrar, 45.

[738] Al Qushayri, *al-Risalah*, 250.

[739] Sirhindi, *al-Maktubat*, I:48.

appropriating Imam Rabbani's views as they are. As will be highlighted, where his views on the subject parallel Imam Rabbani's, Gülen reiterates Imam Rabbani's opinions, giving reference to him; where his views differ, he states plainly his own interpretations and views.

Despite Imam Rabbani's employing different terms, it becomes clear that he refers to the witnessed, visible realm as 'alam khalq (Realm of Creation) and the Realm of the Unseen as 'alam 'amr (Realm of Command). Accordingly, a believer's gaining an awareness of the Realm of Command is contingent upon their working their five faculties which pertain to the spiritual realm. Expressed in Arabic as lataif al-khamsa, these five qualities relating to a person's spirituality are qalb, ruh, sirr, khafi and akhfa. According to Imam Rabbani, entry to the Realm of Command starts from the stage of the heart and then journeying through this realm continues with the dimensions of spirit, secret, secrets of Lordship and secrets of manifestation. Grasping these five jewels and being able to comprehend their truths can be the portion of not every person who follows the Prophet, but of some of those perfected believers among them.[740]

The role of the heart, as the starting point of this journey is pivotal. As Imam Rabbani expresses, the heart—in Sufi epistemology being the organ of cognition, not the brain—is the node that first receives spiritual knowledge. In his work, which constitutes an excerpt from Imam Rabbani's Maktubat, Alam Irshad clearly highlights the connection between the heart and the other bodily organs and faculties:

> The Mujaddid writes in his monograph the Mabda' wa Ma'ad that initially the heart receives a spiritual knowledge and it is only then that the knowledge is transmitted to the sensory faculties. On the other hand, the sensory organs receive a worldly knowledge first and it is only then that knowledge is transmitted to the heart, which is the repository of conviction.[741]

Tariqa, according to Imam Rabbani[742] is comprised of seven steps or stages. Preceding the five faculties listed earlier are the two added facul-

---

[740] Ibid.

[741] Alam, Faith Practice Piety: An Excerpt from the Maktubat-i Imam-i Rabbani, 147.

[742] Literally meaning paths, roads or ways, the word tariqa in the Islamic context refers to the systematized, formalized discipline of Sufism. All the principles of tariqa have their foundation in Prophet Muhammad's practice. That is to say, there is

ties of the 'body' and 'nafs' pertaining to the physical world. In contrast to the other tariqa, the Naqshibandi Sufi order begins the spiritual journey by skipping these two faculties belonging to the Realm of Creation and starts from the Realm of Command, or from the heart.

Starting at the first stage of the Realm of Command are manifestations of God's acts, followed by manifestations of His Attributes at the second and manifestation of His Essence at the third. After mentioning the manifestations pertaining to these three stages, Imam Rabbani does not name the remaining two, instead contenting himself to say that "thereafter, the stages gradually advance in accordance with the degrees of manifestation." In his view, a believer at each of these steps pulls away from himself or herself and nears their Lord; and with the completion of these steps, their closeness to God reaches the ultimate level. At this level, they are honored with the stations of *fana* (annihilation in God) and *baqa* (subsistence with God). [743]

When Imam Rabbani's words are considered within the sequence that he offers, the heart—the first step of the Realm of Command—perceives the manifestations of God's acts; at the stage of the spirit, the manifestations of the attributes appear, while at the level of secret, the person is favored with the manifestations pertaining to God's Essence. As already mentioned, alongside not characterizing the manifestations of the levels of *khafi* and *akhfa* he asserts that these stages increase a believer's nearness to God. If we are to understand what he describes as "manifestation pertaining to action" as the manifestation of God's Names, it can be said that the level of heart is God's Names, the level of spirit is God's Attributes, while the level of secret looks to God's Essence, and that *khafi* and *akhfa*—taking the entirety of all these into consideration—shoulder very important functions with regard to nearness to God (*qurbiya*).

Imam Rabbani also articulates the psychological state experienced at each of these stages. As such, the level of *akhfa* is the level in which the stations of *fana* and *baqa* are felt and perceived. This is, at the same

---

implementation and practice, but its name is not *tariqa*. *Tariqa*'s emergence within a particular system dates back to the third century in the Islamic calendar. Personalities such as Junayd al-Baghdadi and Bayazid al-Bistami are considered to be among the leading figures of *tariqa*. *Tariqa* was in later eras represented by such figures as Naqshibandi, Abd al-Qadir al-Jilani, Ahmad Rufai and Ahmad Badawi.

[743] Sirhindi, *al-Maktubat*, I:70.

time, the definition of *walaya* (sainthood), for he sees sainthood as being comprised of *fana* and *baqa*.[744] The body of a believer who has been able to attain the rank of 'friendship with God' has softened with worship of God, their bosom is in surrender and they are in complete tranquility. Their carnal soul is content and they are pleased with their Lord. Their Lord is also pleased with them. Their heart has become secure in God, the Converter of Hearts, their spirit is purified in its entirety and is now ready for the appearance of the Attributes of Divinity. While secret, being the third of these five faculties is honored with manifestations of His Essence, *khafi* experiences awe before God's freedom from fault and defect, His sacredness and greatness, and *akhfa* reaches an indescribable union whose nature is unknown.

Imam Rabbani purports that in order for a human being to assume the qualities of a true Islamic identity, they must overcome these five stages. He underscores the idea that the heart, secret, arcanum and super-arcanum each have their own particular state and ecstasy, and that there is a need for all of these to be passed one-by-one and for one to be enveloped with the perfection of each. After passing these five stages and the shadows of the Names and Attributes therein, the time then comes for the shadowless manifestations of the Divine Names and Attributes. After these come the manifestations pertaining to God's Essence via the carnal self's finding rest; earning God's pleasure and approval is possible only at this level. The comparison between the previous grace and the point that is now reached is like a drop of water compared with an endless ocean. In explaining that the ultimate aim for a believer is attaining this level, Imam Rabbani says, "It is this undertaking that is the real one; the rest is vain desire."[745]

With these words, he asserts that *qalb*, *ruh*, *sirr*, *khafi* and *akhfa* each have their own particular manifestations, but that there are certain others beyond these. He posits that in addition to each of these five levels or dimensions of the Realm of Command having their own distinct favors, beyond these there are shadowless manifestations of the Names, Attributes and Essence that can be perceived by only those possessing *nafs mutmainna*, or a Soul at Rest, and that attaining these is or should be the true aim.

---

[744] Ibid., I:127.
[745] Ibid., 233.

While Gülen generally accepts Imam Rabbani's views, he does not concur with the former's "heart, spirit, secret, arcanum, super-arcanum" sequence. Gülen sees the spirit an atmosphere which encompasses all the other faculties.[746] The heart is within the province of the spirit and constitutes an inner faculty which possesses all the profundities in question. Within the heart is contained *latifa al-Rabbaniya*, which characterizes *sirr*, *khafi* and *akhfa* all at once, that Gülen calls *fuad*.[747] After this short introduction, these issues will now be considered in depth.

Sirr

In beginning his discussion on the concept of *sirr*, Gülen uses the word 'profound'[748] to describe the nature of the topic. While such an introduction can be read as an indication that detailed and definite information would not be provided due to his humility[749] in this regard, it can also be understood as a way of illustrating that this topic is one that is closed to human perception and grasp. Or alternatively, it is possible to see this as implying that because the issue is not an objective one, it is open to differing interpretations. At any rate, Gülen also indicates elsewhere the difficulty in comprehending such topics as spirit, heart, the mind and perception.[750]

Denoting something that is 'hidden,' *sirr* in Gülen's view is the first of the spiritual faculties in the human being which opens to the 'Reality of Realities.'[751] Secret's being the 'first' of the spiritual faculties is, as a result, indicative of *khafi* and *akhfa* being its deeper dimensions. On this basis, it is possible to suggest that the heart possesses the deeper dimensions of secret, arcanum and super-arcanum, embedded within it. For instance, if the heart is a shell, secret is the first faculty that is encountered upon its being peeled, with the others following. Before getting into the par-

---

[746] Gülen, *Key Concepts in the Practice of Sufism 2*, 261.

[747] Gülen, *Key Concepts in the Practice of Sufism 3*, 191.

[748] M. Fethullah Gülen, *Key Concepts in the Practice of Sufism 4*, trans. Ali Unal (New Jersey: The Light Publishing, 2010), 47.

[749] In Islamic spiritual understanding, those who are capable of feeling in this manner generally do not divulge the secrets that they have attained so as not to reveal that which pertains to their relationship to their Lord. And those who do reveal these secrets often find them to be above the level of the comprehension of most people.

[750] Gülen, *Key Concepts in the Practice of Sufism 1*, 23.

[751] Gülen, *Key Concepts in the Practice of Sufism 4*, 48.

ticulars it should be stated that these three dimensions of the heart are deeper aspects of the heart which ensure that the heart's most important functions, such as belief in God and knowledge of Him, are realized to perfection. This approach can be encountered in many of Gülen's interpretations and analyses. As mentioned in passing earlier, he likens all of these to telescopes and binoculars with progressively increasing diameters. The smallest of these binoculars and/or telescopes is *sirr*, and constitutes the first observation point for the heart which possesses the innate capacity to 'see' God.[752]

While defining secret as "a faculty and dimension of the heart"[753] Gülen also ascribes to it the expression *latifa al-Rabbaniya*. It is evident that Gülen uses this statement for *fuad* and *akhfa* also. From this perspective, it is interesting to note the expansive scope of this expression. A "Divine trust" in the heart,[754] *sirr*'s relationship to the heart is akin to the relationship between the body and the spirit. Just as the spirit is a trust within the body, so too is secret a trust within the heart.

Stating that some who describe *sirr* make reference to the verse, "God knows best whatever is in their bosoms,"[755] Gülen says that they refer to it as the pure bosom that is faithful, loyal and which prefers God and the life hereafter to everything else. For Gülen, this condition has been understood to mean hearts' reaching the level of *sirr*. A heart which believes in God and the other essentials of belief becomes a heart that uses its deeper dimension known as *sirr*. In other words, a heart overflowing with belief puts into motion its quality referred to as secret.

Gülen evaluates the people of secret within three categories. Accordingly, those believers who pursue nothing other than God's approval and pleasure and who resist the urgings of their carnal self make up the first category. The second group is comprised of these who strive to conceal the degree of their relationship with God and their standing with Him. The last and highest level is assumed by those who use everything as a means to invoke God and who, alongside hiding what good they do for others from others, are even careful to hide it from themselves.[756]

---

[752] Ibid.

[753] Gülen, *Key Concepts in the Practice of Sufism 2*, 66.

[754] Ibid.

[755] (11:31)

[756] Gülen, *Key Concepts in the Practice of Sufism 2*, 69.

When listing these three categories, Gülen says that those in the second and third try their utmost not to reveal their closeness to God and their feelings and perceptions, which in turn has been accepted as reference to the correlation between the literal and more specific meaning of secret.

Gülen refers to the heart as the "storehouse of the knowledge of God," and secret as the "system with which we can observe more abstract and profound truths."[757] When the adjectives are removed from this statement, the notion of *qalb* as a repository and *sirr* as a system emerge more clearly. Hence, the heart has been created with the capacity to possess *ma'rifa*, or experiential knowledge of God. When the deeper dimensions pertaining to it are put to work, this "repository" can be filled. That which is to fill it first is secret. When its system is set into motion, secret is able to observe God, beyond even His Names and Attributes.

Gülen's presenting secret as a 'system' is noteworthy. Its ability to fulfil its mission is contingent upon its being worked. When this system is put to work, it is mobilized and is able to fill the heart repository. It is equally possible for secret not to fulfil its duty, due to its not being worked and therefore its being left passive.

When explaining secret, Gülen also lists the characteristics of those people who have attained it. In his view, the people of this 'horizon' are those who, while on the one hand avoiding everything God does not approve of, on the other hand strive to conceal their "inner riches" and "depth of their *ma'rifa*" from all others. In addition to trying their utmost to perform their deeds with sincerity, they do not neglect purification of their heart, spirit and carnal soul. That which makes them people of secret is—as mentioned earlier—their hiding the things that they are spiritually favored with from other people, and not making themselves visible.[758]

It is possible to conclude that when making these evaluations, Gülen makes use of accumulated knowledge on one hand and weaves his own fabric of understanding with the threads of his perception and awareness on the other. This is because in the history of *tasawwuf,* the measured, restrained and intricate style employed by some scholars when putting forth their views has been interpreted as such. That is to say, when artic-

---

[757] Gülen, *Key Concepts in the Practice of Sufism 4*, 48.
[758] Ibid.

ulating issues resting on their own inner perceptions and insights, they feared that those who would not be able to understand them would draw erroneous conclusions and interpretations and, for this reason, they used obscure expressions. It can also be argued that their choice of vague, hazy wording can also be due to their avoiding the possibility of praise by the people and the associated fame that would accompany it.

Khafi

The word *khafi* literally means 'concealed,' while in the context of Sufism referring to the heart's dimension that is deeper than *sirr*, but shallower than *akhfa*. When defining *khafi*, meaning obscure, secret and concealed, and hidden, Gülen says that it is a dimension of the heart that is more imperceptible and hidden than secret, while at the same time being more open to the realms beyond, with a broader horizon of observation.[759] Moving beyond mere definition in making observations with regard to *khafi*, Gülen uses expressions unique to him. These expressions will be relayed and his particular views elucidated.

For Gülen, *khafi*, or arcanum, is the heart's "elevated sense of observation." Among those things that it observes, "perception beyond the Divine Names and Attributes" comes to the fore. As such, looking, observing and looking at something with the purpose of drawing a lesson—the literal meaning of the original Turkish word that Gülen uses—emerges as a characteristic of *khafi*, as was the case with *sirr*. That which *khafi* is to observe with heed is that which surpasses God's Names and Attributes; that is, His Essence.

In Gülen's view, *khafi* is "a system that cannot be perceived with the mind," "design or map of Divine mysteries," an "observatory" given to the heart in order for it to "look on the truths." *Khafi*, moreover, is "another deep dimension of the heart which is turned to the realms and truths beyond."[760] Using such expressions as "observatory" and "horizon of observing"[761], Gülen again uses metaphor to illustrate his point. Accordingly, *khafi*, or 'the private,' resembles a lookout from which realities and the Realms of Existence and the Unseen can be observed. Here, it can be

---

[759] Ibid.
[760] Ibid.
[761] Ibid., 50.

suggested that what Gülen terms 'realities' are those things accepted as absolute in Islam, first and foremost God Himself, and paradise and hell-fire. What he refers to as the "visible and invisible realms of existence" can be evaluated within the same light. That is, we can say that these are matters whose existence the Islamic belief upholds, but which cannot be seen in this world, and again provide the same examples.

When making mention of *khafi*, Gülen again employs metaphor and describes it as a "pair of binoculars" or a "telescope." For him, *khafi*, a profundity more capable and with a wider margin of perception, is a telescope with the capacity to observe the realms beyond.[762] Furthermore, *khafi* is "a mirror where the secrets of Lordship descend in the perfected human being and a pair of binoculars showing that which cannot be seen."[763] It can be understood from this statement that *khafi* is a characteristic that is found in perfected believers. Because people of this level are able to use their heart's dimension of *khafi*, their hearts are as though a point of descent of Divine mysteries, or a site where the Creator's secrets are to be found. It therefore becomes evident that the stage of *khafi* looks to God's Essence and comprehends some of the qualities pertaining to Him. At the same time, *khafi* is such a 'telescope' that with it human beings become aware of the Realm of the Unseen, and see those things that are in existence, but are invisible.

Akhfa

The dimension following the stages of secret and secrets of Lordship, or in other words the deepest and most extensive of all the dimensions of this heart, is the level of *akhfa*, or 'the more private.' In his discussion on this super-arcanum, Gülen uses such terms as *makhfi, makni, mastur* and the expression 'truth whose existence is unknown,' all of which come to mean hidden, covered and closed. Gülen states that only those with elevated spirits can reach this depth and that such people are very small in number. In his view, *akhfa* is a Heavenly faculty "open to the Hidden Treasure" given to only the most special of servants.[764]

---

[762] M. Fethullah Gülen, "Sır, Hafâ ve Ahfâ," *Sızıntı Magazine* 2011, 235.
[763] Ibid.
[764] Gülen, *Key Concepts in the Practice of Sufism 4*, 50.

When expressing this—the heart's deepest dimension—he uses the term *Kanz al- Makhfi*. Denoting 'Hidden Treasure,' this concept is a symbolic nominal describing God and depicting the fact that He cannot be completely comprehended and that He is a Being above and beyond perception.[765] The *akhfa* horizon is the deepest aspect of a heart that has been given a capacity to observe—even if not completely—this Great Being who is beyond comprehension. In reference to this particular quality, Gülen says that it is "the end or end point."[766]

Gülen says the following in relation to the benefits of *akhfa*:

> *Akhfa* is a manifestation like lightning and of essence coming to the true universal human being from realms beyond, and perpetually provides such diverse indications and signs that they drive them, each moment, to deeper observations, closer study, and scrutiny; in so doing, it allows them to experience a continuous hope and exhilaration of union.[767]

As can be seen, Gülen refers here to manifestations "like lightning" and "of essence." Before Gülen, Imam Rabbani used this expression within the context of it being a characteristic of the spiritual station of secret. In his view, a believer who ascends to this station of *sirr* by transgressing the stages of *qalb* and *ruh* reaches the point of being open and receptive to these Divine manifestations.[768] The word *barq* used in this expres-

---

[765] The expression *Kanz al-Makhfi* is cited in the narration, "I was a hidden treasure. I wanted to be known, so I created the universe" (Ismail ibn Muhammad al-'Ajluni, *Kashf al-Khafa,'* 2 vols. (Beirut: Dar Ihya' al-Turath al-'Arabi, 1932), II:132.). Notwithstanding this statement's being related as a Prophetic Tradition, it has not been considered as reliable with respect to the criteria determined in studies of hadith methodology. Even so, from the perspective of validity in meaning and its connotations and expressly following Ibn 'Arabi's use of this expression, it was readily adopted by the Sufis and has been employed intensively in Sufi discourse. For this reason, this expression gradually became one unique to the discipline of Sufism. God's being *Kanz al-Makhfi* has been evaluated not in relation to His Names and Attributes, but as a matter pertaining to His Essence. That is to say, He is never One Who is unable to be known in any respect. He, by virtue of His Names and Attributes—albeit to a certain degree—can be known, but in terms of His Essence, is the Exalted Being Who will never be able to be perceived. Such is the information and meaning concerning this expression that has been expounded.

[766] Gülen, *Key Concepts in the Practice of Sufism 4*, 53.

[767] Gülen, "Sır, Hafâ ve Ahfâ," 235.

[768] Sirhindi, *al-Maktubat*, I:127.

sion is an Arabic word meaning lightning. Implied through the word *dhati*, on the other hand, is in all likelihood God's Essence. This being so, it can be gauged from this statement that certain sensations and perceptions with respect to God's Essence come to a believer's heart in a flash and in a rather forceful way. However, while Imam Rabbani sees these kinds of manifestations as a characteristic of secret, Gülen deems these same manifestations as a feature of *akhfa*. The issue on which they both concur is *akhfa*'s being the final point with regards to union with God. While Gülen defines this as the "hope and rapture of union," Imam Rabbani expresses this as "a matchless union."[769]

As is evident from the abovementioned, there is embeddedness between these three dimensions of the heart. These increasingly deepening dimensions become even more hidden as they deepen, but at the same time, they develop and become more expansive with respect to their serving their particular functions. While *khafi* is deeper when compared to secret, it has less depth than *akhfa*. Notwithstanding the fact that it is not known who gave these dimensions their particular names in Sufi history, it is clear that these names are very well suited to their meanings. It is quite possible that the example of the palace that Gülen occasionally uses stems from this. He illustrates the closeness of a servant to God with the metaphor of a person who enters a palace:

> If a believer feels himself or herself to be very close to God with respect to the scope of their experiential knowledge, this means that they have entered the 'privy chamber' and their every action must befit their surroundings. For they are no longer out on the street, at the gateway, in the corridor or in the waiting room; they have entered the privy chamber and have established their pavilion at the focal point of the Sultan's palace. And there, sitting would be different, as would standing, the nature of speaking would change and of remaining silent... the attitudes and deportment in the privy chamber are completely unique. Moreover, even holding the tongue there is, for the most part, not enough; it is a station that necessitates curbing the inclinations of the heart also.[770]

---

[769] Ibid.

[770] M. Fethullah Gülen, *Ölümsüzlük İksiri* (İzmir: Nil Yayınları, 2011), 161.

According to this example Gülen provides, those who attain a grasp of the heart's dimension of secret are as though at the entrance of the palace. Those favored with the *khafi* dimension are as though in the lobby or the drawing room of the palace. Those who are able to penetrate to the dimension of secrets of manifestation, on the other hand, have been accepted into the most private rooms of the palace and, as a result, have become those who know what no one else is able to know and see what no one else is able to see.

When explaining these mysteries, Gülen uses such terms as 'observation,' 'house of observation,' 'horizon of observation,' 'gaze,' 'binoculars' and 'telescope.' By way of illustrating the embeddedness of secret, secrets of Lordship and secrets of manifestation it can be said that these each resemble telescopes of differing apertures and focal lengths. A heart duly using the telescope of secret believes in God on the horizon of secret, knows and loves Him in accordance with this capacity. A heart using the *sirr* telescope in the best possible way is now given a *khafi* telescope with a much wider aperture and focal length. That heart now looks at its Lord with this telescope knows Him and loves Him. As for the rare heart that uses that this befittingly too, it is now honored with observing God with the "the heart's most important dimension," the *akhfa* telescope which no other surpasses in terms of scope and focal distance. This level now attained is the highest possible degree that a heart can reach.

Another point worthy of mention at this juncture relates to the names given to the heart's different dimensions. As already touched upon, denoted by each of the words *sirr*, *khafi* and *akhfa* is hiddenness, obscurity and secrecy. Perhaps for this reason, Gülen says that those qualified individuals journeying at these depths do not explain overtly everything they sense and experience, but on the contrary, only what they are qualified to convey, and only to those who are able to understand them. It is not appropriate to disclose secrets to those who are not authorized to hear them. That which is not permitted to be revealed should be guarded like one's honor. For Gülen, God has disclosed secrets belonging to Himself to some believers; however, this disclosure is not explicit, but on the contrary, to a certain extent obscure and veiled. For this reason, what falls upon believers with an awareness of Divine mysteries is not to relay what they feel and perceive to people directly, but on the contrary to conceal most of what they experience so as not to give rise to misunderstanding and confusion. For "there is soundness in silence and reverence to God in concealing Divine secrets."[771] Perhaps for these reasons the heart's dimensions have been defined with such words.

Heart-Conscience Relationship

Gülen's views on the heart, his identification and description of it through various metaphors and his approach to the concept of conscience are very similar. This is the reason why such a subheading was deemed appropriate for this section. It is possible to say that there is no difference between the concepts of *wijdan* and *qalb* in Gülen's interpretations with respect to their nature and function. In any case, in the Qur'anic verses and *hadith* and in Islamic literature to the present day, the word heart has always been used in place of conscience. Gülen's preference and use of the word *wijdan* is in all likelihood due to Nursi's use of the word also and because of its richness in meaning.

Gülen sees conscience as what can be expressed as the differing dimensions of thought, *ta'aqqul* (reasoning), *tafakkur* (reflection), *tadhakkur* (recollection), *takhattur* (remembrance), *tahlil* (analysis) and possessing the power of *tarkib* (composition), as well as being the source of knowledge and gnosis. In this regard, just as conscience is that which reasons, thinks, mentions, remembers, interprets, it is also the name of the faculty with the capacity to possess every kind of knowledge as well as experiential knowledge of God.

That Gülen establishes his framework of reasoning on the basis of Nursi's definition of conscience is axiomatic:

> Literally meaning the essence of human existence and a person's perception of themselves, *wijdan* (conscience) is a spiritual mechanism composed of the willpower, which chooses between good and evil, the spiritual intellect (*fuad*), which is the inner, most essential dimension of the heart, the inner power of perceptiveness (sensation or feeling), and consciousness.[772]

Conscience is the essence and core of the human being, while willpower, the subtle inner faculties, the mind and the power of perception

---

[771] Gülen, *Key Concepts in the Practice of Sufism 4*, 50.
[772] Gülen, *Key Concepts in the Practice of Sufism 3*, 188.

are the four components which make up this mechanism. There are two issues that will be underscored here. The first is that in clarifying these four constituents, Gülen starts with the phrase which literally reads "the human spirit's" in the original text. This vividly illustrates his considering conscience and spirit in the same thread.[773] As such, the spirit's being called "the essence of human existence" is not at all erroneous. The second issue is Gülen's understanding *latifa al-Rabbaniya* to be *fuad*. In the first part of this thesis, the concept of *fuad* was examined and that it is a dimension of the heart was emphasized. Tirmidhi's view bears importance within this context. In his view, "*Fuad* is the third of the heart's stations and its comparison to the heart is as the pupil is to the eye, as the Sacred Mosque is to Mecca, as the room in a house is to the house and as the essence of a walnut is to the walnut. It is the place of *ma'rifa*, memory and imagination. When a person encounters something of benefit, first their *fuad* and then their heart benefits from it. Just as the pearl is at the center of the oyster, the heart is at the center of the *sadr* (bosom), and *fuad* is at the center of the heart."[774] It is evident that Gülen, sharing the same view as Tirmidhi, sees *fuad* as a dimension of the heart.

According to Gülen, each of the four components making up the conscience has distinct physical and metaphysical depths. As such, *sadr* constitutes the physical aspect of *latifa al-Rabbaniya*.[775] *Sadr* is a "covering" protecting the metaphysical depths of conscience and "is like a picture of the meaning or spirituality of matter." The heart, which is within this covering, is the observer of both the corporeal and metaphysical realms. *Latifa al-Rabbaniya* is a polished mirror onto which all God's Names and Attributes are reflected, the special observer of the Realm of the Tran-

---

[773] Nursi elucidates this issue as follows: "Will, mind, emotion, and the subtle inner faculties, which constitute the four elements of the conscience and four faculties of the spirit, each have an ultimate aim. The ultimate aim of the will is worship of God; that of the mind is knowledge of God; that of the emotions is love of God; and that of the inner faculties is the vision of God." (Nursi, *The Damascus Sermon*, 117.) As is evident, Nursi considers conscience and spirit within the same thread and has not seen any difference between the two. When looked at from this perspective, it can be said that there is no difference between heart, conscience and spirit.

[774] al-Tirmidhi, *Bayan al-Farq*, 38.

[775] The Qur'anic concept of *sadr* was discussed under the heading "Words close in Meaning to the notion of *Qalb*."

scendental Manifestation of Divine Commands (*'Âlam Jabarut*)[776] and the treasury and source of *iman* (belief), *idh'an* (conviction), *'irfan* (knowledge of the Divine), *kashf* (discovery), *ilham* (inspiration) and Divine gifts and radiance. Its pericardium, or "furnace-like" depth (*shaghaf*) is the source of the fire of love for God, while its depth referred to as *sirr* is its "telescope" and polished mirror that gazes upon God.

It is useful here to recall Tirmidhi's connection between *sadr* and *qalb*. Tirmidhi's system of psychology is built on the three central elements of the carnal self (*nafs*), the source of emotions and passions; the *sadr* (breast), which controls a person's actions; and the heart, which is the origin of esoteric knowledge that he describes as a kind of light from God which every individual has in their heart:

> Now the heart is situated inside the breast and the breast surrounds the heart. The self, on the other hand, is outside the breast...and these desires and passions al-Tirmidhi compares to smoke, which, when the passions are not kept in check, escapes from the self and enters into the breast and fills it. Now this smoke, if it fills up the breast, prevents the heart, which is in the middle of the breast, from filling the breast with its light and knowledge. Thus it is only by controlling these passions that an individual can clear his breast of this smoke and let the light of his heart shine out and fill his breast. It is by means of this light shining out of the heart that an individual is enabled to perceive all sorts of truths which would otherwise be unknown to him.[777]

Hence, the heart, taken under protection in a covering known as *sadr*, possesses inner depths nested one within the other. One of these is

---

[776] Realm of the Transcendental Manifestation of Divinity By immaterial realms, Gülen means the Realms of *Lahut, Rahamut, Jabarut* and *Malakut*, the Realms of the Transcendental Manifestation of Divinity, the Transcendental Manifestation of the Divine Mercy and Compassion, the Transcendental Manifestation of Divine Attributes and Names and the Transcendental Manifestation of Divine Commands respectively. While acknowledging the difficulty of saying anything definite in relation to these topics, he states that all related considerations are statements based completely upon *kashf* (discovering), *mushahada* (observation) and *mukashafa* (disclosure) with faithfulness to the determinative fundamentals of the Qur'an and Prophetic tradition.

[777] Nicholas Heer,. "Al-Hakim al-Tirmidhi's Kitab al-'Ilal," in *1960 Annual Meeting of the American Oriental Society* (Connecticut2006).

latifa al-Rabbaniya, interpreted as *fuad*. This inner depth of the heart is the site of belief in and knowledge of the Divine. Put differently, the human being believes in and acquires experiential knowledge of God with this quality. As for *latifa al-Rabbaniya*—this belief, gnosis and love of God—it is realized by means of its depths, *shaghaf*, secret, secrets of Lordship and secrets of manifestation. With the *shaghaf*, or pericardium, they love God, while with the depths of *sirr*, *khafi* and *akhfa* they gain ground in terms of knowing God. They observe God with telescopes, as it were, with progressively increasing diameters and focal lengths and advance to the state of as though seeing God, in accordance with their scrupulousness and willpower. A very strong believer becomes one who possesses personal and accurate knowledge of God. As secret, secrets of Lordship and secrets of manifestation were discussed in detail earlier, these will not be elucidated in depth here.

Heart-Spirit Relationship

As an individual who has examined and commented on virtually every topic in relation to metaphysics, Gülen has also discussed the spirit and has presented his own interpretations on its nature and functions. Under this subheading, on the basis of the topic at hand, namely Gülen's understanding of *qalb*, his descriptions and definitions of the spirit will be discussed and the connection he makes between the spirit and heart will be evaluated.

The spirit, for Gülen as previously mentioned, embraces all the other spiritual feelings and faculties like an atmosphere and "connects them to the heart."[778] On the basis of such a premise the heart, its inner depths of *sirr*, *khafi* and *akhfa* and conscience—which comes to mean one and the same thing as heart—are elements that need to be evaluated within the spirit, as will be done respectively.

Gülen's defining the spirit to be "the non-material essence of human existence, motion, perception, feelings, and intellectual and 'spiritual'

---

[778] Gülen, *Key Concepts in the Practice of Sufism 2*, 261. There can perhaps be only one exception herein, and that is the *nafs* (carnal soul). Just as there are those who accept the carnal self to be a part of the spirit, there have also been those who have considered it to be a second spiritual mechanism distinct from the spirit. In light of all that has been said so far, the second seems more plausible.

development"[779] suggests that he does not make much of a distinction between the heart and spirit. For in presenting his evaluations in relation to the heart he refers to it as "the center of all emotions and (intellectual and spiritual) faculties, such as perception, consciousness, sensation, reasoning, and willpower."[780] Ascribing similar concepts to both the spirit and the heart, Gülen thus also points to the general-specific difference between them. That is to say, according to Gülen, there is a general-particular relationship between the heart and the spirit. More precisely, while every feature pertaining to the heart is at the same time a feature of the spirit, a feature applying to the spirit may not necessarily belong to the heart. This is due to the spirit's being akin to an atmosphere which takes in the heart also.

Gülen sees the heart and secret as the two eyes of the spirit which look to eternity,[781] believes that that spirit's advancement towards perfection is realized "by journeying in the heart on the way to God,"[782] and states that in much the same way, "the spirit is honored with penetrating the inner dimension through the windows of the (spiritual) heart, and with the observation of what lies behind the manifestations of Divine Attributes and Names through the windows of the secret."[783] The common feature of all these interpretations and approaches is the heart's being a part of the spirit and its complementary element.

Apart from this, Gülen has pointed to the affinity between *qalb* and *ruh* by using similar expressions to describe both. For instance, just as the heart is the fortress of vital matters for human beings such as belief, knowledge, wisdom and experiential knowledge of God and "the human truth,"[784] the spirit "is the basis of the mechanism of learning, discernment, inspiration, and conscience, and it is the essence of humanity."[785] In the same way, Gülen's referring to the spirit as "an important means for the human relationship with God,"[786] is another example that can be offered

---

[779] Gülen, *Key Concepts in the Practice of Sufism 3*, 135.
[780] Gülen, *Key Concepts in the Practice of Sufism 1*, 22.
[781] Gülen, *Key Concepts in the Practice of Sufism 3*, 179.
[782] Ibid., 172.
[783] Ibid., 174-75.
[784] Gülen, *Key Concepts in the Practice of Sufism 1*, 22.
[785] Gülen, *Key Concepts in the Practice of Sufism 2*, 176.
[786] Gülen, *Key Concepts in the Practice of Sufism 3*, 172.

of the spirit's similarity to the heart. This is because Gülen states that God's treatment of human beings is according to "the quality of their hearts."[787]

Gülen also makes mention of the situation whereby the heart, feelings, perception and secret come to harm along with the spirit. So long as life is lived based upon carnality and bodily desire, "this causes the 'death' of the spirit."[788]

In the text where Gülen describes conscience as "most important mechanism of the spirit," he describes conscience as "an observatory for the 'observation' of God,"[789] such that this serves to reinforce the notion of the common nature of heart and conscience. This is because as elucidated earlier, the most important functions of the heart and its inner depths is their each being a telescope or a pair of binoculars with which to observe God.

As is evident in figure 1.1 below, alongside seeing the spirit as an atmosphere or umbrella embracing the heart, Gülen ascribes characteristics of the heart to it and interprets and evaluates it as though seeing no difference between the two. Thus, it is axiomatic that Gülen looks at the spirit not from the perspective of speculative theologians, but with respect to spirituality, and has made his interpretations within this framework.

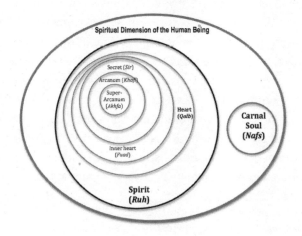

Figure 1.1

---

[787] Gülen, *Key Concepts in the Practice of Sufism 1*, 23.
[788] Gülen, *Key Concepts in the Practice of Sufism 3*, 177.
[789] Ibid., 187.

According to this diagram, a person's spiritual life is comprised of the two elements of spirit and carnal self. Spirit envelops the heart and all of its inner depths like an atmosphere. The heart, in this sense, can be called *sadr*. The first depth of the heart is *fuad*, also known as *latifa al-Rabbaniya*. *Fuad* is the first dimension encountered upon the peeling of the heart shell. *Fuad* possesses interested depths called *sirr*, *khafi* and *akhfa*. These three dimensions are like telescopes with progressively increasing vision capacity, as the seat of belief in and knowledge of God. In addition, these three dimensions serve as a wellspring of a human being's faculties such as willpower, thought, perception and awareness. That is to say, *aql* and all its associated functions are realized by these dimensions of the heart.

There are other functions also attributed to the heart, which are not shown on the diagram in order to avoid confusion. These are *shaghaf*, point of reliance and point of seeking help. The first of these, *shaghaf*, is the source of love and mercy emerging in the heart, while the other two constitute the inner depths of the heart that a person uses to turn to God in times of difficulty and affliction.

Emerald Hills of the Heart

It was mentioned at the outset that the four volume work, Key Concepts in the Practice of Sufism: Emerald Hills of the Heart, to which myriad references have been made throughout this work, would be emphasized separately in and of itself. In any case, failing to refer specifically to this work while focusing on Gülen's understanding of the heart would have truly been a great shortcoming. Therefore, under this heading, I will discuss Gülen's own thoughts on this work, some of his observations pertaining to it and outline my own approach. It ought to be indicated that examining this work at this juncture is of added importance with respect to recognizing the mission that Gülen ascribes to the heart.

In this work, as an individual possessing the conviction that the human being can develop to the extent of their working their heart—the expression of their immaterial existence—Gülen stresses the heart and draws attention to its being amenable to development. In addition, he inspires the curiosity and desire necessary for each individual person to attain the level of perfected human being, as such pointing to a horizon and goal to be reached for the believers. According to Gülen, this work does not suffice with merely expounding the terminology of Sufism, but simultaneously provides certain key principles for the sake of better understanding these concepts and subsequently rendering these an indispensable part of one's life. Such vehicles and means as remembrance of God and mention of His Names, reflection and the prescribed prayer are of great importance in way of ensuring these and scaling these emerald hills. In other words, Key Concepts in the Practice of Sufism: Emerald Hills of the Heart, "instructs in the paths of getting free of the narrow confines of materialism and carnality, walking towards the horizon of the heart and spirit and opening the door to the boundless atmosphere of the spiritual realms beyond matter."

For Gülen, in order to reach the goal that this work presents, there is a need to first know the particular terminology and then to be greatly and constantly preoccupied with these matters. This is at the same time a progression that begins with clarification of concepts and leading to perceiving and feeling them. Saying while elucidating this matter, "There may be a great many truths engraved beyond words and instilled between sentences," Gülen stresses the need to read between the lines. In his view, there is a need to look more deeply at issues, in taking this possibility into consideration, and not getting caught up in only words and expressions. Of even greater importance is the point that reliance and seeking refuge in God in order for these lofty truths to be felt in the heart is an absolute must.

In his article concerning *Key Concepts in the Practice of Sufism: Emerald Hills of the Heart*, Süleyman Eriş states that, "the topics discussed in the work are derived from the Qur'anic verses and Prophetic Traditions, flow in the current of the Ahl al-Sunna tradition, now and again including citations from the great predecessors of Sufism, and are kneaded from the comma to the full stop by the author's heart." Indeed, alongside being based in the Qur'anic verses and Traditions and referenced in the prominent guides among the Companions and their followers, he has imbued and saturated his own thoughts, approaches and beyond these, the sensations and perceptions of his heart into the work. Otherwise stated, in his separate discussions, Gülen has considered the Qur'anic verses and Prophetic Traditions as the body, so to speak, of that chapter, then adding to and clothing it with his own knowledge, perceptions and insights.

Key Concepts in the Practice of Sufism: Emerald Hills of the Heart in the words of Enes Ergene, "is a conversation of the beloved drawing us to our aim of revival and tying all our human interests to the realms beyond." Through this work, Gülen presents the people of today, who have embarked upon the search for identity or who are experiencing a crisis of identity, with the prescription that Islam has presented since the very beginning. This is the human being's search for their own self and God's opening a path leading to Him by showing the Sufi path in response. In other words, the human being is themselves to the extent that they enable themselves to reach their Creator and thus completes their search and their journey.

Key Concepts in the Practice of Sufism: Emerald Hills of the Heart is a road map indicated in the way of the heart of a believer perceiving God. This map lacks only the length of the journey. With it has been expounded virtually every aspect such as the curves in the road, the points of unevenness, descents and ascents, points of narrowness and wideness, stopovers and their features and waiting times, and the itinerary has also been presented with all its particulars.

In this work, Gülen holds the hands, so to speak, of those seeking spiritual development, like the parents of an infant holding their hand as they learn how to walk, he accustoms them to walking without stumbling and falling. Throughout the work, he has prepared the ground for people of all levels and understandings to readily find a place for themselves. Even a novice to the path does not sense the startling disparity between themselves and one who has progressed a great deal along the path. At the same time, the reader is given the hope of reducing this gap with a little more exertion and endeavor and their aim and ardor undergoes not even the slightest offence.

Throughout the work, a method that can be summed up as embarking upon the journey with repentance, seeking God's forgiveness and propriety, being exceedingly mindful of the rules and considerations pertaining to the journey whilst along the way, and making no concessions in self-possession and vigilance in the name of experiencing and maintaining vision and ultimate union, has been cultivated.

To sum up, Key Concepts in the Practice of Sufism: Emerald Hills of the Heart is a journey of intimate knowledge leading the human being to God. This is a journey at the essence of which is sincerity, self-possession, vigilance and propriety. Key Concepts in the Practice of Sufism: Emerald Hills of the Heart is a modern *tekke* (Sufi Lodge), so to speak, which Gülen presents to the people of the modern age. In this way, he carries the concept of the Sufi lodge beyond a physical ground and space and establishes a 'civilization of spiritual knowledge' ('irfan). He offers guidance and instructs in convenances in virtually every aspect, from the formative phase of this civilization and its establishment and construction to its functioning and eventually its continuance.

Social Contribution of a Life of the Heart

This section will examine the impact of a life of the heart on social life, within the framework of Gülen's approach. In Gülen's world of ideas and thought, the notion of the human being's attaining the level of true humanity holds a central position. He believes in the indispensability of spiritual development in the matter of the human being's connection with their Creator, as well as in their being a successful and constructive individuals in the social sphere. That is to say, Gülen sees today's Muslims' overcoming the predicament in which they find themselves as contingent upon the improvement in the life of their heart and spirit. He expresses this matter as follows:

Although some people today disdain moral values, the inner depths of the human being, and the importance of the life of the heart and spirit, there is no doubt that the route to true humanity passes through them. No matter what some people may think, the successful application of these dynamics to life offers the only solution that can save the person of the present. People today must be relieved from the social, political, cultural, economic, and various other depressions that are bending them over double, forcing their back into a misshapen twisted form.

By means of this approach, Gülen evaluates the situation of the Muslims from a sociological standpoint and affirms that they are face to face with a great many problems of the age. It is possible to locate both the malady and diagnosis, as well as the means of treatment in these words. In his view, Muslims of the modern day are experiencing diverse social, economic, political and cultural problems and this can be referred to as a diagnosis of their adversity. Life of the heart and spirit, however, are the "dynamics" and sole solution to their affliction and predicament. This perspective is rather striking with respect to his connecting the solution to the problems that Muslims face in the modern world, to spirituality. Despite the fact that the problems of the Muslims in our day appear outwardly to be scientific and technological backwardness, Gülen's making mention of not these by way of a solution, but referring to spirituality instead, his seeing the answer here and commencing his discussion from this juncture, is significant. According to him, despite the fact that those things which humanity awaits or feels the need for are concerned with spiritual shortage, all exertions being in the way of satisfying carnal desires is a grave delusion. Recovery from this delusion rests in approaching and evaluating the human being with their spiritual as much as with their physical existence. Sincerely believing the solution to lie here, Gülen draws attention to this matter at every opportunity. In this section, an attempt will be made to discuss Gülen's approach specifically, under different sub-headings.

The Inheritors of the Earth

As touched upon, Gülen approaches the situation of the Muslims from a social perspective, on the one hand making an assessment and diagnosis of the situation, while indicating methods of treatment for the illness and problem on the other. Gülen places the "inheritance of the Earth" that the Qur'an refers to and promises to the Muslims, at the locus of his discourse in this context. In his view, due to the failure of Muslims to put forth the performance necessitated by this celestial inheritance, they have been deprived of inheritance by the True Owner and Master of all dominion. The path to deliverance from such deprivation passes through returning to and seeking refuge in God, the Owner of that dominion. The greatest failing experienced by present-day Muslims is, "the deformation that is suffered in both their inner structure (in their hearts and souls) and in their outward structure (their falling behind in contemporary knowledge)." For this reason, Gülen commences his enumeration of the characteristics of perfected believers, which he refers to as "inheritors," with perfected belief.

Gülen compares present-day Muslims to the Prophet's Companions and stresses that they are far beyond and much more profound than the Muslims of our day with respect to life of heart and spirit. It can be said that through the use of this language, he indicates the characteristics required for believers in order for the success which the Companions achieved in the Age of Happiness to be repeated in our day. Gülen's conviction that the revival in our day will be realized by devout servants of

God with sound feeling, thought, perception, consciousness and willpower, is unwavering. As is evident, in mentioning the attributes of those righteous servants, he again makes mention of matters concerning the functions of the heart.

Gülen correlates success in the social, financial, economic and political dimensions of life with a sound reading of the 'book of the universe.' Just as Islam regulates a believer's belief and actions in this world and in the Hereafter, it simultaneously holds the human being "in a position to intervene in natural phenomena, and in a position to comprehend and examine the mysteries of the laws of nature." The phrases, "intervene in natural phenomena" and "comprehend and examine the mysteries of the laws of nature" express humanity's capacity of disposal in the world. Again within Gülen's interpretations, humanity, being God's vicegerent on earth, realizes this vicegerency as possessing the power of disposal on earth, in the Name of God. In other words, the human being has been conferred a position of dominance in the world and everything, on principle, has been subordinated to them. Accordingly, humanity is in a position of rebuilding the world by means of discovering the laws that God has placed in the universe. This being thus, the situation of the believer exhibiting such high performance assumes importance also. In depicting the archetype of precisely such a human being, Gülen puts forward the life of their spirit and heart as their most salient characteristic.

After ascribing faith as the first attribute of the inheritors of the earth, Gülen expounds it further, stressing its indicators. In his view, the purpose of the human being's creation is to possess a perfected belief, deepen in experiential knowledge of God and attain love of God. Once the human being has been favored with these, spiritual ardor and spiritual delight will ensue, even if these are not sought. In the same place is also Gülen's definition of belief. Belief is bringing into the open of the human reality hidden within the spirit of the human being. It can be said that through this definition, Gülen points to the level that the human being who is in a position of inheritor of the earth needs to attain in their own inner world. Consequently, the inheritors of the earth, "who plan to build the world of the future," must first construct their own inner world. And this is possible only by carrying the requirements of Islam to their own private world in the best possible way. Gülen describes those believers realizing such a task as, "spiritual physicians."

To the extent that Gülen describes the human being as an individual member of society as being a possessor of perfect faith, he also connects their responsibilities and action within the society to their spiritual life and, broadly speaking, considers spiritual life together with religious thought. According to this assessment, that which directs both the thoughts and societal duties of a believer is their religious and spiritual life. For Gülen, the advancement of a believer in their own inner world as well as their contribution and success in the social sphere is directly proportional to the life of their heart and spirit. In other words, the spiritual life of a believer, which develops in parallel with their endeavor in worship, remembrance of God and reflection, makes a positive contribution to both their personal world and their place within society as, for Gülen, spiritual life is the key dynamic of public life as much as it is for personal life. In short, it can be said that there exists a relationship of direct proportionality between the matter of connection with God and being a productive member of society, and the vitality and dynamism of a life of the heart.

People of Heart

One of the expressions that Gülen employs in presenting the prototype of the believer is "people of heart." By means of such phrases as "whole-hearted volunteers," "hero of the heart" and "person of heart," he considers the human being along with their heart. The people of heart he depicts are with sound heart, elevated will and resolve, noble manner, active patience and insight. Only those believing by means of them will be able to regain their own disposition, character, and brilliance.

Highlighting the same theme, Gülen again weaves his fabric of discussion using the same expressions:

Indeed, the hero of the heart is, as the Qur'an and the Messenger of God have told us, the person of truth, who sees, thinks, and acts with all the faculties of such a conscience; whose sitting and standing are mercy, whose words and speech are mildness and agreement, and whose manners are politeness and refinement. They are the people of heart and truth who reveal and teach others the secret of knowing and perceiving the Creation from the inside, who can express the true meaning and purpose of the Creation.

Here, Gülen sketches the portrait of a believer without direct reference to Qur'anic verses and Prophetic Traditions but through extracting them and in doing so again uses the word heart adjectivally. In accordance with this approach, heroes of the heart who take heed of the voice of their conscience in their every thought and action and who are compassionate, clement and courteous, are able to express the true meaning and purpose of life and deliver the people of the modern world—by God's leave—of the suffering and misery in which they find themselves.

In Gülen's discourse, the good of society is contingent upon the good of the individual. The same issue upon which many thinkers before him experienced suffering of thought and stressed the importance of, Gülen too emphasizes. In his view, a community "in exemplary order," is one most refined in its spiritual immensity and which is comprised of individuals who have transcended their corporeality again based upon these values. Only such a society can ensure "universal harmony" and its continuity and permanence.

Marriage of Heart and Mind

Another one of Gülen's expressions directly related to the subject at hand and upon which he devotes wide discussion is the "marriage of heart and mind." It is fair to say that he views it as the first condition in the solution to the problems of our day. Gülen emphasizes the issue using diverse turns of phrase and articulates exactly what he means by this in connection with each context.

According to Gülen, while human reason pursues logic, reasoning and the rational sciences in its preoccupation with the natural sciences, the human heart seeks the religious sciences and the Divine gifts coming with a spiritual life. Gülen believes that the line of Islamic thought emerges with the convergence of both of these and that a departure would otherwise result, due to bigotry, incertitude and doubt. He posits that having a voice in such disciplines as physics, chemistry and mathematics can only be possible through embracing the religious sciences and draws attention to the notion that advancement can only be realized via a strong command of book the book of the universe as well as the Qur'an. His "marriage of heart and mind" expression indicates the joint treatment of religion and knowledge or belief and science. He holds the view that this is not a need, but a necessity.

Within such a context, the heart must not fall behind the mind in order to preserve its vitality. In the inability of a person with a highly advanced logic and dialectic to develop to the same degree in heart is the risk of dry logic and dialectic consuming and killing their heart, and this results in their failure in constant self-renewal. The heart's being put to use and developed at least as much as the mind and the eventual marriage of heart and mind is absolutely essential for this to be realized.

In describing those succeeding in the marriage of heart and mind, he underscores their simultaneously being the true inheritors of the earth. People who have been able to realize such a marriage are the righteous servants of God who are sound in thought and feeling, perception and willpower, systematic with respect to their pursuit of knowledge lives and reliable in their undertakings and behavior.

Gülen succinctly relates what is meant by the marriage of heart and mind in the following manner:

The purpose of our creation is obvious: to reach our utmost goals of belief, knowledge, and spirituality; to reflect on the universe, humanity, and God, and thus prove our value as human beings. Fulfilling this ideal is possible only through systematic thinking and systematic behavior. Thought will provoke action, and thereby start a "prosperous cycle." This cycle will produce more complex cycles, generating between the heart's spirituality and the brain's knowledge, and thereby develop ever-more complex ideas and produce larger projects.

As is evident, Gülen expresses his purpose on the basis of the human being, universe and God triad. Accordingly, the human being can strive to achieve the level of true humanity by advancing along the corridor comprised on belief, intimate knowledge of God and spiritual delight. On the other hand, they attempt to understand the universe, develop a great many projects with the interconnection of thought and action and, as such, build their world hereafter, construct their life in this world and realize their purpose of creation.

Metaphysical Thought

The issue that will be addressed under this heading is the meaning implied in Gülen's use of such expressions as "metaphysical thought" and "universal metaphysics." The province of the concept of metaphysics, a branch of philosophy and denoting that which remains 'beyond the physical sciences,' are such themes as existence, coming into being, the universe, singularity, relationship and cause. Gülen perceives this concept in his own discourse as spirituality and uses it in this sense. For instance, he sees metaphysics as the foundation and essence of the Muslim identity and evaluates this term in connection with all the associations of the concept of spirit.

The reason behind a discussion of metaphysics here is Gülen's belief that an accurate grasp of existence is possible only through looking at it with the eye of the spirit. Always considering the human being with their inner world together with their outward-oriented aspect, he places metaphysics in a very important position with respect to perceiving and understanding the physical world. To his mind, those who, "pit modern scientific thought against spirit and meaning are people lacking in sound reasoning who comprehend nothing from the visible and invisible dimensions of things, who are unable to grasp the limits of the physical and metaphysical and who do not possess the capacity of reflection." However, the most important source of science and scholarship is metaphysical thought and the horizon of the spirit.

Gülen draws attention to the necessity of metaphysics for interpreting existence in its own interrelated dimensions and in a manner befitting its reality. In so doing, he stresses the need to examine existence "through the prism of metaphysics," to know the universe, grasp what this knowledge means in practice and observe and evaluate all things with all their facets.

Gülen refers to the indispensability of applying to two key sources in way of penetrating into "the ever-fresh essence of the Qur'an" which he defines as "universal metaphysics"—the Qur'an and the Prophetic example. Arriving at a universal metaphysics will only be possible by taking refuge in the balancing principles of these sources and their boundlessness which opens onto metaphysics. Gülen is of the conviction that those who turn to these two sources with pure intention and in realization of their need, blending modern methods and styles, will reach this Qur'anic spirit.

Conclusion

As is evident, the most salient aspect of the heart is its being the center of all emotions and intellectual and spiritual faculties, such as perception, consciousness, sensation, reasoning, and willpower, reminiscent of Nursi's categorization in relation to *wijdan*. With such an approach, Gülen considers the heart within a rather broad framework. Accordingly, the heart is the center of perception, awareness, reason and willpower, or these together make up the heart. When the heart uses these capacities in the proper way and sufficiently, it elevates a person to the level of true humanity. For it is always the heart that thinks, learns, knows, perceives, comprehends, understands, feels and discerns.

While the heart, secret and the spirit may appear as discrete elements making up human spirituality, it becomes evident that these are each different dimensions pertaining to human spirituality. Gülen, like his predecessor Nursi, more often than not mentions the word heart in conjunction with the word spirit. While this juxtaposition evokes a sense of the synonymity of these terms, it also serves as an indication of the spirit's encompassing the heart and all its associated faculties, like an umbrella.

In Gülen's works, it is possible to see the extent to which Gülen was influenced by Ghazali. This becomes most prominent in his appropriation and elaboration of the *latifa al-rabbaniya* concept. It is possible to state that Gülen was influenced in the general sense by Ghazali and in particular by Imam Rabbani.

Notwithstanding Ghazali's turn to the heart in the latter period of his life, he is accepted generally as a theologian. As such, he naturally considers the heart from a broader perspective. Ahmad Sirhindi's concern, however, is not to merely describe the heart and its functions. As the founder of the Mujaddida branch of the Naqshband Sufi order, his aim is not to refer to the heart, or elucidating its nature and functions for their own sake; his mission, in presenting the profundities of the heart, is to facilitate those aspirants of this Sufi path to advance spiritually by means of knowing their heart and developing it.

Gülen brings together the theological and Sufi standpoints to form a collective understanding of the heart. This is why it is possible to see the respective standpoints of the religious sciences such as theology and Sufism in Gülen's understanding of the heart charted above. In considering Gülen's position relative to Nursi, Ghazali and Sirhindi, the following emerges: Nursi looks at the heart from Imam Ghazali's vantage point. In so doing, he elaborates in detail on the concept of the Divine subtle faculty, which he rephrases as 'Divine gift,' and the heart's being the seat of love and knowledge of God. Gülen, while also articulating these in his works, finds a window through which Imam Rabbani looked at the heart, within a narrower ambit, looking in particular at its secret, arcanum and super-arcanum dimensions. Gülen's contribution is most strongly evident when the fabric of his understanding of the heart is understood as woven with these key fibers, surpassing his predecessors in delineating and describing the separate elements making up the heart and explaining how these inter-layered depths relate to one another. Thus synthesizing the views of Ghazali and Imam Rabbani, Gülen offers a broader and more encompassing view of the heart.

Drawing from the thoughts and views of such personalities as Ghazali, Imam Rabbani and Said Nursi, the most important figures of their own respective times whose impact transcended the era in which they lived, Gülen has voiced his own views on the heart. The factor setting Gülen apart from the above named figures is his possessing the wish and will to build a civilization with people of the heart and spirit.

In addition to approaching the human being as a whole with their physical as well as spiritual facets, like his predecessors, Gülen connects their physical wellbeing to their spiritual wellbeing. Just as this is the case in a person's private life, this is also thus in the societal sense. He aims to develop the human being by weaving his thoughts with a view to their advancing towards perfection in terms of their spiritual life. He constructs a spiritual structure which begins with belief, is kneaded with knowledge and love of God, maintains its consistency with spiritual ardor and joyful zeal and which exhibits continuity. I have defined this as a "civilization of spiritual knowledge." We can also refer to this as a civilization that can only be reached after a long and arduous journey by means of using to the utmost the heart, which is in the position of commander, and all its subtle faculties such as the mind. Alongside taking up the subject specifically in his work entitled, "Key Concepts in the Practice of Sufism: Emerald Hills of the Heart," he has emphasized the same issue in a great many articles published in Turkish under the series entitled *Çağ ve Nesil*.

Not settling merely with this, Gülen has set his sights on establishing another universal civilization along with people succeeding in developing themselves with respect to the life of their heart and spirit. I suspect that there is no harm in describing this civilization on a global scale as a "civilization of morality."

By means of such an approach and thought pattern, we can say that he has aspired to build the statue of the human soul. He aims for those individuals possessing the ability to travel along the emerald hills of the heart, so to speak, to construct their own statues. In addition to virtually all his works being aimed at this purpose, his *Key Concepts in the Practice of Sufism: Emerald Hills of the Heart* calls out to and revives human spirituality, while his work The Statue of Our Souls: Revival in Islamic Thought and Activism approaches and constructs the human being on the material and social plane. The issue to which Gülen draws persistent attention, however, is that those who are to build a civilization of morality in a social and material sense must first be able to establish a civilization of spiritual knowledge for themselves. In other words, this second civilization is the product and even the necessary result of the first. Those who develop the life of their heart in the 'Sufi lodge' named *Key Concepts in the Practice of Sufism: Emerald Hills of the Heart*—those believers who know God intimately alongside believing in Him with an unwavering conviction—will reflect this developed state of their hearts in their practical lives and construct the 'statue' of their own souls. This is because, "for a person to become a human in the full sense of the word, and to the extent to which we aspire, depends on their being under the command of the heart and on their listening to the soul despite their sensual and bodily concerns and their concern for earning a livelihood." It can be argued that this approach is the succinct expression of all Gülen's ideas and endeavor.

General Conclusion

One of the first things to come to mind at the mention of Sufism or spiritual life in Islam is undoubtedly the heart. The heart, with respect to its nature and functions, has preoccupied Muslim scholars and thinkers since Islam's beginnings. The topic's being left somewhat obscure in the Qur'anic verses and Prophetic traditions can be viewed as an indication of the difficulty of expressing it with complete lucidity. As maintained by Fethullah Gülen, the heart concept is as vague and hazy as the spirit and willpower. However, these considerations should not evoke the notion that the heart is something that cannot at all be understood. This current study, at any event, is the result of an endeavor to plumb the meaning of the heart as it appears in the literature of Islam. The obscurity of the topic arises from the fact that 'heart' pertains to a person's spiritual life rather than their corporeal one. It being possible to consider this thesis as a 'thematic tafsir' from the perspective of the Principles of Qur'anic Exegesis (*Usul al-Tafsir*), the results can be summarized as follows:

Literally meaning to invert, turn upside down, turn so as to make something's uppermost part its undermost, *qalb* in Sufi terminology is, in short, the "expression of a human being's spiritual existence." Possessing an enigmatic disposition, the heart has been defined in the Qur'an with such words as *fuad*, *lubb* and *sadr* and sometimes with their plural forms. The heart's being presented with different terms is significant with respect to its being an expression of the interlaced depths in its structure.

Just as the most important organ of a person's physical and corporeal aspect is their heart, the most important dimension of a human being's spiritual and ethereal aspect has been given the same name. In the same way that the material heart pumps blood to the human body and gives it life, so to speak, the spiritual heart breathes life into the human's spiritual being. As the center of perception, conscience, comprehension, feeling, intellect and willpower of the human being, the heart constitutes the human essence and reality. As shown in this thesis, the heart in Islamic belief is the name given to the jewel which the Creator accepts as His addressee, holds responsible for its actions and either rewards or punishes. It is the inner world of the human being, the arena of struggle and contest between both celestial and satanic forces. Indeed, it is the heart which either gives a person peace or causes them remorse and anguish due to what they have done. Because it is always the heart which denies, is sincere, becomes duplicitous, has mercy, takes pity, is angry, wants revenge, becomes greedy, turns to goodness, inclines to evil, it has been referred to as the sum of the capabilities belonging to the human being.

It is possible to speak of a very close connection between such concepts pertaining to a person's immaterial world as intellect, spirit and conscience, and the heart. As it is the heart which thinks, understands, grasps and perceives, the intellect has been considered one of its deeper dimensions. One of the general conclusions reached as a result of our study is that there is no difference between *wijdan* (conscience) and *qalb* (heart) and that *ruh* (spirit) envelopes *qalb* (heart) like an atmosphere.

The second issue that we have sought to underscore in this thesis is the meaningful interaction that God has with the heart. In brief, God treats the human being by virtue of their heart and according to the level of the life of their heart. Moreover, He intervenes between His servant and their heart, contracts and expands the heart of His servant, leads the heart to guidance, gives it tranquility and steadfastness and purifies it. The most natural result of this Divine operation over the heart is the formation of belief and action therein and, through knowledge, love, fear and invocation of Him. In sum, the heart's inclination is to its Creator.

Another issue emphasized in this study relates to the various conditions that the heart is subjected to. However tender and clement the composition of the heart may be, it—when exposed to certain situations— becomes hardened, sealed, stricken with illness and can even die. It is meaningful that all of these issues coming into question in relation to the heart are a demonstration of the changeability inherent in the word's semantic repertoire. Another salient result of this study is the fact of this mutability of the heart sometimes occurring as part of a process, and at other times emerging instantaneously. When looked at from the Qur'anic perspective, while the heart's change oriented towards God is accepted as "development or growth," its other propensities are considered "digression or deviation." Within this framework, we approached the heart's being believing and tender as positive and its disbelief and hardness as being negative.

Both scholars of the classical period as well as contemporary scholars have preoccupied themselves with the heart. Ghazali, one of the most prominent scholars of the classical period, has defined the heart as a "Divine subtle faculty" and this view has constituted one of the significant approaches examined in this study. By use of the word 'Divine,' Ghazali associates this human organ with God and this sets the course for our analysis. Placing the heart in such a position, Ghazali analyzes its functions too from this standpoint. In his view, the heart is an organ which knows God and has the capacity to draw near to Him. However, this characteristic of the heart in Ghazali's view is also susceptible to engendering the exact opposite result. That is, just as the heart can gain proximity to its Creator, it is simultaneously of the disposition to become estranged from Him. Ghazali's approach within this context can be summarized as his viewing the human as virtually being composed of their heart, because in Ghazalian theology, it is none other than the human heart which is the direct addressee of God. We attempt to explain in this study that all of Ghazali's endeavors are aimed at substantiating this premise. A second argument consolidating this view of Ghazali especially is also worthy of note: in his view, the relationship between the heart and the other organs is akin to that between a sultan and his subjects, a commander and his soldiers, and a master and his slaves and servants. In other words, the other organs and faculties fulfil without delay or hesitation the heart's every command, good or evil. This vividly evokes Mawlana's allusion to the heart's command over the five senses:

> Similarly, all the five senses are passing (in movement) according to the will and command of the heart, like the spool (in the hand of a weaver). All the five senses are moving and trailing their skirts (sweeping along) in whatever direction the heart indicates to them.[790]

The heart, for Ghazali, possesses a neutral standing; it is equally open to receiving angelic inspiration as to being subjected to satanic promptings. In order for the heart not to be defeated in the face of satanic urg-

---

[790] Rumi, *The Mathnawi of Jalalu'ddin Rumi*, 194.

ing and suggestion, Ghazali presents remembrance of God as an alternative or a means to prevailing over Satan. Hence, the heart takes shape in accordance with the attributes that are dominant therein. When Satanic attributes prevail, the heart becomes estranged from God and reaches the point of being a helper to Satan and the enemies of God. In so far as the angels are dominant, however, it does not pay heed to the enticements and deceptions of Satan and, despite his ceaseless persistence, inclines towards worship and devotion.

Contemporary Muslim scholar Said Nursi, in his description and definition of the heart, makes frequent reference to Ghazali's *latifa al-Rabbaniya* expression. In this thesis, we explored in detail Nursi's stressing *wijdan* (conscience) and *dimagh* (mind) in his characterization of the heart in particular. In Nursi's view, concisely, *wijdan* (conscience) is the dimension of the heart where the feelings and perceptions occurring to it are manifested, while *dimagh* (mind) constitutes the dimension where thoughts and ideas occurring to the heart are reflected. In a period during which positivism gained exceptional value, especially in Turkey, Nursi strikingly asserts that "The Light of Reason Comes From the Heart" and "There can be no reason without the heart," thus treating the intellect as a dimension of the heart. In effect, Nursi like Ghazali, has expressed a person's essentially being made up of their heart in a different way. In other words, it can be argued that Nursi looks at the heart with Ghazali's outlook.

That Nursi defines the site of Satan's intervention on the heart as *lümme-i şeytaniye*, or satanic center, was also elucidated. As far as we are aware, there is no other scholar or thinker who has employed this term. Satan's 'point' being the center wherein he whispers every kind of thought, fancy, suggestion, intention, baseless fear and urging aimed at wickedness and wrongdoing was presented.

Fethullah Gülen, one of the prominent scholars of the modern age, however, in contrast to his predecessors, focusses more on the functions of the heart. Furthermore, using language readily accessible to human beings of the modern age, he presents his view by means of tropes that are easily comprehensible. For instance, when articulating the notion of the protection of the heart, he uses the term 'quarantine' and has again addressed the understanding and comprehension of the modern person using such terms as 'stairway,' 'projection,' 'door,' 'laboratory' and 'test center.'

While Gülen concurs with Ghazali's defining the heart as *latifa al-Rabbaniya*, it is noteworthy that he does not employ the term in the same way, instead understanding it to mean the inner depth of the heart known as *fuad*. As such, when the heart is considered as a shell, so to speak, it is possible to suggest that that which will show itself from directly beneath that shell is *fuad* (inner heart). Naturally, of course, there are inner profundities and depths beneath *fuad* including *shaghaf* (pericardium), *sirr* (secret), *khafi* (arcanum) and *akhfa* (super arcanum), such that Gülen, with this approach, sees development of the heart as a life-long process.

Gülen, moreover, when describing the heart, uses expressions such as 'point of observation,' 'special observatory,' 'repository of *ma'rifa*' and 'system of observation' and underscores its possessing a function like a pair of binoculars or a telescope. In so doing, he frequently emphasizes the aforementioned inner depths of the heart known as *sirr*, *khafi* and *akhfa*, provides information pertaining to these and offers his own particular interpretations.

While there is a distinct similarity between the approaches of Ghazali, Nursi and Gülen, there is virtually no point on which their opinions diverge. It is as though each of them completes the one who came before. The important factor distinguishing Gülen from his predecessors is his making mention of the innermost layers of the heart. In this, taking Imam Rabbani as reference, he goes beyond Ghazali and Nursi. From this perspective Gülen reworks their ideas with his own accumulation of knowledge, charting a rather original map of the heart.

The main contribution of this thesis to Islamic Scholarship is that it represents the first work in the English language to take as its focus the human heart. While there are innumerable studies that touch upon the importance of *qalb* and beyond this, situate it at the center of Sufism, we have come across none that deal with the heart directly, in and of itself. In so doing, we have attempted to piece together the information pertaining to *qalb* in the extant literature and have sought to add the great legacy of the heart concept in Islamic scholarship to the current literature. We have endeavored to present the views, interpretations and evaluations of Ghazali in the classical period with respect to their standing and influence, as well as the approaches of Said Nursi and Fethullah Gülen, whom we believe to have had an enormous impact in the modern age.

Glossary

'Alam Ghayb:	Unseen Realm
'Alam Shahada:	Visible Realm
'Amal al-jawarih:	Works of the limbs
'Amal:	Action
'Alam 'amr:	Realm of command
'Alam Jabarut:	Realm of the transcendental manifestation of Divine commands
'Alam khalq:	Realm of creation
'Alam Lahut:	Realm of Divinity
'Alam malakut:	Angelic realm
'Alam mulk:	Realm of dominion
'Alam nasut:	Realm of physical reality
'Alim:	Knower
'Amal al-birr:	Works of piety
'Arif:	Gnostic
'Ayn al-yaqin:	Certainty coming from direct observation or seeing
'Ilm al-qulub:	Knowledge of Hearts
'Ilm al-yaqin:	Certainty coming from knowledge
'Ilm:	Knowledge
A'ma:	Blind, The antonym of basira
Ahl al-Haqq:	The People of Truth
Ahl al-qulub:	The People of Hearts
Akhfa:	Super arcanum
Al-insan al-kamil:	Perfected human being
Al-Wadud:	The One who is best-loved
Amana:	Divine trust
Aql:	Intellect
Arbab al-qulub:	Masters of Hearts
Arsh:	Supreme Throne
Ashab al-qulub:	Companions of Hearts

Asma al-Husna: The Most Beautiful Names, is used to refer to the ninety-nine Names of God

Awam: Common people

Awba: Turning to God in contrition

Baqa: Subsistence with God

Barzakh: Intermediate Realm between Visible and Unseen Realms

Basira: Eye of the heart

Basit: The Reliever

Bast: Openness

Batini: Inner, Esoteric

Buraq: The name of the horse-like creature that is said to have carried Prophet Muhammad during his Ascension to Heaven

Dalala: Transgression or misguidance

Damara: Intellect, Intelligence

Damir: Mind, Secret thoughts

Dhikr al-qalbi: Recalling God with the heart

Dhikr: Remembrance

Dimagh: Mind

Dirayah tafsir: Commentaries

Diyq al-sadr: Inner suffering, stress, grief, sorrow and sadness

Fana: Annihilation in God

Fard: Religiously obligatory

Fasad: Corrupted, vitiated, perverted, marred, spoiled, deteriorated

Fayd: Ease

Fi'l: Action

Firar: To escape, the natural consequence of fear

Fitna: Putting a person through various trials to know fully or to reveal the aspects that are unknown

Fuad: Inner heart

Ghadab: Anger

Ghishawa: Veil

Hadith Qudsi: Divine hadith

Hadith: Prophetic Tradition

Hal: State

Haqiqa al-insaniyya: Human Reality

Haqq al-yaqin: Certainty coming from direct experience

Haqq: Truth, a thing whose existence is so certain that it cannot be denied

Hayba:	The necessary condition of experiential knowledge such that only those who know God can possess this kind of fear
Hayra:	Experience of utmost astonishment
Hilm:	Intellect
Hidaya:	Guidance
Hijr:	Intellect
Hijra:	Emigration; The beginning of the Islamic calendar
Hiss:	Feeling
Hubbat al-qalb:	Grain of the heart
Ibtila:	Retrieving mud or soil from the bottom of a well
Idh'an:	Conviction
Idrak:	Awareness
Ihata:	Encompassing and understanding a topic in all its facets and fields
Ihbat:	Tranquility and submission
Ikhlas:	Sincerity
Ilham:	Inspiration
'Ilm laduni:	Esoteric and spiritual knowledge
Iman:	Belief
Inaba:	A degree deeper and more comprehensive than tawba, or repentance
Inaya:	Providence
Inkishaf:	The secret of the unseen is revealed to
Intibah al-qalbi:	Awakening of the heart
Irada juz'iyya:	Minor human will
Irada:	Will
Irfan:	Personal and accurate knowledge of the Divine
Ishraq:	Light shines in the heart
Islah:	Correcting something and removing vice
Istiqama:	Straightforwardness
Itmi'nan:	Tranquility
Jahiliyya:	The Age of Ignorance
Jamil:	The Beautiful
Jawhar:	Jewel, substance
Ka'ba:	God's Sacred House
Kanz al- Makhfi:	Hidden Treasure
Kashf:	Discovery
Khafi:	Arcanum

Khashya: Fear grounded in knowledge, weighted in calm and tranquility

Khatir: Passing thought that occurs to the heart involuntarily

Khatm: Heart's being sealed,

Khawf: Fear of punishment in return for something committed

Kürsi: Chest to the Divine Seat

Lataif al-khamsa: Five Subtle Faculties: Heart, Spirit, Secret, Arcanum and Super-arcanum

Latifa rabbaniya ruhaniya: Subtle tenuous substance

Latifa: Subtle faculty

Lin: Soft

Lubb: Bosom

Lümme: Mark, insignia, stamp, point, evil suggestion and delusion

Ma'lumat: Information or knowledge.

Ma'rifat al-qulub: Gnosis of Hearts

Ma'rifa: Experiential knowledge

Mahabbat Allah: Love of God

Mahw: Spiritual annihilation

Makhafat Allah: Fear of God

Maqam: Station

Maqamat al-qulub: Stations of the Hearts

Masiwa: Used to refer to everything other than God

Masmu': Acquired mind

Matbu': Imprinted or innate mind

Mu'minun: Believers

Mudrik: Perceiver

Muhasaba: Self-criticism

Muraqaba: Self-supervision

Mushahada: Observation

Mustahab: Religiously recommended

Mutasawwifun: Sufis

Nafs al-natiqa: Reasoning or Articulating Soul

Nafs: Carnal soul

Naqshibandiyya: Sufi order

Nazargâh-i İlahî: Focus of God's sight

Niyya: Intention

Nuha: Intellect

Nur: Divine light

Qabd:	Contraction
Qabid:	The Constrictor
Qalb:	Heart
Qalb al-salim:	Sound heart
Qast:	Clear decision
Qudrah:	Power
Qulub, Eqlab, Qilaba, 'Aqlub: Plural forms of Qalb	
Qur'an:	Holy Book of Islam
Qurbiya:	Proximity to God
Quwwa al-qudsiya: Transcendental power	
Rahba:	To dread the realization of one's fears, escaping with all one's strength
Raja:	Hope
Rayn:	Heart's being sealed
Rij'sa:	Filth
Riqqat:	Tender
Ruh:	Spirit
Rusukh:	Steeping in a topic and mastering
Sahw:	Spiritual sobriety
Sakina:	Serenity
Salih:	Righteous
Samad:	Self –Sufficient
Sayr u suluk al-qalbi: Journeying with the heart	
Sayr u suluk:	Journeying and Initiation
Shaghaf:	Pericardium
Shahwa:	Appetence
Sharh al-sadr:	Chest's opening and expansion by means of Divine light and serenity
Sharh:	Cutting opening, splitting, expanding the flesh and explaining a vague or inexplicit expression
Shawq:	Joyful zeal
Shirk:	Associating partners with God
Shu'ur:	Consciousness
Sirr:	Secret
Sū':	A worldly or incorporeal thing which causes a person grief and sorrow
Subhan:	All Glorified
Sulh:	Peace

Sunna:	The Prophetic Way
Suwayda':	The black dot
Tadabbur:	Contemplation
Tafakkur:	Reflection
Tafaqquh:	Penetrating to the essence of a matter
Tafsir:	Qur'anic exegesis
Taghut:	Deities
Tahlil:	Analysis
Taqlid:	Purely blind imitation
Taqwa:	Piety
Tarkib:	Composition
Tasawwuf:	Sufism
Tasdiq:	Affirmation
Tawba:	Repentance, turning to God due to wrongdoing or transgression
Tawhid:	Divine unity
Tazakkur:	Remembrance
Thabat:	Steadfastness
Ulu al-albab:	The People of Discernment
Wajal:	Being afraid of punishment
Wajd:	Ecstasy
Wajib:	Religiously prescribed
Wakr:	Deafness
Wali:	Friend of God
Wijdan:	Conscience
Wuquf:	Full comprehension
Yaqin:	The closeness or distance to certainty in knowledge
Zahiri:	Outward
Zann:	Presumption, doubt, suspicion
Zaygh:	To be inclined, to swerve
Zulumat:	Darkness

References

'Abduh, Muhammad. *Tafsir al-Manar*. 12 vols. Cairo: Matba'at al-manar, 1931.

(TDK), Turkish Language Association. *Great Turkish Dictionary*. Edited by Mehmet Doğan. Ankara: Vadi Yayınları, 2001.

Abrahamov, Binyamin. "Al-Ghazali's Supreme Way to Know God." *Studia Islamica*, no. 77 (1993): 141-68.

Abu al-Faraj 'Abd al-Rahman ibn 'Ali, Ibn al-Jawzi. *Zad al-Masir Fi 'Ilm Al-Tafsir*. 8 vols. Beirut: Dar al-Kutub al-'Ilmiyya, 1414 [1994].

Abu Dawud, Sulayman ibn Ash'as al-Sijistani. *Sunan Abi Dawud*. 4 vols. Jeddah: Dar al-Qibla, 1998.

Al Qushayri, 'Abd al-Karim. *al-Risalah al-Qushayri fi al-'Ilm al-Tasawwuf*. Beirut: Dar al-Kitab al-'Arabi, 2005.

al-Nawawi, Muhy al-Din Abu Zakariyya Yahya b. Sharaf. *Sharh Sahih Muslim*. 18 vols. Beirut: Dar al-Qalam, 1997-1993.

al-'Ajluni, Ismail ibn Muhammad. *Kashf al-Khafa.'* 2 vols. Beirut: Dar Ihya' al-Turath al-'Arabi, 1932.

al-'Ayni, Badr al-Din. *'Umdat al-Qari*. 25 vols. Beirut: Dar Ihya' al-turath al-`Arabi, 2001.

al-Bayhaqi. *Shu'ab al-Iman*. 7 vols. Beirut: Dar al-Kutub al-'Ilmiyya, 1990.

al-Dihlawi, Shah Wali Allah. *Hujjat Allah al-Baligha*. 2 vols. Beirut: Dar Ihya' al-'Ulum, 1990.

al-Firuzabadi, Muhammad Ibn Ya'qub. *al-Qamus al-Muhit*. Cairo: Mu'assasaturri'salah, 1951.

_____. *Basa'ir dhawi al-tamyiz fi lata'if al-Kitab al-'Aziz*. 6 vols. Beirut: al-Maktabah al-'Ilmiyyah, n.d.

al-Ghazali, Abu Hamid Muhammad ibn Muhammad. *Mishkat al-Anwar*. Cairo: Matba'a al-Sidq, 1904.

_____. *Al-Munqiz min al-Dalal*. Beirut: Muassasa al-Kutub al-Saqafiyya, 1987.

_____. *Ihya' 'ulum al-din*. 5 vols. Beirut: Dar al-Kutub al-'Ilmiyya, 1996.

_____. *Wonders of the Heart*. Translated by Walter James Skellie: Islamic Book Trust, 2007.

_____. *The Marvels of the Heart: Book 21 of the Ihya' 'Ulum al-Din*. Edited by Walter James Skellie. Louisville: Fons Vitae, 2010.

al-Hujwiri, Ali B. Uthman. *The Kashf al-Mahjub (The Revelation of the Veiled) An Early Persian Treatise on Sufism*. Translated by Reynold A. Nicholson. Cambridge: Gibb Memorial Trust, 2000.

al-Isfahani, Raghib. *Al-Mufradat fi Gharib al-Qur'an*. Cairo: al-Anjilo al-Misriyya, 1970.

al-Jawziyya, Ibn Qayyim. *Madarij al-Salikin*. 3 vols. Cairo: Dar al-Hadith, 1983.

al-Jaziri, Ibn al-Athir. *an-Nihaya fi Gharib al-Hadith*. 2 vols. Cairo: Dar al-Ihya' al-Kutub al-Arabiyya, 1963.

al-Jurjani, Sayyid Sharif. *Kitab al-Ta'rifat*. Beirut: Dar al-Kutub al-'Ilmiyya, 1983.

al-Kashani, 'Abd al-Razzaq. *Istilahat al-Sufiyah*. Cairo1981.

al-Kashmiri, Muhammad Anwar. *Fayd al-Bari ila Sahih al-Bukhari*. 6 vols. Beirut: Dar al-Kutub al-'Ilmiyyah, 2005.

al-Mahalli, Jalal al-Din, and Jalal al-Din al-Suyuti. *Tafsir al-Jalalayn*. Riyadh: Dar-ussalam, n.d.

al-Makki, Abu Talib. *Qut al-qulub fi mu'amalat al-mahbub*. 2 vols. Beirut: Dar al-Kutub al-'Ilmiya, 2005.

al-Mawlawi, Tahir, ed. *Sharh al-Mathnawi*. Edited by Ali Güleryüz, Mehmet Atalay and Kadir Turgut. Istanbul: Dehliz Books, 2008.

al-Mubarakfuri, Muhammad Abdul Rahman b. Abdul Rahim. *Tuhfat al-Ahwazi*. 10 vols. Beirut: Dar al-Fikr, 1995.

al-Muhasibi, al-Harith. *Kitab ar-ri'ayah li huquq Allah*. Cairo: Dar al-Kutub al-Haditha, 1970.

al-Munawi, 'Abd al-Ra'uf. *Fayd al-Qadir*. 6 vols. Beirut1682.

al-Muttaqi, Ali. *Kanz al-'Ummal*. 19 vols. Hyderabad: Da'irat al-Ma'arif, 1953.

al-Nasa'i, Abu 'Abd al-Rahman b. Shu'ayb. *Sunan al-Nasa'i*. 8 vols. Beirut: Maktab al-Matbu'at al-Islamiyya, 1930.

al-Nuri, Abu al-Husayn. *Maqamat al-Qulub*. Beirut1968.

al-Qari, 'Ali. *al-Mawdu'at al-Kubra*. Beirut1986.

al-Qashani, 'Abd al-Razzaq. *Istilahat al-Sufiyah*. Cairo1981.

al-Qastallani, Ahmad b. Muhammad. *'Irshad al-Sari li Sharh Sahih al-Bukhari*. 15 vols. Beirut: Dar al-Kutub al-'Ilmiyya, 1996.

al-Razi, Fakhr al-Din. *Kitab al-nafs wa al-ruh*. Islamabad: Islamic Research Institute, 1985.

_____. *Tafsir al-Kabir (Mafatih al-Ghayb)*. 32 vols. Beirut: Dar al-Kutub al-'Ilmiyya, 1990.

al-Suhrawardi, 'Abu Hafs 'Umar. *'Awarif al-Ma'arif*. Edited by Adib al-Kamdani and Muhammad Mahmud al-Mustafa. Mecca: Al-Maktaba al-Makkiya, 2001.

al-Tabari, Abu Ja'far Muhammad ibn Jarir. *Jami' al-Bayan fi Tafsir al-Qur'an*. 30 vols. Beirut: Dar al-Ma'rifa, 1986.

al-Tahanawi, Muhammad 'Ali. *Kashshaf istilahat al-funun*. Beirut: Dar al-Sadir, 1745.

al-Taymiyya, Ibn. *Majmu'at al-Fatawa*. 37 vols. Riyadh: Maktabat al-'Ubaykan, 1997.

al-Tirmidhi, Abu 'Isa Muhammad b. 'Isa. *Sunan al-Tirmidhi*. 4 vols. Beirut: Dar Ihya' Turath al-'Arabi, n.d.

al-Tirmidhi, Hakim. *Bayan al-Farq bayn al-Sadr wal -Qalb wal-Fu'ad wal-Lubb*. Cairo: Dar Ihya' al-Kutub al-'Arabiyya, 1958.

_____. *Nawadir al-Usul*. Beirut: Dar al-Kutub al-'Ilmiyya, 1992.

al-Zabidi, Murtada. *Taj al-'Arus min Jawahari'l Qamus*. 10 vols. Cairo1888.

_____. *Ithaf al-Sada al-Muttaqin Sharh Ihya' 'Ulum al-Din*. 10 vols. Beirut: Dar al-Kutub al-'Ilmiyya, 1989.

al-Zamakhshari, Mahmud. *Asas al-Balaghat*. Beirut: Dar al-Tanwir, 1984.

_____. *al-Kashshaf 'an haqa'iq ghawamid al-tanzil wa-'uyun al-aqawil fi wujuh al-ta'wil*. 6 vols. Riyadh: Maktabat al-'Abikan, 1998.

Alam, Irshad. *Faith Practice Piety: An Excerpt from the Maktubat-i Imam-i Rabbani*: Sufi Peace Mission, 2012.

Albayrak, Ismail. *Klasik Modernizmde Kur'an'a Yaklaşımlar*. Istanbul: Ensar Neşriyat, 2004.

Alusi, Mahmud ibn 'Abd Allah. *Ruh al-ma'ani fi tafsir al-Qur'an al-'Azim wa al-sab' al-mathani*. 30 vols. Beirut: Dar al-Fikr, 1997.

Ansari, 'Abd Allah, ed. *Manazil al-Sa'irin (Resting Places of the Wayfarers)*. Edited by 'Abd al-Hafiz Mansur, Knowledge of God in Classical Sufism: Foundations of Islamic Mystical Theology. Tunis: Dar al-Turki lil-Nashr, 1989.

Asad, Muhammad. *Message of the Qur'an*. Gibraltar: Dar Al-Andalus, 1980.

Asım Efendi. *Translation of Al-Qamus*. 4 vols. Istanbul: Cemal Efendi Matbaası, 1305.

at-Tabarani, ed. *al-Mu'jam al-Awsat*. Edited by Mahmud al-Tahhan. 10 vols. Riyadh: Maktaba al-Ma'arif, 1985.

Aydın, Hüseyin. *Muhasibi'nin Tasavvuf Felsefesi*. Ankara: Pars Yayıncılık, 1976.

Baldick, Julian. *The Essence of Sufism*. Edison, NJ: Chartwell Books Inc., 2004.

Bashir, Shahzad. *Sufi Bodies: Religion and Society in Medieval Islam*. New York: Columbia University Press, 2011.

Baydawi, Nasr al-Din. *Anwar al-Tanzil wa Asrar al-Ta'wil*. 2 vols. Istanbul: Şirket-i Sahafiye-i Osmaniye, 1884.

Berelson, Bernard. *Content Analysis in Communication Research*. New York: Free Press, 1952.

Bukhari, Muhammad b. Ismail. *al-Jami' al-Sahih*. 4 vols. Beirut: al-Maktaba al-'Asriya, 2002.

Burckhardt, Titus. *An Introduction to Sufi Doctrine*. Translated by D. M. Matheson. Bloomigton (IN): World Wisdom, 2008.

Bursawi, Ismail Haqqi. *Ruh al-Bayan*. 10 vols. Istanbul: Mektebetu Eser, 1969.

_____. *Kitab al-Natija*. Edited by Ali Namlı and İmdat Yavaş. 2 vols. Istanbul: İnsan Yayınları, 1997.

Chittick, William C. *The Sufi Path of Knowledge*. Albany, NY: State University of New York Press, 1989.

_____. *Faith and Practice of Islam*. Albany: White Cloud Press, 1992.

_____. *Sufism - A Short Introduction*. Oxford: One World, 2000.

Coope, Jessica A. "With Heart, Tongue, and Limbs: Ibn Hazm on the Essence of Faith." *Medieval Encounters* 6, no. 1-3 (2000): 101-13.

Derin, Süleyman. *Love in Sufism: From Rabia to Ibn al-Farid*. Istanbul: Insan Publications, 2008.

Draz, M. Abdullah. *The Moral World of the Qur'an*. London: I.B. Tauris, 2008.

Ergül, Adem. *Kur'an ve Sünnette Kalbî Hayat (Spiritual Life in the Qur'an and Sunna)*. Istanbul: Erkam Yayınları, 2000.

Esposito, John L. *The Oxford Dictionary of Islam*. New York: OUP, 2003.

Foundation, Turkiye Diyanet. *TDV Encyclopedia of Islam*. 37 vols n.d.

Frembgen, Jürgen Wasim. *Journey to God; Sufis and Dervishes in Islam*. Translated by Jane Ripken. London: Oxford University Press, 2008.

Garnard, Ibrahim W., and A. G. Rawan Farhadi. *The Quatrains of Rumi: Ruba 'iyat-i Jalaluddin Muhammad Balkhi-Rumi*. New York: Sophia Perennis, 2008.

Gülen, M. Fethullah. *Key Concepts in the Practice of Sufism 1*. Translated by Ali Unal. Fairfax, Virginia: The Fountain, 1999.

_____. *Prizma 3*. Izmir: Nil Yayınları, 1999.

_____. *Zamanın Altın Dilimi*. Izmir: Nil Yayınları, 2002.

_____. *Key Concepts in the Practice of Sufism 2*. Translated by Ali Unal. Somerset, New Jersey: The Light, Inc, 2004.

_____. *The Essentials of the Islamic Faith*. New Jersey: The Light Publishing, 2006.

_____. *Prizma 6*. Izmir: Nil Yayınları, 2006.

_____. *Kalbin Solukları*. Izmir: Nil Yayınları, 2009.

_____. *Kalbin Zümrüt Tepeleri 4*. Istanbul: Nil Yayınları, 2009.

_____. *Key Concepts in the Practice of Sufism 3*. Translated by Ali Unal. New Jersey: Tughra Books, 2009.

_____. *Gurbet Ufukları*. Istanbul: Nil Yayınları, 2010.

_____. *Key Concepts in the Practice of Sufism 4*. Translated by Ali Unal. New Jersey: The Light Publishing, 2010.

_____. *Speech and Power of Expression: On Language, Esthetics, and Belief.* Istanbul: Tughra Books, 2010.

_____. *Ölümsüzlük İksiri.* İzmir: Nil Yayınları, 2011.

_____. "Sır, Hafâ ve Ahfâ." *Sızıntı Magazine,* 2011, 234-36.

Hayyan, Abu. *al-Bahr al-Muhit.* 10 vols. Beirut: Dar al-Fikr, 1992.

Heer, Nicholas. "Al-Hakim al-Tirmidhi's Kitab al-'Ilal." In *1960 Annual Meeting of the American Oriental Society.* Connecticut, 2006.

Helminski, Kabir. *The Knowing Heart: A Sufi Path of Transformation.* Boston: Shambhala Publications, 1999.

_____. *The Book of Language: Exploring the Spiritual Vocabulary of Islam.* Bristol: The Book Foundation, 2006.

Ibn al-'Arabi, Muhy al-Din. *Tafsir al-Qur'an al-Karim.* 2 vols. Beirut: Dar al-Andalus, 1981.

_____. *al-Futuhat al-Makkiyya.* Cairo: al-Hay'a al-Misriyya al 'Amma, 1985.

_____. *Fusus al-Hikam.* Algiers: Mufam li al-Nashr, 1990.

_____. *Kitab al-Masa'il.* Damascus: Dar al-Mada, 2004.

Ibn Hajar, al-Asqalani. *Fath al-bari sharh Sahih al-bukhari.* Beirut: Dar al-Kutub al-'Ilmiyyah, 1997.

Ibn Hanbal, Ahmad. *al-Musnad.* 6 vols. Beirut1969.

Ibn Kathir, Abu al-Fida. *Tafsir ibn Kathir.* 10 vols. Riyadh: Darussalam, 2000.

Ibn Majah. *Sunan Ibn Majah.* 4 vols. Beirut: Dar al-Ma'rifa, 1996.

Ibn Manzur, Abu Fadl Muhammad b. Mukarram. *Lisan al-'arab.* 18 vols. Beirut: Dar al-Sadir, 1997.

Ibn Sa'd. *al-Tabaqat al-Kubra.* 8 vols. Beirut: Dar Sadir, 1960.

Izutsu, Toshihiko. *Creation and the Timeless Order of Things.* Ashland, Oregon: White Cloud Press, 1994.

_____. *Ethico-Religious Concepts in the Qur'án:* McGill-Queen's Press, 2002.

_____. *God and Man in the Qur'an.* Kuala Lumpur: Islamic Book Trust, 2002.

Jawhari, Abu Nasr Ismail. *Taj al-Lugha wa sahah al-'Arabiyya.* 2 vols. Beirut: Dar al-Fikr, 1998.

Kalabadhi, Abu Bakr Muhammad ibn Ibrahim, ed. *al-Ta'arruf li-madhhab ahl al-tasawwuf.* Edited by Ahmad Shams al-Din. Beirut: Dar al-Kutub al-'Ilmiyya, 1993.

Kalın, Ibrahim. "Reason and Rationality in the Qur'an." In *The 2nd Muslim - Catholic Forum.* The Baptism Site, Jordan, 2011.

Karamustafa, Ahmet T. *Sufism: The Formative Period.* Los Angeles: University of California Press, 2007.

Kılavuz, Ahmet Saim. *İman Küfür Sınırı.* Istanbul: Marifet Yayınları, 1997.

Knecht, Tariq. *Journal of a Sufi Odyssey: A True Novel, Book 3*: Tauba Press, 2010.

Koren, J., and Y.D Nevo. "Methodological Approaches to Islamic Studies." *Der Islam*, no. 68 (1991): 87-107.

Krippendorff, Klaus. *Content Analysis: An Introduction to Its Methodology*. California: Sage Publications, 2004.

Kübra, Necmeddin-i. *Tasavvufi Hayat*. Translated by Mustafa Kara. Istanbul, 1980.

Lane, Edward William. *An Arabic-English Lexicon*. 8 vols. Lebanon: Librairie Du Liban, 1968.

Lings, Martin. *What is Sufism?* London: Unwin Paperbacks, 1988.

Majma' al-Lughah al-'Arabiyyah. *Al-Mu'jam al-Wasit*. 2 vols. Cairo: Arabic Language Academy, 1962.

Makki, Abu Talib Muhammad ibn 'Ali, ed. *Qut al-qulub fi mu'amalat al-mahbub wa wf tariq al-murid ila maqam al-tawhid*. Edited by Sa'id Nasib Makarim. 2 vols. Beirut: Dar Sadir, 1995.

Massignon, Louis. *Essay on the Origins of the Technical Language of Islamic Mysticism*. Translated by Benjamin Clark. Notre Dame, IN: University of Notre Dame Press, 1997.

Mawdudi, Sayyid Abul A'la, ed. *Tafhim al-Qur'an*. Edited by Ali Bulaç. 7 vols. Istanbul: İnsan Yayınları, 1996.

Murad, Abdal Hakim. "Fath al-Bari: Commentary on Sahih al-Bukhari." Al-Sunnah Foundation of America (ASFA), http://www.sunnah.org/history/Scholars/fath_al_bari.htm.

Muslim, Abu al-Husayn Muslim ibn Hllaj al-Qushayri. *Sahih al-Muslim*. 4 vols. Cairo: Dar Ihya' Kutub al-'Arabiyya, 1956.

Napora, John A. "Love and Lover Transformed: The Sufi Path to God." In *Metanexus Conference on Works of Love*. Philadelphia, 2003.

Nasr, Seyyed Hossein. *Sufi Essays*. Chicago: ABC International Group, 1999.

Nicholson, Reynold A. *The Mystics of Islam*. London: Routledge And Kegan Paul Ltd, 1970.

_____. *Studies in Islamic Mysticism*. London: Cambridge University Press, 1980.

_____. *Sufism: The Mysticism of Islam*. Los Angeles: IndoEuropean Publishing, 2009.

Nursi, Said. *The Damascus Sermon*. Translated by Şükran Vahide. Istanbul: Sözler Publications, 1996.

_____. *A Guide for the Youth*. Translated by Şükran Vahide. Ankara: Ihlas Nur Publications, 2003.

_____. *Münazarat*. Edited by Abdullah Aymaz. Izmir: Şahdamar Yayınları, 2006.

_____. *The Staff of Moses*. Istanbul: Sözler Publications, 2006.

_____. *Mathnawi al-Nuriya*. Translated by Huseyin Akarsu. New Jersey: The Light, Inc., 2007.

_____. *The Rays*. Translated by Şükran Vahide. Istanbul: Sözler Neşriyat, 2007.

_____. *Signs of Miraculousness: The Inimitability of the Qur'an's Conciseness*. Translated by Şükran Vahide. Istanbul: Sözler Publications, 2007.

_____. *The Letters*. Translated by Şükran Vahide. Phoenix: Nur Publishers, 2008.

_____. *The Reasonings*. Translated by Huseyin Akarsu, The Risale-i Nur Collection. New Jersey: Tughra Books, 2008.

_____. *The Words*. Translated by Şükran Vahide. Istanbul: Sözler Publications, 2008.

_____. *The Flashes*. Translated by Şükran Vahide. Istanbul: Sözler Neşriyat, 2009.

_____. *Emirdağ Lahikası (Emirdağ Letters)*. Istanbul: Şahdamar Yayınları, 2010.

_____. *Tarihçe-i Hayat*. Istanbul: Şahdamar Yayınları, 2010.

Pavlis, Natalie A. "An Early Sufi Concept of Qalb: Hakim al-Timidhi's Map of the Heart." McGill University, 2001.

Pazarlı, Osman. *Din Psikolojisi (The Psychology of Religion)*. Istanbul: Remzi Kitapevi, 1982.

Qurtubi, Abu 'Abd Allah. *al-Jami' Li-ahkam-il Qur'an*. 20 vols. Beirut: Dar al-Kutub al-'Ilmiyya, 2004.

Rabbani, Wahid Bakhsh. *Islamic Sufism*. Aligarh, India: Premier Publishing Company, 2001.

Rida, Rashid. *Tafsir al-Manar*. 12 vols. Beirut: Dar al-Kutub al-'Ilmiyya, 1999.

Rumi, Jalal al-din. *The Mathnawi of Jalalu'ddin Rumi: Translation of Books I and II*. Translated by R. A Nicholson. Cambridge: E. J. W. Gibb Memorial Trust, 1982.

Rumi, Mawlana Jalal al-Din. *Diwan-ı Kabir*. Vol. 6. Istanbul: Remzi Kitabevi, 1958.

Sarraj, Abu Nasr 'Abd Allah ibn 'Ali. *Kitab al-luma' fi'l tasawwuf*. Edited by Reynold A. Nicholson. London: Luzac & Co, 1914.

Sayyid Qutb. *Fi Zilal al-Qur'an*. 5 vols. Beirut: Dar al-Shuruq, 1986.

Schimmel, Annemarie. *Mystical Dimensions of Islam*. Chapel Hill: The University of North Carolina Press, 1975.

Schuon, Frithjof. "The Quintessential Esoterism of Islam." edited by Jean-Louis Michon and Roger Gaetani, 251-75. Bloomington, Indiana: World Wisdom, Inc., 2006.

Sirhindi, Ahmad Faruq (Imam Rabbani). *al-Maktubat*. 3 vols. Cairo: Matba'a al-Miriyya, 1899.

Stoddart, William. *Sufism: The Mystical Doctrines and Methods of Islam*. New Delhi: Taj Company, 1994.

Taylan, Necip. *Ghazali'nin Düşünce Sisteminin Temelleri*, TDV Encyclopaedia of Islam. Istanbul: Marmara Üniversitesi İlahiyat Fakültesi Vakfı (İFAV), 1989.

_____. "Bilgi." In *TDV Encyclopaedia of Islam*, 157-61. Istanbul: Turkiye Diyanet Foundation, 1992.

Ünal, Ali. *The Qur'an with Annotated Interpretation in Modern English*. New Jersey: Tughra Books, 2008.

Yamani, Salman Zayd Salman. *al-Qalbu wa Wazaifuhu*. Dammam: Dar Ibn al-Qayyim, 1994.

Yazır, Elmalılı Muhammed Hamdi. *Hak Dini Kur'an Dili*. 10 vols. Istanbul: Azim Dagitim, 1979.

Yeğin, Abdullah, Abdulkadir Badıllı, Hekimoğlu İsmail, and İlhan Çalım, eds. *Ottoman Turkish - Turkish Encyclopaedic Great Dictionary*. 2 vols. Istanbul: Türdav, 1981.

Yıldırım, Suat. *Kur'an-ı Hakim ve Açıklamalı Meali (The Holy Qur'an and its Translation with Commentary)*. Istanbul: Define Yayınları, 2006.

Zuhayli, Wahba. *Tafsir al-Wajiz*. Damascus: Dar al-Fikr, 1991.

Index